ONE SHINING MOMENT
SPORTS HEROES FOR A DAY

BURNHAM HOLMES

HarperTorch
An Imprint of HarperCollinsPublishers

HARPERTORCH
An Imprint of HarperCollins*Publishers*
10 East 53rd Street
New York, New York 10022-5299

Copyright © 2003 by Burnham Holmes
ISBN: 0-380-79879-4

First HarperTorch paperback printing: March 2003

HarperCollins®, HarperTorch™, and ❦™ are trademarks of HarperCollins Publishers Inc.

Printed in the United States of America

Visit HarperTorch on the World Wide Web at www.harpercollins.com

10 9 8 7 6 5 4 3 2 1

For my own one shining moment,
Vicki Reid (1947–1998):
friend, wife, mother of our son.

"At least for that one time in his life, that one shining moment, he was the best player. That should be meaningful to somebody. That should have some merit if you were the best."

—Don Newcombe

Acknowledgments

This book has been more of an undertaking than I at first thought it would be. I would like to express my appreciation to Roger Harris for his kindness in letting me use his extensive sports library and his private collection of letters from athletes, and to Michael Shohl, my editor at HarperCollins, who stepped in and made it all happen. I would also like to thank Randy Kniffin, Louis Phillips, and my agent, Ivy Fischer Stone, for their encouragement. And finally, thanks and a great big hug to my son, Ken, who read a lot while I was working on this book.

I looked through many libraries and bookstores during the course of this project, but a couple of books stand out: *The Baseball Encyclopedia* for hard facts, and *The Great American Sports Book* for fun, off-beat reading.

Contents

Introduction	xiii
Auto Racing	1
Baseball	8
Basketball	121
Bicycling	146
Bowling	151
Boxing	157
Coaches and Officials	172
Fans	180
Football	197
Golf	216
A Grab Bag of Fame	232
Hockey	239
Horse Racing	267
Running	273
Soccer	289

Swimming   291

Tennis   302

Track and Field   309

Walking   334

Water Sports   340

Weightlifting   347

Winter Sports   348

Introduction

The future is now, and fifteen minutes in the limelight is as much as most anyone can expect. In sports, especially, this seems to be the name of the game. *One Shining Moment* captures the fleeting nature of fame that is the world of sports.

Traveling through the landscape of sports both major and minor, the reader will encounter here relatively well-known athletes as well as figures known only to long-suffering family members and trivia buffs. What follows combines the poignancy and pathos of human life itself. These are athletes, coaches, and fans glimpsed through the other end of the looking glass. Some are the stories of Everyman in striped socks and numbered jersey, the stories of you and me if we had been so lucky as to have enjoyed a brief moment of glory.

These pages feature the accomplishments of sports figures ranging from Lizzie Arlington, the first woman to sign a minor league baseball contract, to Louis Zamperini, the high-school miler who qualified for the

Olympic Games. There is an emphasis on baseball, but there are also pages aplenty about basketball, boxing, football, golf, hockey, running, swimming, tennis, and track and field, as well as a healthy sprinkling of other pastimes. The common denominator is that most of these athletes were plunged into the spotlight for a flickering moment before the fade to black.

Why do sports seem to matter to us as much as they do? "American spectators are frustrated athletes," once observed high jumper John Thomas. "In the champion, they see what they'd like to be." Perhaps it is this identification with athletes, this participation in their ups and downs that is unlike so much of the day's news—news that leaves us dehumanized, demoralized, and at a remove from the human experience. Sports have the capacity to generate empathy, the feeling of being present in the other guy's shoes. As the esteemed sportswriter Red Smith observed: "Sports is the real world. People we're writing about, they're suffering, living and dying, loving and trying to make their way through life just as bricklayers and politicians are." Or, as United States Supreme Court Chief Justice Earl Warren once put it: "I always turn to the sports page first. The sports page records people's accomplishments; the front page has nothing but man's failures."

Furthermore, many of us have enough experience in sports to appreciate what the athlete is undergoing. For instance, we may remember a time when, standing in the batter's box, we were almost able to count the stitches on the ball as it was leaving the pitcher's hand, then swinging and hitting the ball cleanly, solidly. The sense of the ball against the bat reverberating all the way down the arms to the shoulders and chest and torso and legs, then spinning around, dropping the bat and running to first base, eyes on the ball as it rises up and up, disappearing over the outfielder's head. All these long years later, there lingers that memory cascading through the body. From time to time it pops up when watching a ballgame or even when there doesn't seem to be any logical explanation. It is just a memory of one shining moment that falls into position unbidden. Another recollection, equally poignant, is the long walk back to the bench after striking out with the bases loaded.

Yes, an athlete's one shining moment may not be rolling out and throwing a touchdown pass, but dropping the ball in the end zone. The image in the mind's eye may be the undercard, the underbelly of success. As we reflect in the winter of our souls, when we have finally gained a mature perspective, we often realize that we can glean as much from our almosts, our might-have-beens, our what-ifs, our failures, as we can from our unbridled successes. Also, the passage of time tends to be kind. As Joe Cleary, a pitcher for the 1945 Washington Senators who left his only Major League appearance after only getting one out and with the highest ERA of all time, 189.00, once remarked years later, "I just don't think about it much anymore."

As to the lasting importance of the role of heroes in sports, whether of the 15-minute variety or longer term, it may shed some light to remember the words of the captain of the US hockey team that won the gold medal at the 1980 Winter Olympics.

"Hero?" pondered Mike Eruzione. "Vietnam vets

are heroes. The guys who tried to rescue our hostages in Iran are heroes. I'm just a hockey player."

Whether flashes in the pan, the proverbial cup of coffee, or someone who boasts a long illustrious career—it all matters little when you get right down to brass tacks. For even victory, as A. E. Housman reminds us, represents "The garland briefer than a girl's."

As great as he was, the Irish runner Eamonn Coghlan could sign on as a symbol for the need to try hard again and again. Although holding the indoor mile world record, he never won a medal at the Olympic Games. At the 1976 Olympics, he was fourth in the 1,500; at the 1980 Olympics, he was fourth in the 5,000; at the 1984 Olympics, he could not compete because of a stress fracture; and at the 1988 Olympics, he finished twenty-eighth out of 30.

"I can hold my head up high, I think, for the rest of my life and say I really tried," Coghlan mused at the end of his career. "I tried honestly. I tried fairly. I had a tremendous life out of my sport, but it wasn't to be. I went to the Olympic Games because that's what it's all about. Making the effort . . . being a sportsman . . . being a true sportsman."

Eamonn Coghlan had a beloved high-school track coach, Gerry Farnan. Coghlan had visited his coach's grave several times before finally reading the epitaph:

"Don't quit when you're beaten. Fight back to an even more glorious victory. Not only in competition, but in life."

And that's what a shining moment is really all about.

Auto Racing

"Racing is like smoking. It gets into your blood and you have to carry on."
—Jim Clark, English racer

On September 7, 1896, at the Rhode Island State Fair in Cranston, Rhode Island, **A. H. Whiting** rode to victory on the five-lap mile-long dirt track. Driving a Riker electric car at an average speed of 24 miles per hour, Whiting completed the course in just over five minutes to edge out the seven others, six of whom were driving gasoline-powered engines.

Long before there was a 24-hour race at Daytona, the team of **Joe Brown** and **John Archfield** drove an Autocar for one night and day on May 25, 1907, to win the Endurance Derby at Point Breeze in Philadelphia. The winners completed a total of 791 miles at an average speed of 33 miles per hour.

On February 12, 1908, six cars wended their way out of Times Square in New York and headed west. A boat took them across the Pacific and then the race continued across Manchuria and Siberia to Germany and finally Paris. The winner was an American team driving a four-cylinder **Thomas Flyer**, who completed the journey in 170 days.

Nineteen-year-old **Blanche Stuart Scott** became the first woman to attempt to drive across the United States by herself when she started out in an automobile on May 16, 1910. Scott completed her journey 109 days later, on September 2.

The first women to cross the US on a motorcycle were the team of **Adeline Van Buren** and **Augusta Van Buren**. Vrooming out of New York City on July 5, 1916, the two sisters puttered into San Diego on September 12, 1916.

In 1927, **Violet Cordery** set out to become the first woman to drive an automobile around the world. Starting off in a three-liter Invicta, Cordery drove across five continents, 10,266 miles in all. Her average speed was an amazing 24 miles per hour.

On November 15, 1965, racing veteran **Craig Breedlove** thundered across the Bonneville Salt Flats in Utah in his jet-powered "Spirit of America" car to become the first man in history to achieve a land speed record of over 600 miles per hour. (Speed is clocked over one measured mile of the 12-mile course in both directions by the United States Auto Club and then averaged.)

Afterward, Craig invited his wife to challenge the women's land speed record of 270 miles per hour. Although **Lee Breedlove** had only experienced practice runs, she powered the 8,000-pound, 34-foot behemoth to a new woman's land speed record of 308.56 miles per hour.

On October 23, 1970, **Gary Gabelich** set a world land speed record of 622.407 mph in the revolutionary Blue Flame at the Bonneville Salt Flats in Utah. This broke the previous record of 600 mph set by Craig Breedlove.

Here is Gary Gabelich's account of what happened that day:

> I'm looking through a small window and can see five miles ahead and it looks like I can see the curvature of the earth, but it's a mirage. I'm in a world of my own and even though I try to remain calm, the adrenaline starts pumping and I'm self-hypnotized. I push the throttle to the floor and my head is forced back. No longer is it man and machine. I'm part of the Blue Flame.

Gabelich's Blue Flame was 38 feet long. From the ground to the top of the tailfin, it measured eight feet, and there were two 12-inch stabilizers on each side. Powered by a rocket engine similar to the one that landed men on the moon, it used a fuel mixture of liquefied natural gas and hydrogen peroxide.

"I can see the markers," recalled Gabelich, "even though within 22 seconds I've gone from zero to six hundred and fifty miles per hour. My oxygen mask is tightly fastened, but my hearing goes completely at six hundred. I smell the heat of the engine and the heat of the wires.

"It is six hundred and thirty at the measured mile and I become more confident than ever that I am going to break Craig Breedlove's mark. At the halfway point, it's six hundred and fifty and I'm all out of fuel, which is the way it's supposed to be. I'm pulling seven Gs and the blood seems to be rushing to the top of my head like a waterfall.

"I release the chute and begin to brake at one hundred and fifty mph and almost immediately I pitch forward from seven Gs to four Gs and I feel the straps on my harness tearing at my shoulders. I turn off the cameras, the tape recorder, everything. It's unreal, fantastic."

"In company with the first lady ever to qualify for the Indianapolis 500 Mile Race," announced Tony Hullman, the owner of the speedway, "Gentlemen, start your engines." And they were off—32 gentlemen and one lady, **Janet Guthrie**. It was a first. And firsts don't always go smoothly. Just being there was the main event. As Woody Allen once said, "Life is eighty-five percent just showing up."

Guthrie had passed her rookie test in 1976 with checkered flags by covering 50 miles at speeds of over 170 miles per hour. But during the qualifying trials her car developed mechanical problems and she had to drop out.

On May 7, 1977, Guthrie was back again, establishing the fastest time of the day, 185.6 miles per hour.

Three days later, she beat that with a 191 but lost control on a turn and her Lightning-Offenhauser was badly damaged. Back on the track in time for the final weekend of qualifying on May 22, Guthrie recorded a four-lap average of 188.404.

"It was certainly the most significant accomplishment of my career," said a relieved Guthrie. "I think a lot of drivers will tell you that making the show here is such an achievement that the race itself is almost an anticlimax."

After just sixteen laps of the Memorial Day race, Ms. Guthrie rolled in for a pit stop. There was something wrong, terribly wrong. Fuel was spilling into the tub and into her bucket seat. Her driving suit was dark with ethanol. Not only was this uncomfortable, it was extremely dangerous. Fireproof suits soaked in fuel do not ward off flames. The crew washed out the tub and seat and sprayed her suit with water. After a fill-up Guthrie was back on the track. But soon she was back in the pits again. The mechanics worked furiously on the racer, trying this, trying that.

But then, Guthrie wasn't the only one with problems. Former champion Johnny Rutherford was already out of the race after only twelve laps. Still, it was a difficult situation for Janet Guthrie.

Back out on the track, back in the pits. Back out on the track, back in the pits. In all, Ms. Guthrie tried six times.

"My mind was pretty well into the race," explained Guthrie. "You have to do whatever is needed as long as there is still a chance to run." Eventually, however, she and the crew made the difficult but inevitable decision to give up any dreams of a checkered flag. Fixing the valve seal was too major a repair.

How did Janet Guthrie view her accomplishment of being the first woman to race at the Indy 500? Was it one small step for Janet Guthrie, or one giant step for womenkind?

"I don't think I had to prove anything," explained Ms. Guthrie. "I think it's a tremendous accomplishment for any driver to drive at Indianapolis." Spoken like the true race car driver that she is and then some. The following year Janet Guthrie became the first woman to finish the 500, placing ninth out of 33.

In December 1979, **Stan Barrett** broke the sound barrier on land, the first time this had ever been accomplished. Driving a three-wheel vehicle propelled by a rocket engine and a Sidewinder missile, Barrett reached a speed of 739.666 miles per hour on the dry lake bed at Edwards Air Force Base in California.

Derrike Cope began his sports career hoping to latch on as a catcher in the majors, until a collision at home plate put an end to that dream. Next he turned to race car driving. His first Winston Cup race was in 1982 at Riverside Raceway, and by 1986 he was racing full-time. Although he can brag that he has been a rookie of the year twice (NASCAR Late Model in '80 and Winston West in '84), the wins have been long in coming. His big one was on February 18, 1990, in the Winston Cup Daytona 500. Interestingly, he only led four laps (54, 180, 194–195), until the final one. With only two laps to go, Dale Earnhardt's car blew a tire. Cope surged into the lead and held off Terry Labonte to the finish line. For leading the two hundredth lap to the checkered flag, Cope captured $188,000.

Baseball

"Never win 20 games, because then they'll expect you to do it every year."
—Billy Loes, Brooklyn Dodgers pitcher

Here is a brief glint of glory, not for an individual but for baseball in general. The year 1947 is usually credited with being the turning point for the entry of African Americans into organized baseball. But on July 9, 1871, a game was held before a crowd of 500 between the **Uniques**, a black team and the Alerts, a white team. According to an article in the *San Francisco Chronicle* dated July 23, the "first time that a colored club engaged in a game with a nine of white players was July 9 in Chicago. . . . The play was creditable on both sides and the contest quite exciting and close throughout. The colored boys won the game by one run, the score standing 17–16."

In 1878, **Bud Fowler** became the first African American to be paid for playing for a white team when he played second base for a team in New Castle, Pennsylvania. Fowler played for over a score of teams in a career that lasted over 30 years.

* * *

The first no-hit game on record took place in the college ranks between Princeton and Yale on May 29, 1875. Here's a recap of the pitching performance of **Joseph McElroy Mann** as it appeared in the *New York Mercury*:

The game between the Princeton and Yale clubs in New Haven yesterday was one of the finest of the season. Mr. Mann's pitching for the Princeton nine was so effective that the Yales did not make a single base hit. The Princetons won by a score of 3 to 0. Woods and Duffield of the Princetons particularly distinguished themselves, the latter taking several beautiful flies after hard runs.

On July 28, 1875, **Joe Borden** of the Philadelphia Whites pitched the first no-hitter in pro baseball when he beat the Chicago White Stockings, 4–0, in the National Association (the first professional league). The next year, pitching for the Boston Red Caps in the National League, Borden tinkered with his pitching motion but still only managed a record of 11–12. But his experimentation with his pitching mechanics never made him consistently effective, and he wound up as the groundskeeper for the club.

Dave Rowe usually played in the outfield and sometimes in the infield. He seldom pitched, but that's where he achieved his fame. His lifetime record was 1–2, but it was the game he pitched on July 24, 1882, for the Cleveland Blues against the Chicago White Stockings that remains lodged in memory. At the end of the fourth inning, Rowe was behind 18–3. Chicago continued to score: two runs in the fifth, four runs in the sixth, once in the next inning, seven times in the eighth, and three in the final frame. Rowe had given up 29 hits and 7 walks. The result didn't sound like a baseball game: Chicago, 35, and Cleveland, 4.

Jack Rowe, the brother of Dave, played 75 games for the National League Buffalo Bisons in 1882. He did not strike out even once in his 308 at-bats.

The record for the most wins for a team starting off a season is 20. And the man who began this streak for the St. Louis Maroons of the Union Association was **Charlie Hodnett**. It took place on April 20, 1884, a rainy opening day with Hodnett on the mound. Charlie completed six innings before the rain halted the game, but it was enough for the win. Hodnett went on to a 12–2 record that year (he was 2–2 the previous year) and a 2.01 ERA. Unfortunately, an ulcerated foot brought his career to a premature end.

Another outstanding achievement from the year 1884 sometimes goes quite unnoticed. It was then that the color barrier was broken in the major leagues. Thirty-five years before Jackie Robinson was born, there was **Moses (Fleet) Walker** of Mt. Pleasant, Ohio. Walker played catcher for the Toledo Blue Stockings of the American Association, the rival of the National League.

The well-educated Fleet Walker had studied at

Oberlin College for three years and the University of Michigan Law School for one. It was in 1881, while at Oberlin, that Walker became the first black athlete to play college varsity baseball. In college as well as the majors, Walker was popular with most of the fans and his teammates. But not all. He was not well received when Toledo played in Louisville, Kentucky, and Richmond, Virginia. As Adrian "Cap" Anson of Chicago put it: "Gentlemen do not play baseball with niggers." Toledo's own star, Tony Mullane, was also difficult. The switch-hitting, ambidextrous pitcher, who played every position except catcher, once admitted that Walker was "the best catcher I ever worked with, but I disliked a Negro and whenever I had to pitch to him I used to pitch anything I wanted without looking at his signals." Even so, the barehanded catcher was able to throw baserunners out. Walker was batting .263 after 42 games when he broke a bone and was later released. Walker never made it back to the majors, but he was part of the first African-American battery when he caught pitcher George Stovey when they played for the Newark Little Giants in 1887. Walker also caught for Syracuse when they won the International League championship in 1889.

The second African American to appear in the Major Leagues, Fleet Walker's brother **Welday Wilberforce Walker**, also played in five games for the Toledo Blue Stockings in 1884. When the Ohio State League issued their official ban in 1888, Walker protested with these words: "There should be some broader cause—," he wrote, "lack of ability, behavior, and intelligence—to bar a player, rather than his color."

Fourteen-year-old **Fred Chapman** from Little Cooley, Pennsylvania, got his big chance to pitch in the major leagues in 1887. Going five innings for Philadelphia in the American Association, Chapman gave up eight hits and two walks and was saddled with a 7.20 ERA; however, he did manage to strike out four batters. Although he never pitched another game in the majors, Fred Chapman lives on as the youngest player ever to play in the major leagues. (Joe Nuxhall, who was 15 years old when he pitched his first game for the Cincinnati Reds, was the youngest player in the twentieth century.)

After a sterling minor league record of 27 wins, **Bumpus Jones** started the last game of the 1892 season for the Cincinnati Reds and threw a no-hitter. The next year when the pitching distance was moved from 50 feet to 60 and a half feet, Jones could not adjust and managed only a 1–4 record and a 10.19 ERA.

Bill Hawke was only a so-so pitcher for the Cardinals and the Orioles, but on August 16, 1893, he became the first pitcher to hurl a no-hitter from the present-day distance of 60 and a half feet. After Hawke's 5–0 victory over Washington, there would be the longest drought in modern-day baseball history—over four years before the next no-hitter.

* * *

Danny Friend was a 32–29 pitcher for the Chicago Colts for four years in the 1890s, but it is what he did or didn't do on August 30, 1897 that sticks in the craw. The New York Giants were ahead, 7–5, as the ninth inning began. Colts' manager and first baseman Cap Anson was thrown out of the game for arguing too vociferously about the growing darkness. In the top of the ninth, the Colts scored five runs. Because Anson was out of the game, the left fielder came in to play first and a player was needed to play left. Friend was selected. The crowd started to laugh as soon as he took the field. Friend had already showered and was wearing a bathrobe. The Giants manager, Bill Joyce, argued about his not being in uniform, and in the delay night fell. It was too late to continue, so the score went back to 7–5 in favor of the Giants.

In 1898, a young woman who went by the name of **Lizzie Arlington**—it might have been improper to use her real name, Elizabeth Stride—appeared as a pitcher in the Class A Atlantic League. She was the first woman to sign a professional baseball contract, a contract that paid her $100 a week.

On July 2, 1898, Lizzie Arlington pitched four innings for the Philadelphia Reserves in an exhibition game. On the mound she gave up six hits and three unearned runs. At the plate she managed two hits off Mike Kilroy, who had pitched four games in the majors some years earlier.

"For four or five innings," wrote Ed Barrow, the president of the league and future head of the New York Yankees, "she had plenty of stuff and control. She knew all the fundamentals of the game, having been taught by a fellow townsman, old Jake Stivetts, who pitched many years in the National League in the 1890s." (Happy Jack Stivetts, a power pitcher, won 35 games for Boston in 1892.)

In her next outing on July 5, 1898, Arlington pitched the last inning of a regulation game for Reading versus Allentown. As was reported in the *Reading Eagle*:

> Miss Arlington was put in in the 9th when Reading was 5 tallies to the good. Joe Delahanty, the first batter to face her, fouled to Heydon. Lyons shoved a little grounder to the female twirler, who threw him out at first. Seagrave and Jim Delahanty made safe cracks and Boyle walked. With the bases full, Cleve gave Newell a foul. "Good for Lizzie," shrieked the crowd.

Lizzie Arlington had performed well. As the newspaper account went on to state: "She went about it like a professional, even down to expectorating on her hands and wiping her hands on her uniform." But attendance had not increased sufficiently, so the team could not justify her high salary. Lizzie was let go. Although her short stint in the minors was over, this first woman to play men's professional baseball continued to play baseball for women's teams for many years.

Minor league teams would wisely employ local high school heroes to draw more fans to the ballpark. One such local boy was 15-year-old **Willie McGill** of

Evansville, Indiana. On July 26, 1889, playing in the Central Inter-State League, McGill threw a no-hitter as the Evansville nine blanked the team from Davenport, Iowa, 3–0.

Canadian and future major leaguer **Nig Clarke** smacked eight home runs in as many at-bats as Corsicana sank Texarkana by the outrageous score of 51–3. (Some telegraph operators thinking the news to be a mistake transmitted the score as 5–3.) This tall tale, even by Texas League standards, was played out on June 15, 1902. By the by, Nig Clarke only hit six home runs in nine seasons in the Major Leagues.

Jim St. Vrain was a pitcher on the 1902 Chicago Cubs. For his one year in the majors, St. Vrain had a won-lost record of 4–6 and an ERA of 2.08. He issued 25 walks, registered 51 strikeouts, and gave up 88 hits. But what he absolutely couldn't do was get a hit himself. Whenever St. Vrain was at the plate: Nothing. Nada. Zip. He couldn't even get a piece of the ball. Swish . . . swish . . . swish. Every time.

Since St. Vrain threw lefthanded, manager Frank Selee wondered one day, why did he bat righthanded? Why not bat lefthanded? It couldn't be any worse, he reasoned. So the next time up, St. Vrain stood on the other side of the batter's box. And wouldn't you know, he hit a grounder out to Honus Wagner. The great Pirate shortstop fielded it cleanly, then stopped, and looked at the runner. Jim St. Vrain was running to third base. After a few seconds of hesitation, the Flying Dutchman threw to Kitty Bransfield at first.

In a subsequent at-bat, St. Vrain made contact with the ball, this time running to first base. He even got three hits, ending his career with an average of .097.

It was the second of a doubleheader in the heat of a July day in a 1903 Minnesota summer and the town teams of Benson and Willmar were heading into extra innings. In the top of the tenth, Benson scored a run. Now it was up to Willmar. **Thielman**, the pitcher for Willmar, went up to the plate and stroked a single. The next batter, O'Toole, hit the ball past the center fielder. As O'Toole was rounding second he saw an exhausted Thielman crumpled on third base. O'Toole picked up their star pitcher and carried him home, letting Thielman's foot drag across the plate before his own. Then he placed Thielman gently on the grass. A doctor climbed down from the stands to bend over the silent form. "This man," the doctor said, "died back there on third base. His heart broke down under the strain."

Thielman may have been dead, but his run counted and Willmar had won the game.

The youngest player ever in organized baseball was nine-year-old **George Diggins**. Actually, he was the mascot for the Concord, New Hampshire minor league team in the New England League. But on June 25, 1904, when one player was injured and another was kicked out, there weren't enough players to field a team. Little Georgie was needed in order to have nine players. No one objected on the team from Lowell, Massachusetts, so George Diggins played three innings. In his only at-bat he struck out.

* * *

On September 1, 1906, **Joe Harris** was on the mound for the Boston Red Sox versus Jack Coombs of the Philadelphia Athletics. The two rookie righthanders battled 24 innings—the longest game ever in the American League—until Colby Jack (the Athletics acquired him off the Colby campus in Maine) won 4–1. Harris had more than one heartbreak that year. There were no fewer than eight shutouts pitched against the Red Sox when Harris was on the mound. He not only lost 14 in a row but ended the year with a 2–21 record. He finished his career with a 3–30 record.

How many pitchers throw a shutout in their first major league appearance? That's what **Tex Neuer** did in his debut for the 1907 New York Highlanders. In fact, Neuer hurled three shutouts in the six games he played in, and departed the scene with a 4–2 record and a 2.17 ERA. He never pitched in the Major Leagues again.

Long before the All-American Girl's Professional Baseball League during World War II, there was **Alta Weiss** of Ragersville, Ohio. The daughter of a doctor, Alta started playing baseball with boys at 14; and in 1907, at the age of 16, she made her debut as a pitcher for a men's semiprofessional team called the Vermilion Independents. Going five innings, Ms. Weiss gave up five hits and one run. When she wasn't on the pitcher's mound, she played first base. Vermilion won the game that day 4–3 in 11 innings.

As reported the next day in the *Lorain Times Herald*, "Miss Weiss can easily lay claim to being the only one who can handle the ball from the pitcher's box in such style that some of the best semi-pros are made to fan the atmosphere."

Weiss's next seven outings led to the game with the Vacha All-Stars of Cleveland. In this game she was spellbinding. "She is there with chimes and bells. In the second inning she showed up best. She struck out the first batter. The next man drove a sizzling liner at her. She made a catch that increased the cheers three-fold. It was a beauty that would do credit to any pitcher. Then she fanned the next batter, retiring the side."

In 1908 her father, Dr. George Weiss, bought a base-ball team and called it the Weiss All-Stars. His daughter fell into a routine of pitching five innings and then playing first base the rest of the game. If she had a weakness it was at bat.

Alta Weiss became the first woman ever to help put herself through medical school by playing baseball. After becoming a doctor of medicine in 1914, she hung up her bloomers and hung out her shingle.

On July 9, 1909, Cleveland shortstop **Neal Ball** had one transcendent inning in a game against the Boston Red Sox. After catching an Amby McConnell line drive for the first out, Ball touched second to get Heine Wagner of Boston, who had strayed too far off the bag for the second out, and tagged Jake Stahl still coming from first for the third out—for the first unassisted triple play in the major leagues. As if that weren't enough, that same inning Ball hit an inside-the-park home run. This was one extraordinary inning for a player who had topped all shortstops the previous year by committing 80 errors and who hit only four home runs during his entire seven-year career.

The most outstanding thing that **Larry LeJeune** did on a major league field came on October 12, 1910. It was then, at a Field Day exhibition in Cincinnati, that LeJeune uncorked a throw of 426 feet 9 inches. Although he was a batting champion five times in the minors, LeJeune played only 24 games in the majors.

On July 19, 1911, **Walter Carlisle** made an unassisted triple play. This was unusual enough, but Carlisle was an outfielder. Playing in the Pacific Coast League for Vernon, Carlisle was playing a very shallow center field. With men on first and second, he caught the ball, touched second, and ran to first to tag the bag before the runner could scurry back.

One of the most fascinating of all the mascots was a man from Marion, Kansas, who showed up one July day in 1911 at League Park when the Giants were playing in St. Louis and announced to manager John McGraw that he was destined to become a great pitcher for the Giants. He had been told by a fortune-teller that if he could pitch for them, they could win the pennant that year. McGraw immediately realized that this 31-year-old man, **Charles Victor Faust**, was not mentally balanced; he let him try out anyway. Faust's pitches were so soft that McGraw could catch him barehanded, and when the man from Kansas came up to bat and hit a soft grounder, the infielders misplayed the ball to first, and second, and third, and home, allowing Faust to slide across the plate before the ball arrived. In some circles Faust would be institutionalized, but McGraw put a Giants' uniform on him.

The Giants went on to win four straight from St. Louis. The Giants left on a road trip, leaving Faust behind. The Giants started to lose. McGraw had Faust join the team and the Giants started to win again.

Victory Faust, as he became known to the Giants' players, had become an important part of the team. He not only cheered from the sidelines, but he warmed up before games. As a matter of fact, McGraw even put him in to pitch in the ninth inning of two games when the games were out of reach for the other team. (The Giants had to get permission from the other team because Faust wasn't officially on the roster.) How did Victory Faust do? In the last game of the season, against the Dodgers, Faust pitched one inning, allowing one hit and no runs. And at the plate (the other team was in on the ruse, as there were already three outs), Faust was hit by a pitch. He stole second, he stole third, he scored. "Who's loony now?" he asked his laughing teammates. Indeed, John McGraw would write: "I give Charlie Faust full credit for winning the pennant for me—the National League pennant of 1911."

The Giants were also champions of the National League in 1912 and 1913. But eventually, Faust's luck wore off. In 1914, he wasn't well and wound up in a ward for the insane in a hospital in Portland, Oregon.

The next year, on June 18, 1915, Charles Victor Faust died there. The Giants finished in last place that year.

Playing in New York has always been a baptism of fire for ballplayers. It can be a trying experience, even for a player of the stature of Ty Cobb. On May 15, 1912, the Detroit Tigers were in New York for a game with the Highlanders at Hilltop Park. This matchup usually spelled a good game, but that day most of the tension seemed to be between the fans and the Tigers. By the fourth inning Cobb's chief heckler, Claude Leuker, had moved him to climb into the stands and beat him up. (It was reported that he had been calling Cobb a "half-nigger.") Cobb was not the only one to leave the field. Some of his other teammates also climbed into the stands. But it was Cobb who was ejected from the game by Umpire O'Loughlin.

"Everybody took it as a joke," said Cobb. "I was only kidding that fellow, and I frightened him to death, but I would not take from the United States Army what that man said to me, and the fans in New York cheered me to the echo when I left the field. I don't look for applause, but for the first time in my life I was glad that the fans were with me."

When President Ban Johnson of the American League heard of the incident, Cobb was suspended from baseball indefinitely. His teammates did not let him slip off by himself. Until their star was allowed to play, they vowed not "to ever wear the colors of the Detroit team again."

The *New York Times* sided with management: "The sole underlying cause is the growing resentment of all authority and discipline throughout the world. If the president of the American League expels the entire Detroit team for breach of contract he will do right."

For the game on May 18, the players assumed that the suspension would be lifted. When it wasn't, they refused to play. The Detroit management did not want to forfeit the game because it would cost them in those days the astronomical sum of $5,000. So they quickly drew up some one-day contracts and signed up players from St. Joseph's College in Philadelphia and a sandlot team called the Park Sparrows. Pitcher Allan Travers, center fielder Bill Leinhauser, third baseman Jack Smith, second baseman Jim McGarr, and left fielder Dan McGarvey were from St. Joseph's; right fielder Hap Ward, third basemen Billy Maharg and Ed Irvin, and shortstop Pat Meaney were the sandlotters; first baseman Joe Sugden and catcher Deacon McGuire were Tiger scouts. Each man made $10; the pitcher made $25. As one onlooker recalled: "Any ballplayer who could stop a grapefruit from rolling uphill or hit a bull in the pants with a bass fiddle was given a chance of going direct from the semi-pros to the Detroits and no questions asked."

Aloysius "Allan" Travers, a seminary student, took the mound for Detroit. It wasn't long before things got out of hand. The Athletics were bunting. (Anyone who has worked with young ballplayers knows how much time and effort has to go into learning how to handle bunts.) By the third inning several thousand fans out of the 20,000 at the ball park that day had unsuccessfully demanded a refund. For those who stuck around for the hour and forty-five-minute game—including the real Detroit team sitting in the upper deck—the Philadelphia third baseman had two teeth knocked out by a ground ball and the center fielder was knocked out by a fly ball to account for two of the Amateurs' nine errors. Travers served up 26 hits as the Philadelphia A's trounced the Detroit Amateurs, 24–2. He walked seven and struck out one. Not every brief exposure to fame ends in a shutout or a runner circling the bases.

Although Travers pitched a complete game, he allowed the most hits and runs in one ball game. He also wound up with a lifetime ERA of 15.75. (In his defense, 10 of those runs were unearned, and he was pitching against a team that had won the two previous World Series.) By game's end each player was given an additional $20, perhaps for having endured an afternoon of humiliation.

Ban Johnson wanted to put an end to the travesty and also prevent this team baseball strike from spreading to the rest of the league. He had no desire to allow a repeat of the Player's Revolt of 1890. Before their next game, in Washington on May 21, Johnson said he would ban every Detroit player from the game of baseball unless each paid a $100 fine and returned to the lineup. With Cobb's encouragement, each one did. By the date of their next game, May 26, Cobb had served his 10-day suspension. After paying his $50 fine, he was back in the outfield and Allan Travers was back to studying for the priesthood. But nothing will ever erase the Detroit Amateurs' day in the majors. As Yogi would say, you can look it up.

* * *

In 1912, **Bill Otis** got one hit for the New York Highlanders in 20 plate appearances, but even at the age of 100, he could remember it. It happened at Griffith Stadium in Washington on July 5, 1912. Walter Johnson was pitching and Otis tagged a line drive over second base. "I was very flattered to get a hit off him," recalled Otis of the long ago memory. "He was a great pitcher." Otis died nine days before reaching 101. He seemed to have no regrets.

George Shears gets only one line in *The Baseball Encyclopedia*. His appearance in only four games in 1912 contains none of the excitement that is in his letter to Roger Harris:

"The first time I was called in to pitch (I was a left-handed pitcher) was against the Philadelphia Athletics. They were leading the league. It was in the ninth inning, we were ahead 3 to 2. The bases were 'loaded,' no one out and with Home Run Baker at bat. The first pitch I made, Baker popped up to the second baseman. The next batter hit into a double play to end the game.

"My manager, Harry Wolverton, came running out to the mound and hugged me. The next day the New York papers heralded the new 'find' of the Highlanders. Soon after, I injured my pitching arm.

"The next year I was sent to Jersey City to see if I could work the soreness out of my arm. The first game I pitched there was against Baltimore. I was beaten 3 to 2 in 11 innings by a lefthanded pitcher named Babe Ruth. This was Babe's first year in baseball. I spent six or seven years in the minors after that."

* * *

In 1913, **Walter Malmquist** hit .477 for York in the Nebraska State League. This is the highest batting average in professional baseball. For purposes of comparison, Hugh Duffy hit .440 for Boston in 1894; Nap Lajoie hit .426 for Philadelphia in 1901; Ted Williams hit .406 in 1941. Unlike these three, however, Malmquist never made it to the majors.

Clarence Garrett was 2–2 for Cleveland in 1915. "The highlights of my career all happened in a minor league," confessed Garrett. "While at Madison, I pitched a doubleheader. Winning the first game 1–0 in 11 innings and the second game 4–1 in 9 innings, I struck out 20 and allowed 6 hits."

On June 17, 1915, pitcher **George Zabel** came off the bench and into a game between the Chicago Cubs and the Brooklyn Dodgers. When he entered the game there were only two outs in the first inning. Zip Zabel finally won the game for the Cubs in the nineteenth inning, 4–3. Zabel's eighteen-and-one-third-inning relief performance is the longest in major league history. The rest of his three-year career was a so-so 11–14.

Jack Nabors pitched from 1915 to 1917 for the Philadelphia Athletics and at one time had 19 straight losses. In fact, he lost a total of 25 games while only winning one. But he did win one. He did win one.

When a pitcher starts his first major league game any number of things may happen. But the final outcome of what happened to young **Henry Heitman** was nothing even the most seasoned of managers could have foreseen.

On July 27, 1918, the twenty-one-year-old Heitman took the mound for the Brooklyn Robins in a game against the St. Louis Cardinals. He got the first batter out. The next batter up hit safely. So did the third. The pressure was on as Heitman bore down on the fourth batter. Another hit. It was a time for adjustments, but can a manager or catcher settle down a rookie who is feeling vulnerable to the point of being incompetent? The fifth batter came to the plate. And yes, it was another hit, and then, Henry Heitman was out of the ball game with only one out. The Dodgers went on to lose; Heitman picked up the loss with an astronomical 108.00 ERA.

However, it was to be the only loss of Henry Heitman's career. He never returned to the ballpark. On the way home he stopped off at the recruiter's office and enlisted in the United States Navy. Perhaps his thinking was that if you're going to get swamped, it's better to do it in a boat.

Hank "Lefty" Thormahlen was 29–30 during his six-year career, but it is for a game he pitched in 1918 that he is mainly remembered. With a no-hitter going for the Yankees into the ninth inning, Lefty had only one out to go when he weakened, giving up two singles and a walk. Well, Lefty still had the shutout. The next batter up lofted a pop fly to Ping Bodie in the outfield. Bodie dropped it and Thormahlen lost the game 1–0.

Johnny Jones appeared in a total of 5 games and had a 1–0 record. He saved a 1–0 New York Giants victory in the eleventh inning on July 4, 1919. The next year for the Boston Braves he did something even grander in an exhibition game. "I struck out Babe Ruth with the bases full, the first time I ever saw him."

On May 1, 1920, baseball history was made. It began quietly enough with the Brooklyn Robins' **Leon Cadore** facing the Boston Braves' **Joe Oeschger** through a scoreless first four innings. Brooklyn scored in the fifth; Boston scored in the sixth. And that was it. There was no more scoring, even though they continued inning after inning.

"I think the most critical inning for me was the seventeenth," said Oeschger. "The Dodgers filled the bases with only one out, but a great play by Hank Gowdy saved my neck." The ball was hit to Oeschger, who threw it to the plate for one out; Gowdy, the catcher, threw to first, but it pulled Walter Holke off the bag, who threw it back to the catcher. "Hank took the throw at full reach, flung himself bodily across the baseline, and tagged [Ed] Konetchy out as he came barreling in. This brought the small crowd to its feet with a cheer that could be heard to the Charles River."

After 26 innings, three hours and 50 minutes, the game was called because of darkness. Cadore had faced 95 batters, given up 15 hits, and pitched 20 consecutive scoreless innings. Oeschger had faced 85 batters, given up nine hits, and pitched 21 straight scoreless innings, the major league record.

"I don't say I wasn't a little tired after those 26 innings," continued Oeschger, "but I have been more fatigued in some nine-inning games, when I got into a lot of jams. They are what wear a pitcher out. There weren't too many tight situations in this long game."

Cadore was 68–72 during his 10-year career; Oeschger was 82–116 during his 12-year career. But nothing else they ever did rivaled the historic significance of the game neither of them won nor lost. In honor of that moment a New York haberdashery had placed in its window "the longest tie in history." On the cravat was stamped the batteries and the score inning by inning.

Cliff Brady played second base for the Boston Red Sox in 1920. In 53 games he had 41 hits in 180 at-bats. It wasn't a distinguished career, but it did include a memorable moment, his first game in St. Louis, a moment that he describes in a letter to sports collector Roger Harris.

Tommy Connolly, who umpired the first game in the American League on April 24, 1901 (and had a career that lasted 58 years), believed in helping young players and he showed it in Cliff Brady's first game in St. Louis. A local undertaker by the name of Mr. Donnelly was in the habit of picking up the umpires at the hotel and taking them to the ballpark. Mr. Donnolly was also honoring Cliff Brady, a local boy who had made it to the big leagues, by presenting him with a suit and a bouquet. Wanting to repay a favor, Connolly instructed the catcher to give Brady something good to hit.

"The catcher told me a fastball, and I took it and then he said it again and it was a good one and I got a base hit and you would have thought the ump got the hit," wrote Brady. "This is the truth."

* * *

There was another catcher in the 1920s who caught two of the famous pitchers of the day, and this was a woman, **Mabel Schloen**. While playing for the East Rutherford Cubs, Schloen caught Walter Johnson for three innings of an exhibition game at Fenway. Later, with the Eastern League Providence Grays, she caught Rube Marquard. The versatile Mabel Schloen was in vaudeville, too. One of her routines poked fun at baseball.

Claude Noel was a pitcher for Marshfield in the Wisconsin Valley Baseball League. In 1921, Noel threw two no-hitters with only two days rest between games. When the St. Louis Browns got wind of this, they immediately signed him to a contract. The Browns must have had second thoughts about their new player, though, for Claude Noel never threw a pitch in the major leagues.

Southpaw **Bert Cole** played for the Detroit Tigers from 1921 to 1925 before moving to Cleveland during the 1925 season. In 1927, he pitched for the White Sox. In his six-year career, he was 28–32.

But it is one pitch in particular that Cole recalls. "I threw the pitch that the great Babe Ruth hit for the longest home run, traveling over the flag pole in center field," wrote Cole. "At that time it was over five hundred feet to the flag pole in center and the Babe whacked it over the top of the pole, which was ninety feet high, an estimated drive of six hundred feet."

Byron "Rube" Yarrison fooled a few batters with his natural sinker for the Philadelphia Athletics in 1922

(1–2) and for the Brooklyn Robins in 1923 (0–2). "The one outstanding moment in my career recalls the time Mr. Mack asked me to pitch the last inning versus the Yanks. Without even warming up, I pitched to Meusel, Ruth, and I don't recall the other player. Anyway, all three of them I got out—two to third base and a fly to right field. Connie said, "Rube, you pitch better if you don't warm up."

In 1922, a rookie pitcher named **Hub Pruett** seemed to cast a spell over Babe Ruth. How did this man whose nickname was "Shucks" (that was as salty as his language ever got) come to dominate one of the greatest hitters in the game?

Pruett certainly had an inauspicious beginning. As a kid he was assigned to the pitcher's mound because his throws would sail off target from other positions. When he was a student-athlete at the University of Missouri, he only threw a curve and a screwball— nothing that ever made him think he might be major league material. Basically, Hub wanted to make money so he could go to medical school. However, in his first year with St. Louis, in 1922, the 5 foot 10, 165-pound southpaw helped the Browns challenge the Yankees for the pennant. And if his stats against Ruth in 1922 were representative of his whole career, Hub Pruett would be bound for Cooperstown.

On May 22, Pruett in relief struck out Ruth once and walked him. On June 10, again in relief, Pruett struck out Ruth. In his first start against the Yanks on June 12, Pruett walked the Bambino, then struck him out three times. On July 12, Pruett retired Ruth on a ball hit back to the box and struck out Ruth three times, the last time with the bases loaded. On August 25, Pruett again fanned Ruth with the bases loaded. On September 17, Pruett walked Ruth, struck him out, then gave up a home run and a single. Aw, shucks! The spell of his screwball seemed to have been broken. Still and all, Pruett had held the most feared batter in baseball to a batting average of .158. (Ruth batted .315 overall for 1922.) Even though the Bronx Bombers went on to win the pennant, St. Louis had given the Yanks a scare.

The next season the Brownies' lefty struck out Ruth three times and gave up a homer and a walk. In 17 official at-bats, Hub Pruett had struck out Ruth 13 times. After that his record against Ruth was lackluster, as was his overall record, a career 29–48 with a 4.63 ERA. Eventually, Hub Pruett hung up his spikes in favor of a stethoscope around his neck. Upon running into Ruth some years later, Pruett expressed his appreciation. "I want to thank you for putting me through medical school. If it wasn't for you," Pruett said, "no one would have heard of me."

Charlie Robertson was pitching for the Chicago White Sox on April 30, 1922, in only his third start in the major leagues. His opponent that day at Navin Field in Detroit was the potent Tigers. That was the year Ty Cobb batted .401 and Harry Heilmann hit .356. Indeed, the whole lineup had an average of .306. It was a tough team to play, but the twenty-six-year-old rookie righthander was more than up to the challenge. The Tigers couldn't hit him all day. They kept complaining that he was throwing a spitter, but umpire Dick

Nallin couldn't find anything wrong with the ball. In fact, in the ninth inning player-manager Cobb insisted Nallin go out to the mound and inspect the rookie's uniform. After Nallin found nothing suspicious, Robertson resumed with the help of a diving catch from left fielder Johnny Mostil in setting the Tigers down in order.

Charlie Robertson had thrown the sixth no-hitter in major league history, the third in the twentieth century, and the first ever on the road. After such high promise, Robertson had arm problems for the next six years, and left the game in 1928 with a record of 49–80.

On August 14, 1922, a young woman named **Lizzie Murphy** filled in at first base for an all-star team made up of American Leaguers. Their opponent was the Boston Red Sox. It was a charity game, but the third baseman wasn't feeling charitable. When a sharp grounder was hit to him, he held it for a few moments, then fired a bullet to Murphy. She caught it without batting an eye and threw it around the infield. The third baseman was impressed. "She'll do," he said.

Six years later Murphy played for the National League All-Stars in another charity game. Not only was Lizzie Murphy the first woman to play in a major league exhibition game, she was also the only person to play for the all-star teams of each league.

Hank Hulvey was playing for Connie Mack's son Carl at Martinsburg, West Virginia, and doing so well in 1923 that Hulvey was sent up to see Carl's dad in

Philadelphia. Connie Mack asked the 24-year-old if he wanted a tryout. Certainly, he replied.

"Well, son, I'm glad to hear you're eager," said Mr. Mack. "We'll pitch you against the Yankees this afternoon."

"Connie Mack told me not to get excited about pitching against the Yankees," said Hulvey. "He said they were just human beings. I told him I'd just pitch 'em the way I would anybody. I was a little nervous, but I guess I didn't have enough sense to be scared."

Hulvey did just fine his one afternoon in the big leagues. He struck out Babe Ruth twice and had a 2–2 game when Ruth came up for the third time. The catcher called for a change-up. Hulvey didn't even have one, so he just threw a pitch slow.

"He knocked the ball out of the park. When I got back to the dugout, Connie Mack said, 'Don't worry, he does that to everybody.'"

The Yankees went on to win the game and Hank Hulvey went back to the minors, where he enjoyed a 21-game career.

In 1923, manager John McGraw of the Yankees wanted a counterbalance to The Sultan of Swat, Babe Ruth, and thought he had found it with **Moses Solomon**, "The Rabbi of Swat." Solomon had picked up that nickname while clouting 49 home runs in the Southwestern League earlier that year. The other goal was for Solomon to be a drawing card for more Jewish people to come out to the ballpark. Returning to his hometown, the outfielder certainly performed at the plate. In two games Moses Solomon cracked two singles and a double in eight times at bat for a lofty .375 batting average. But in the field he was a disaster, a liability in left or anywhere else. This good-stick, no-glove player was quickly given a one-way ticket back to the minor leagues.

Ernie Padgett played in only four games during his first year in baseball. But on October 6, 1923, this shortstop for the Boston Braves made only the fourth unassisted triple play in major league history. Padgett went on to play 267 more games spread out over five years, but he never again recaptured the excitement he generated during this one play his rookie year.

Dutch Levsen pitched for Cleveland from 1923 to 1928 and had a record of 21–26. But what really set Levsen apart was what happened on August 28, 1926. Levsen had started the game against Boston and four-hit the Red Sox for a 6–1 victory. But Levsen's teammates, George Burns and Joe Sewell, started kidding him about how he'd had it too easy. Perhaps it was because the game had only lasted an hour and twenty minutes. Whatever the reason, this got under Levsen's skin enough that he asked manager Tris Speaker if he could pitch the second game, too. In the second game Levsen four-hit Boston again in a complete game 5–1 victory that lasted an hour and thirty minutes. He did not have a strikeout in either game. It's a safe bet that this will be the last time a major league pitcher will have two complete game wins on the same day. Unfortunately, the next spring he hurt his arm and only won three more games.

Johnny Schulte played 192 games, mostly as a catcher, from 1923 to 1932 for the Browns, Cards, Phillies, Cubs, and Braves. Twice after he had been released, Schulte was sitting in the stands watching the game. Bill McKechnie of Boston needed a catcher and Schulte was enlisted to strap on the tools of ignorance (the nickname for the catcher's equipment). The other time, Joe McCarthy of Chicago had to ask Schulte to play catcher. "It paid to go to ball games," was how Johnny Schulte expressed it.

Carl Yowell was 3–4 for Cleveland in 1924–25. "Once I pitched one ball and won a game," Yowell said. As this lefthander nicknamed Sundown would have agreed, sometimes timing is everything.

"Big Ben." "Lefty." **Ben Shields** had the nicknames and the winning percentage (1.000) that legends are made of. But the 6–1, 195-pound southpaw didn't play much in the majors. In 1924, he appeared in only two games for the Yankees with no decisions. The next year, he started two games for the Bronx Bombers, went the whole nine innings, and won both. He also won another game he appeared in. The next time Shields appeared in the majors was for three games in 1930 in a Red Sox uniform. And then in 1931, Shields switched leagues and won one for the Phillies. And there you have it. Big Ben's perfect 4–0 record.

* * *

Mel Kerr scored one run in one game for the Cubs in 1925. But in 1926 he set a minor league record. "In one game I had ten putouts playing center field for Bloomington in the Three I League. This made *Ripley's Believe It or Not.*"

Ken Ash was 6–8 over four years first for the 1925 White Sox and then for the Reds from 1928 to 1930. But his most satisfying moment came on July 4, 1925, when he struck out the Yankees' Murderer's Row. "The 40,000 in Chicago gave me a standing ovation."

You would think if you turned an unassisted triple play, you'd have the spotlight to yourself. But not so for **Jimmy Cooney**, a shortstop in the 1920s. On May 30, 1927, this Cubs shortstop nicknamed "Scoops" snared Paul Waner's line drive, stepped on second to get brother Lloyd Waner, who had wandered off the bag, and tagged out Clyde Barnhart, who was barreling down from first. But the very next day, May 31, Detroit first baseman Johnny Neun snagged a line drive off the bat of Cleveland's Homer Summa, tagged out Charlie Jamieson before he could get back to first, and ran all the way to touch second before Glenn Myatt could scurry back to the bag. A single weekend had witnessed the executions of major league baseball's sixth and seventh unassisted triple plays.

Foster "Babe" Ganzel played in 23 games as an outfielder and a pinch hitter for the Washington Senators in 1927–28, posting a nifty batting average of

.311. But it was as a minor league player and manager that he left his mark. Once when he was managing Selma, the fans were getting on his case because his team seldom bunted. Just to show those hecklers, Ganzel had the first nine batters bunt. All reached base safely.

In his seven-year career for the Cards and Tigers beginning in 1927, **Heinie Schuble** had 935 at-bats. But it was one of his first trips to the plate in 1927 that mattered the most to him. He and his wife were married on home plate his rookie year.

Overton Tremper played 46 games for the Brooklyn Robins in 1927 and 1928, a time that is sometimes referred to as the Dark Ages for the team that became the Dodgers. Wilbert Robinson was managing a lot of older players to a lot of second-division finishes. But the 21-year-old Tremper provided a breath of fresh air during a doubleheader in September 1928 when he woke everyone up with three singles, a double, and a triple. For the rest of his major league career he only had 15 more hits in 86 at-bats.

Bill Windle was a little-used first baseman from a wide spot in the road, Galena, Kansas. In 1928, he only played in one game for the Pittsburgh Pirates and he only came to bat one time. Windle whacked a double, ending the year with a 1.000 batting average.

The next year Windle went into a tailspin. Although he played in twice as many games, again this left-handed batter came to the plate only once and he struck out. His season ending average was .000. His career average, though, was a loftier .500.

Ray Boggs had been a teacher in Colorado and traveled in the summertime to Wyoming to play baseball. It was there that a friend of Rogers Hornsby saw Boggs and gave him a chance to play for the 1928 Boston Braves. Boggs appeared in five innings in four games in August and September, allowing two hits and seven bases on balls.

"My biggest thrill," said Boggs, "was when I came off the mound after pitching two innings of shutout ball to have George Sisler, who was playing first base for the Braves, tell me that my start in the majors was more impressive than his. I did not realize at that time he broke into the majors as a pitcher. Regrettably, a nerve at the point of my left shoulder blade took me out of baseball forever."

On April 27, 1929, pitcher **Clise Dudley** came to the plate for the Dodgers. It was the first time he had ever batted in the major leagues. On the very first pitch Dudley hit it for a home run. This was the first time any player had ever done this. For the rest of his five-year career, Dudley hit a dismal .185 and had an unspectacular record of 17–33.

Jim Mosolf played for the Pirates and the Cubs from 1929 to 1933, but it was as a pinch hitter for the Cubs that he made the record books. In a game with the Cardinals in 1933, "Dizzy Dean had sixteen strikeouts when I went up to the plate," remembered Mosolf. "I worked him to a full count, then he buzzed one past my ear, obviously too high. I started for first base but Ted McGrew, the umpire, called the pitch a strike." Ol' Diz had set a new major league record.

On Independence Day (July 4), 1929, former major leaguer **Roy Edward "Dizzy" Carlyle** launched a 618-foot rocket at the Emeryville Ball Park in California. Carlyle's blast is the longest home run ever actually measured. (Some of the other tape busters are merely calculated.)

Playing every infield position except shortstop during his 318 games spreading out from 1929 to 1934 for the Giants, Reds, and Cardinals, **Pat Crawford** hit a pinch hit home run in his first at-bat in the majors and hit another pinch hit homer with the bases loaded before a packed Polo Grounds, also in 1929. (He only hit seven more homers during his career.) Crawford's other personal highlights were playing with the Gas House Gang in 1934. Crawford's 11 pinch hits led the league and helped get the Cards into the World Series.

Harry Rosenberg appeared in nine games for the New York Giants in 1930. "My most exciting experience was when I threw my bat up in the air on a bad third strike," he recalled. "The umpire informed me that if the bat comes down I'm out of the ball game." It was easy to understand this outfielder's frustration. He struck out in four of his five at-bats.

* * *

In 1930, **Biff Wysong** started a single game for Cincinnati and lost. The next year he started two games and lost both. But in 1933, his last year in the majors, Wysong finally got his victory in relief. What a relief!

Jimmy Reese played second base with the Yankees ('30 and '31) and the Cardinals ('32). Of his 232 games there was one that stood out. "While with the New York Yankees, I walked up to bat with the bases full and one out. Bob Shawkey walked over to remind me not to hit into a double play, for a fellow by the name of Babe Ruth was the next batter. Well, a dream did come true! I hit the first ball pitched by Cleveland's great Wes Ferrell for a home run into the right field bleachers. We won the game, 7 to 6."

Jackie Mitchell (born Virne Mitchell) may not be a household name, but this pitcher was a real phenom. For starters, this pitcher struck out two of the greats of the New York Yankees in an exhibition game on April 2, 1931. The kicker is that Mitchell was a woman. Here's how it happened.

The seventeen-year-old Mitchell was a good basketball player, but she also knew how to throw a baseball, having learned from her next-door neighbor back in Memphis, Dazzy Vance. Indeed, she was good enough to garner the attention of Joe Engel, the manager of the Chattanooga Lookouts of the Southern Association. Engel signed her to a contract, and Mitchell became only the second woman to play on a men's professional baseball team. (See **Lizzie Arlington** to read about the first.)

The Yankees were down South for spring training, and Engel knew a good thing when he saw it. Why not have his club play the Bronx Bombers and have Mitchell face the meat of Murderer's Row? Engel thought his young pitcher had what it took. As her father once stated: "Her best asset is control. I've seen her strike out the side on nine pitched balls, every one over the middle of the plate." In any case, the prospect of a young woman versus the mighty Yankees was sure to sell a mess of tickets.

Even though Mitchell hadn't pitched since the previous season, she still felt confident about facing the Sultan of Swat. "Yes, I think I can strike him out," she said on the eve of the game.

A rain out created even more interest. When the two teams finally got together in Chattanooga, far from The House That Ruth Built, there were 4,000 people in the small rickety stadium. Clyde Barfoot started the game. After giving up a single and a double, the score was 1–0. Manager Bert Niehoff had seen enough. He signaled for Mitchell to enter the game to face the third batter in the lineup, Babe Ruth. The Bambino was not particularly happy about this turn of events. "I don't know what's going to happen if they let women in baseball," he had told a reporter. "Of course, they will never make good. Why? Because they are too delicate. It would kill them to play ball every day."

Mitchell wasn't exactly delicate, but at five-seven and 130 pounds, she was one of the smallest pitchers Ruth would face that year. Not to mention the only woman.

After a few warmups, Mitchell was ready. Ruth took

the first pitch for ball one. Mitchell's next pitch was right over the plate. Ruth swung and missed for strike one. The third pitch was also a swing and a miss. Mitchell was getting Ruth on her "drop pitch." Ruth dug in and took the fourth pitch for the third strike. He looked back at the umpire in disgust. Imagine, the Sultan of Swat, the future holder of the immortal record of 60 homers (before Maris, McGwire, and Bonds, of course) being struck out by a young woman.

As usual, Ruth was followed by the Iron Horse, Lou Gehrig. Mitchell struck out Gehrig, too. Three swings at three sinkers. Always the gentleman, Larrapin Lou calmly returned to the dugout.

The next batter up was Tony Lazzeri. Lazzeri fouled off the first pitch. After having thrown seven strikes to the heart of Murderer's Row, Mitchell's control suddenly vanished. The next pitch was a ball, as were the next three. With runners on first and second, Engel strode to the mound; Mitchell was through for the day. But what a day it had been.

"I don't expect to become a World Series hero," said Mitchell, her elation tempered by realism. "To tell the truth, all I want is to stay in professional baseball long enough to get money to buy a roadster."

The Lookouts lost to the Yankees that day 14–4, but Jackie Mitchell deserved something fast on four wheels for being the woman who struck out both Babe Ruth and Lou Gehrig.

It wasn't to be with the Lookouts, for Commissioner Kenesaw Mountain Landis saw to that by voiding her contract. Her next stop was with the Lookout Juniors, then playing exhibitions, and finally she appeared with the House of David baseball team from 1933 until 1937. Jackie Mitchell finally got her roadster.

Lou Polli may have been 0–2 in the majors (Browns in '32; Giants in '44), but he played a ton of AAA ball and in high school he really made some news. Playing for Goddard Seminary in Barre, Vermont, Polli pitched a 10-inning game and struck out a record 28 batters.

After his rookie year, lefty **Tony Freitas** was 12–5, but he had four years of losing records after that in the majors. In 1937 Freitas was back in the Pacific Coast League to stay. Even when Branch Rickey tried to lure him back to the majors, Freitas was a no-go. One of his best years was his last; in 1953, he was 22–9 for Stockton. In his very last game, the 45-year-old threw a shutout.

At the age of 39, **Alex McColl** was called up to Washington in 1933. After relieving a game, McColl got a chance to start. Here is what happened, in his own written account:

"The game went along zero and zero for five or six innings when we got two men on bases and me at bat. The pitcher was wide with two pitches and the coach on third gave me the hit sign. I doubled to left center. I drove in two runs and then scored myself. We won three to one.

"But the next morning I couldn't lift my arm. Pulled a chip of bone loose in my elbow so did not pitch again until the World Series, when I pitched two perfect innings in the second game in New York—seventh and eighth innings. We lost the series four to one to the Giants."

McColl had his arm operated on during the off-season and was 3–4 for the next year for the Senators. Then it was off to the minors until he retired at the age of 47.

John "Spike" Merena was only 1–2 in his career, but his one win was a big one. In September 1934, he shut out New York on four hits to win 5–0 and eliminate the Yankees from the American League pennant.

On July 31, 1935, **Kitty Burke**, a nightclub singer from Cincinnati, was heckling Cardinal outfielder Joe Medwick about his hitting ability. (Hardly the case as Muscles hit a Ducky Wucky .353 that year.) In any case Medwick invited her to bat, and she accepted. Grabbing Babe Herman's bat out of his hands, Kitty Burke went up to the plate to face Cardinal pitcher Paul Dean. Dean underhanded the ball; Burke slapped it between the mound and first; Dean fielded her grounder and easily beat her to first. Getting his bat back, as well as his at-bat, Herman for the one and only time in his life followed Miss Burke in the batting order. So, how long do you think it will be before the next woman comes up to bat in the major leagues?

Sometimes ballplayers date events in their lives the way the rest of us do. Where were you when Kennedy was shot? John Lennon? **Dino Chiozza** couldn't have had a much shorter cup of coffee. Two years out of high school he played two games at shortstop for the

1935 Phillies. One assist. No at-bats. But the time stuck in his mind. "I was present the day Babe Ruth played his last game," wrote Chiozza. "The last ball Ruth fielded was a triple by my brother Lou." (Lou Chiozza played six years in the majors, batting .277 in 616 games.)

Lefthanded pitcher **Harry Eisenstat** was 25–27 from 1935 to 1942 (Dodgers, Tigers, and Indians). But his biggest thrill was in 1938 while pitching for the Tigers against the Indians' Bob Feller. Feller set a record with 18 strikeouts, but Eisenstat won the ballgame, 4–1.

On September 7, 1936, **Frances Dunlop** filled in at right field for the Fayetteville Bears in a minor league game. No balls came her way in the outfield and she didn't get a hit, even though the young woman with the nickname of "Sonny" hit the ball sharply all three times at the plate. The final result of this game in the Class D Arkansas–Missouri League was Bears 5, Cassville 1.

Two years later, on August 8, 1937, it was the opposite story. Playing second base this time, Sonny handled four chances without a miscue and was one for two at the plate. The Bears lost 6–5 in extra innings.

After 52 games and 173 at-bats in 1936, rookie outfielder **Eddie Wilson** was hitting a high-flying .347 for the Brooklyn Dodgers when he was hit in the head by a pitch from the Pirates' Mace Brown. Wilson was through for the year with a fractured skull. The next year he tried to come back, but after 54 at-bats in 36 games he was hitting only .222. Sold to Portland, Wilson never appeared in another major league game.

Coming off a 20–10 year in 1936, righthander Johnny Allen of the Indians was having a spectacular year in 1937. Riding the crest of a 15–0 season, in Allen's next start he was matched with **Jake Wade** of the Tigers. "Whistlin' Jake" had never been much to shout about. He suffered control problems. (Basically, he had trouble getting people out; during his 668-inning career, Wade gave up 690 hits and 440 walks.) But it all came together in this one game against Allen. Wade one-hit Cleveland as he beat the Indians, 1–0. It was the high point of his career. Wade played six more years in the majors, putting together a career record of 27–40.

Olympic champions often don't pan out as professionals. Just such a case was that of **Bill Sayles**. Things looked good for the 6 foot 2, 175-pound righthander for a while, the only member of the 1936 gold-winning US baseball team to make the majors. Sayles won a game for the New York Giants in 1943, but then lost three. He was 0–0 in short stints for the Boston Red Sox and the Brooklyn Dodgers.

Fabian Gaffke was an outfielder from 1936 to 1942 for the Red Sox and the Indians. His biggest thrill was hitting a homer in his first at-bat. He hit six others among his 73 hits in 129 games.

Charley Suche has one of the shortest careers in the majors. For the 1938 Cleveland Indians, he pitched one and one-third innings, giving up four hits, three bases on balls, and striking out one. (Before arriving in Cleveland, he did have a no-hitter in the Eastern League.) "I can't lay claim to a lot of fame," said Suche, "however, I do own a 1.000 lifetime major league batting average." Suche was one for one.

Right-hander **Ed Cole** was 1–7 for the St. Louis Browns in 1938–39; his biggest thrill came earlier. On July 10, 1935, in Galveston, Cole pitched a perfect game, facing only 27 Tulsa batters. But it wasn't until there were two out in the ninth and Galveston teammate Bill McGhee hit an inside-the-park home run that Cole won the game.

After graduating from Holy Cross on June 9, 1938, **Bill LeFebvre** went to Fenway Park the next day. He signed a contract, was given a uniform, and sat on the bench with such future Hall of Famers as Jimmy Foxx and Lefty Grove. That day the White Sox were beating the Red Sox 12–1 and in the fifth inning Joe Cronin told LeFebvre to go warm up. Had he heard correctly? He had. The brand-new rookie got hit hard, giving up eight hits in four innings. But it was his first at-bat in the majors that really stands out.

"The first ball that was ever thrown to me in professional baseball I hit over the left field wall there in Fenway Park. I was a left-handed hitter—I swung a little late. Monty Stratton was a pretty good pitcher."

Cronin thought he might use LeFebvre as a pinch hitter, but after 10 games he was sent to the minors and didn't get back up to the Red Sox until the middle of

1939. LeFebvre started a game against Cleveland and won. In his second at-bat in the majors he almost hit another homer.

But after that beginning, it was back to reality. In a career that saw him in Boston in '38 and '39, and in Washington in '43 and '44, LeFebvre was only 5–5. But it was as a batter that he entered the record books. Pinch hitting in '44, LeFebvre was a league-leading 10 for 29. And his career batting average was .276.

"I look at these guys on TV now," said LeFebvre. "I know I was a better hitter than these guys." Maybe LeFebvre should've been a slugger.

Don Lang played 21 games in the infield for the Cincinnati Reds in 1938 and 117 games for the St. Louis Cardinals in 1948. "When I was with the Cardinals," Lang wrote, "I hit a home run when my mother and dad were in the stands—quite a thrill." Even though his two stays were 10 years apart, his batting averages were .260 and .269.

For some, playing in the majors is a dream come true. For others it can be a nightmare. When you hear **Bill Hoffman** describe his experience, it sounds like he might have awakened in a tangled, sweaty pile of sheets.

"I was scared to death," said Hoffman. "The place was packed. And I'd never faced hitters like those guys in my life. I didn't know what to do."

Bill Hoffman had been discovered by Gerry Nugent, the owner of the Phillies, playing in an industrial league in Philadelphia. He seemed like just the ticket to bolster the 1939 flagging Phillies pitching corps. Nugent signed Hoffman to a contract and two days later the raw southpaw was facing the New York Giants. Fifth inning, seven runs behind. Not the greatest of situations for a nervous beginner. Hoffman began with a wild pitch. Then another. And another. He was already in the record books for tying the wild pitch record. Then he worked the count to give up three straight bases on balls. Then he hit a batter. But to his credit Hoffman hung in there and finally got the Giants out. Before exiting the majors, Hoffman appeared in two more games. In six innings he had thrown seven bases on balls, eight hits, and one strikeout.

In 1939, **Harry O'Neill** played in one game in the majors, appearing as a catcher for the Philadelphia Athletics. He didn't even get a chance to come to bat. He also didn't have a chance to play in another game. Harry O'Neill was killed on March 6, 1945, at Iwo Jima.

"As a rookie in 1940 in spring training, I won the shortstop position over four other fellows," said **Ulysses A. Redd** of the Birmingham Black Barons in the Negro Leagues. "I will never forget the feeling on opening day in Birmingham when I heard my name called out before 50,000 people. 'And playing at shortstop and batting in the number two spot. . . .' We played a doubleheader and split with the Kansas City Monarchs. After that Sunday, it was all in a day's work. We played for the love of the game."

* * *

Willard Hershberger was a player who found his 15 minutes of fame intolerable. Playing behind the future Hall of Fame catcher Ernie Lombardi, Hershberger did well enough whenever he got into a game for the Cincinnati Reds. From 1938 to 1940, he played in 160 games and batted .316. But he had trouble dealing with the pressure. When Lombardi got injured during the 1940 season, Hershberger filled in but told manager Bill McKechnie he didn't like to start and felt he wasn't playing well. There was one game in particular that apparently haunted him. With the Reds ahead 4–3, Hershberger called for the wrong pitch for Harry Danning and the Giants' catcher hit a grand-slam home run. The Reds went on to lose the game.

On August 3, 1940, Willard Hershberger didn't show up for the first game of a doubleheader with the Boston Braves. Between games, a friend named Daniel Cohen was sent back to the Copley Plaza Hotel to check on him. Cohen found the body in the bathtub. Hershberger had cut his throat, the twentieth century's only major leaguer to kill himself during his playing days.

Except for one game, **Floyd Giebell** of the Detroit Tigers did not make much of a splash during his career. And that game was on September 27, 1940, when Giebell got the start for the Tigers in the crucial first game of the three-game season-ending series against the Cleveland Indians. Up to that point, the 30-year-old rookie sported a total of only 24 innings' experience and a 2–1 record. Now, he was facing the cream of the American League, Bob Feller, the flamethrower with a sizzling 27–10 record. As if that weren't pressure enough, the American League pennant was on the line. Detroit was leading the Indians by only two games, so they had to win at least one of their three games. When asked why he started Giebell, Detroit manager Del Baker replied: "I figured it would be to my best advantage to start Giebell against Feller, because if Feller is right, nobody beats him. So why waste a good pitcher trying?"

Well, that day Giebell was more than just a good pitcher.

Floyd Giebell pitched a complete game and shut out Feller and the Indians, 2–0. Of his six strikeouts, three were by Ben Chapman, who was a career .302 hitter.

"I was a control pitcher, more or less," explained Giebell, "and I could throw around 91–92 miles per hour. I came inside on Chapman just to show him a fastball, then I struck him out two of the three times on a slider on the outside of the plate."

Giebell's victory clinched the American League pennant for the Tigers. "As far as I'm concerned," said Giebell, "I think the Cleveland team overall was the best team in the league." (Even that day Feller had given up only three hits; unfortunately, one of them was a two-run homer to Rudy York.) But not on that day. Sometimes it's not so much what you do as when you do it.

Giebell hung on the next year, appeared in 17 games, but didn't come up with any wins. He finished out his career at 3–1, with a 3.99 ERA over 67 and two-thirds innings. Nothing much sparkles for Giebell except that gem of a game against Feller.

*   *   *

Outfielder **Don Manno** played in only 25 games for Boston (the Bees in 1940 before they became the Braves in 1941). His first game, though, was the one to remember. Playing in Ebbets Field, Manno came up to bat in the eighth inning with the bases loaded. Bingo! He hit a homer to win the game, 5–4. It was the only home run he ever hit in the majors.

Third baseman **Hilly Layne** appeared in 107 games for the Washington Senators in 1941, 1944, and 1945. "My greatest thrill in baseball," Layne wrote, "was getting five hits in five times at bat against the St. Louis Browns shortly after joining the Washington Senators."

White Sox outfielder **Bill Mueller** threw out both Joe DiMaggio and Charlie "King Kong" Keller trying to score from second base, both in the same inning. After passing his rookie test that day, Mueller played 39 games for the '42 and '45 White Sox.

In 1943, **Chris Haughey** pitched in his only major league game, seven innings against The Dutch Master, Johnny Vander Meer. Haughey gave up five hits and ten bases on balls in his losing effort. The 17-year-old righthander was barely in the bigs long enough for his teammates to learn his nickname, Bud.

Outfielder **Guy Curtright** played in 331 games for the White Sox from 1943 to 1946. In his rookie year, Curtright hit safely in 26 consecutive games, a major league record for rookies that stood for 54 years.

*   *   *

Chet Covington had several nicknames: Lefty, Chesty, The Great. They all described him at various times during his 22-year minor league career. His highlight came on May 23, 1943 at Scranton in the Eastern League, when he pitched a perfect game against Springfield, 5–0. That year he was 21–7. His major league debut with the Philadelphia Phillies came the next year, at the age of 33. He lasted 19 games and was 1–1. His last day with the Phillies he was ordered to walk Musial. "Imagine telling a guy with my stuff to walk Musial," he groused after the game. The next day he was told to pack his stuff and report to Utica. As if 22 years in the minors weren't enough, Covington also boxed in 216 professional fights.

"He'd be certain for the Hall of Fame if the plate were high and outside," wrote Bob Cooke of the New York *Herald-Tribune* of the Dodger righthander **Rex Barney**. Barney played from 1943 to 1950 and appeared in four games in two World Series, but he never lived up to the future that had once been predicted for him. Even today, if pitchers are fast, they are sometimes said to have a Rex Barney fastball.

"I was scared to death," said Barney, "because in April I was pitching in high school and in July I was pitching in the major leagues. I didn't think I was going to pitch very much but I did. I won two games and lost two, but I did it completely scared to death. Then I went into the Army in World War II and was even more scared."

One day as Sergeant Barney was in command of the lead tank, a jeep decorated like it was ready for a parade drove up. It was General George S. Patton.

"Sergeant," said Patton, "where is the front?"

"General," said Barney, "the front of this tank is the front."

"That's too goddamn close for me! Carry on!" said the general and ordered the jeep to turn around and drive him away.

Barney also drove people away with his blazing fastball and his lack of control. But there was a time when it all came together, and that was the fifth game of the 1947 World Series.

"I remember warming up. People were yelling, 'Get that wild bum out of there.' They didn't know what I'd do against the Yankees. Neither did I.

"Well, I walked the first three guys, that's what I did. Rizzuto, Stirnweiss, and Henrich. And out comes Clyde Sukeforth from the bench.

"Clyde told me all I had to do was strike out the next guy and then get the next batter to hit into a double play. Easy? Well, the next hitter was Joe DiMaggio.

"I struck out DiMaggio, Billy Johnson, and George McQuinn and you should have heard those people at Ebbets Field. And believe me, I ate it all up. Every second of it. I can still hear 'em cheering.

"DiMaggio beat me with a home run in the seventh. I lost 2–1 to Spec Shea, but all winter I kept telling myself that I belonged, that I was a big leaguer if I could have done that well against the world champions."

But the next year, again he couldn't find the plate. The Dodgers even sent him to the Karl Menninger

Clinic in Topeka, Kansas, and Menninger himself tried to help Barney. His diagnosis was that Barney was frustrated. And the more bases on balls he issued, the more frustrated he became.

Rex Barney continued in a Dodger uniform until 1950. By then he had 336 strikeouts and six shutouts. But it was nothing compared to what he might have had. After all, he had a Rex Barney fastball.

Other than Satchel Paige, **Chuck Hostetler** at 40 was one of the oldest rookies ever to play in the major leagues. This came during the war years, when you could find players older or younger (Joe Nuxhall) than usual or just plain unusual (like one-legged pitcher Bert Shepard and one-armed outfielder Pete Gray). But Hostetler put on a good show. The outfielder made 137 put outs and 3 errors, and batted .278 in '44 and '45. In his 309 at-bats, he had 86 hits (including 12 doubles and 2 triples), stole 4 bases, scored 45 runs, and knocked in 22. Not bad for a person starting out when most players have long been retired.

In 1945, **Don Fisher** had a short but sharply focused career for the New York Giants. The righthander started one game and pitched a shutout. Indeed, he blanked the Braves 1–0 in 13 innings. He only appeared in one other game in the majors.

Sammie Haynes of the Kansas City Monarchs once admitted he was just an average player. He was not a good hitter because curve balls drove him crazy. But he had a good mind and could remember the habits and characteristics of opposing players. That helped him when he crouched behind the plate and called for a particular pitch. He also had a good arm, and either kept base runners close to the bag or threw them out.

"The first time I ever played in Kansas City was one of my career highlights," said Haynes. "I came up to bat in the third inning with two men on. Alex Smith of the Cleveland Buckeyes was pitching. He threw me a fastball letter high and I hit the ball off the wall. I was going to second and the belt on my pants broke and my pants went all the way down to my knees. I'll never forget that. Nor will I ever forget the first time I caught Satchel Paige. We finished warming up and then sat down in the dugout. He came up to me and said, 'Look, you are the boss. You tell me how and what to pitch. I'm working for you.' That scared me to death; here was the greatest pitcher around telling me to tell him how to pitch, and I had just got there. We went out there and had no problems. He never shook a sign off, not even once.

"The final thrill of my career came when I was playing against the Homestead Grays at Griffith Stadium in Washington, D.C., during the 1945 season. Satchel was pitching. It was about the sixth inning and we were leading 1–0. Cool Papa Bell was on first base with one out and Josh Gibson was at bat. We had two strikes on Josh. It was a 2–2 pitch; I called for a fastball. Satchel threw it right down the middle. Josh looked at the called third strike; I threw to second baseman Jackie Robinson, who put the tag on Cool Papa as he was trying to steal. That really stood out in my memory. I caught the greatest pitcher against the greatest hitter, then threw out the greatest runner. I went back to the dugout and was just floating on air."

During World War II more than 340 major league ballplayers served in military uniforms. Among them were Joe DiMaggio, Bob Feller, Warren Spahn, and Ted Williams. That left a big gap for older players to return, such as Babe Herman and Paul Waner, and players who might not otherwise have gotten a chance to play, such as Bert Shepard and Pete Gray.

Bert Shepard was a lefthanded pitcher who had lost the lower part of his right leg during World War II when he was shot down while piloting a P-38 over a Berlin airfield. When Shepard, a prisoner of war, returned to the States and was fitted for an artificial leg for what was missing below the knee, Clark Griffith heard that Shepard wanted to pitch in the major leagues. Shepard had played in the minors before becoming a pilot, and Griffith wanted him for his Washington Senators, perhaps as much for his pitching prowess as for doing a good deed or even for the publicity.

Shepard was hired to pitch batting practice. It turned out to be a good thing because it gave him time to work on his control and confidence. Quickly, he found out that he had what it took not only to get the ball over but also not to get shelled on every pitch.

On July 10, 1945, Shepard started an exhibition game with the Brooklyn Dodgers. After walking the first two batters, he retired the side. He held the

Dodgers scoreless on one hit until the fourth inning. Then on four straight singles, the Dodgers scored two runs to make the score 3–2. Shepard left the game then but wound up being the winning pitcher.

On August 4, 1945, Shepard came in as a reliever for **Joe Cleary** in the fourth inning of the second game of a doubleheader. Cleary was another pitcher making his Major League debut. But if Shepard was to be the ecstasy, Cleary was the agony. In one-third of an inning, Cleary had allowed 12 Red Sox runs to score in his first and last appearance in the majors. Cleary's 189.00 ERA stands as the highest ever in the record books—except for pitchers who never retired a single batter.

The Senators were in a pennant race and their pitchers were tired. There was little point in bringing in one of the regulars. From the beginning, Bert Shepard was a different story. Entering the game with two outs and the bases loaded, Shepard ran the count to 3 and 2 before striking out George "Catfish" Metkovich. Shepard stayed in and finished the game. In his five and one-third innings, he allowed only three hits and one base on balls, while striking out two. He even threw out two batters who hit the ball back to the pitcher. No one had bunted, but fielding bunts and throwing out the runner was something that Shepard could do, too.

Even though his ERA was a respectable 1.69, it still proved to be his only major league appearance. Shepard was only 25, and he stayed around in minor league baseball until 1955. He retired after also giving up 12 runs in a couple of innings.

Why did Bert Shepard not get another chance to

pitch in the majors? Shepard's own explanation was that "Nobody wanted to see me go in and get clobbered."

Pete Gray was a one-armed outfielder from Nanticoke, Pennsylvania. The righthanded Gray had lost his right arm to a few inches below the shoulder at the age of six when he fell off a truck and his right arm became entwined in the spokes of the wheel. It took an immense adjustment and determination to learn to throw and bat with only his left arm. But Pete, who changed his name to Gray from Wyshner (his brother used that name as a professional boxer), did just that. He also had the moxie to play football, basketball, and hockey, yet it was baseball that became his major love.

In 1942, Gray hit .381 in 42 games for Three Rivers in the Canadian-American League; and for the Memphis Chicks in the Southern Association, he had posted a .289 average in 1943 and a .333 in 1944. That last year Gray had also hit five homers, stolen 69 bases (including stealing home 10 times), and pulled off an unassisted double play. To the surprise of few he was voted the Most Valuable Player in the Southern Association.

In 1945, this son of a coal miner got his chance to play in the majors and appeared in 77 games for the St. Louis Browns.

"He's no sideshow freak," said manager Luke Sewell of his twenty-eight-year-old rookie. "He's a fine player, fast, courageous, and he can hit. We use him when he can help us win, the same as any two-armed player." But he was a strong drawing card. Sixty-five thousand showed up at the stadium in Cleveland when he was in the lineup.

In the outfield Pete Gray was something to behold. He would track down a fly ball, snare it in his glove, snap the glove and ball under his right stump, grab the ball, and fire it back to the infield with his left hand. To field grounders he would stop the ball, drop the glove, then pick up and throw the ball. All of these operations he would accomplish in just a fraction of the time that it takes to tell about it.

One of his best outings was a doubleheader at Yankee Stadium in May 1945. Leading off in the lineup, Gray collected four hits and two RBIs, scored two runs, and had nine putouts, one on a drive to the left field wall with the bases loaded and two outs.

The crowds loved him, too. It wasn't unusual for him to get standing ovations in ballparks at home and on the road. As J. Roy Stockton of the *St. Louis Post Dispatch* wrote: "It was a great exhibition of courage and you can use that word without restraint or blush, even in these war-torn days, when you sing of a gamester like Peter Gray."

One of the stellar statistics in his major league record is that he struck out only 11 times in 234 at-bats. He also hit safely 51 times with 6 doubles and two triples for a .218 batting average, scored 26 runs, knocked in 13 more, received 13 passes to first base, and stole 5 bases.

"I knew I couldn't stay up too long," said Gray about his career in the majors. "I didn't have the power. I . . . hit a lot of line drives that they'd catch ten or fifteen feet from the fence. Just not quite far enough."

With the war over, Gray's contract was bought by Toledo. He knew he would never get a chance to move up to the majors again. "The pitching is a little bit too tough for me up there," he said. Also, because he had to start his swing early, he was vulnerable to change-ups.

After Toledo, Gray played for Elmira and Dallas before retiring at the end of the 1949 season. No matter what, Pete Gray had gone a long way in changing a lot of people's minds about what it means to be handicapped.

Frank Wurm didn't even get his 15 minutes of fame. It was more like 10. During that time, in 1944, he pitched one-third of an inning for the Brooklyn Dodgers. One hit, one strikeout, and five walks later, he was going-going-gone from the game with his 108.00 ERA.

"In 1945, the Cincinnati Reds played against the Chicago Cubs at Fort Knox, Kentucky, during an exhibition game," wrote outfielder **Dick Sipek**. "I started to play after the seventh inning. When I came to bat in the ninth inning with two out, I hit a home run. We won by the score of 5 to 4. It was also a thrilling moment for me because my parents had their silver anniversary on that day." In his 156 at-bats in 1945, the only season he spent in the majors, Sipek hit six doubles and two triples but no more home runs.

Frank Dasso set the one-year strikeout record in the Pacific Coast League with 256 in 198 innings. However, the righthander's two years at Cincinnati in 1945 and 1946 were pretty tame in comparison. In 18 games Dasso was 4–5 with only 40 strikeouts in 96 and two-thirds innings.

Joe Tepsic was a bonus baby for the Brooklyn Dodgers in 1946. His record wasn't much to talk about: in five plate appearances he had one walk, one strikeout, and two runs, for a batting average of .000. The Dodgers understandably wanted to send him down to the minors the next year for some seasoning, but for this outfielder, 1946 was his last season. Tepsic quit. To many fans, Tepsic was a traitor. (See **Hilda Chester** in the Fans section.)

When the name **Jackie Price** comes to mind, one might think of an entertainer. Price could toss a ball back and forth while standing on his head; he could pitch a fastball and a curve at the same time; he could entertain the fans before a game. Bill Veeck was the man behind Price's landing on the Cleveland Indians during the 1946 campaign. Lou Boudreau, his manager, was less than charmed, but he went along with it long enough to have Price play shortstop four times and appear in a total of seven games. For a comedian Price gave a pretty fair account of himself. He had a total of three hits in his thirteen trips to the plate.

The name of **Eddie Klepp** doesn't resonate the way Jackie Robinson does, but they both had a somewhat similar purpose. Klepp was a pitcher and a white man hired by the Cleveland Buckeyes in 1946 in an attempt to integrate the Negro Leagues. Klepp, however, was forced by the sentiment of the day to eat in different restaurants and stay in different hotels than his black teammates. In some ballparks he wasn't even allowed to sit on the same bench as his teammates. As far as talent was concerned, though, Robinson and Klepp were definitely in different leagues. After a few games Klepp vanished.

Tommy Fine had a wonderful year for Scranton in 1946. The righthander won 17 straight and was 23–3 as they won the Eastern League pennant by 18 and a half games. The Red Sox had been keeping tabs on him and called him up in 1947.

Things went differently in the Big Show. He was only 1–2 for the year; in 36 innings he gave up 41 hits, 19 walks, with only 10 strikeouts. Three years later for the Browns his record was even worse. He was 0–1 with an ERA of 8.10. And then it was off to the minors.

"I guess my biggest thrill in baseball," Fine once said, "was pitching a no-hitter in the Caribbean World Series in Panama in 1952."

Lou Brissie saw a lot of action before he joined the Philadelphia A's in 1947. A veteran of World War II, he had been wounded by a shell in 1944 (Brissie was the only survivor of his unit) and had to undergo 23 operations on his leg and foot. After much rehabilitation, Brissie was able to start a game at the end of the '47 season.

"I lost the game, 5–2, but it was a great occasion," he said. "It was in Yankee Stadium on the first Babe Ruth Day. Honus Wagner, Ty Cobb, Tris Speaker, all the great players I had read about were there. You talk about a guy not being in the real world. I thought I'd died and gone to heaven."

But in the coming years it was hard for the left-hander to play on his bad right leg. "Some days I hurt and some days I didn't. You just have to make the adjustment. It was kind of like going to the office. Some days you don't feel like doing it, but you do it anyway."

Brissie really enjoyed pitching to the great hitters like Williams and DiMaggio. But the real problem, as he saw it, was letting the lesser-known hitters get on base.

Brissie ended his career with two years in Cleveland. He was 44–48 over seven seasons.

"I guess a man who goes to war and sees what he sees learns something about life," said Lou Brissie. "I always felt thankful just to be around."

The first Little League World Series Tournament was held in Williamsport, Pennsylvania, on August 21, 1947. In the championship game the Maynard Midget League played Lock Haven Little League. **Ed Ungard**, the pitcher for the Midgets, gave up eight hits and struck out seven, while giving up only four walks, as he beat Lock Haven 16–7 before 2,500 cheering fans.

Bill Bevens, the Yankee pitcher, was one out away from the first no-hitter in World Series history. It was Game 4 of the 1947 World Series and the score was Yanks, 2, Dodgers, 1. Ninth inning. After getting the first batter, Bevens walked Carl Furillo and got Spider

Jorgensen to foul out. Running for Furillo, Al Gionfriddo scampered down to second. Manager Bucky Harris had Bevens intentionally walk Pete Reiser. Eddie Miksis went in to run for Reiser. Cookie Lavagetto was sent in to pinch hit for Eddie Stanky. Lavagetto took the first pitch, then hit Bevens's second pitch against the wall in right-center to break up the no-hitter and score both Gionfriddo and Miksis for the 3–2 win. It was to be Cookie's last hit in the major leagues: The Yankees went on to defeat Brooklyn in seven games.

Bob "Dutch" McCall had a lackluster record of 4–13 for the 1948 Chicago Cubs. His one shining moment came in the minors when he struck out 17 Atlanta Crackers batters in the Southern Association.

Catcher **Earle Brucker, Jr.,** was the son of catcher Earle Brucker. The father belted .290 over five years for the Philadelphia Athletics (1937–43). His son had a single in six at-bats for the A's in 1948.

Lou Boudreau of Cleveland made what seemed an unusual by-the-seat-of-the-pants move in the summer of 1948. Deadlocked with the Boston Red Sox at the end of the season, the Cleveland manager bypassed the team's stoppers, Bob Feller and Bob Lemon, to give the nod to twenty-seven-year-old rookie **Gene Bearden** to start the one-game playoff. Not only was Bearden a rookie knuckleballer and a southpaw pitching in Fenway Park, but he was also taking the mound only two days after his last start. But Bearden was riding high on a 20–7 season and an American

League–leading 2.43 ERA and proved Boudreau right. Bearden and the Indians put down the Red Sox 8–3 to take the American League title. Bearden went on to win a game of the World Series, 2–0, facing only 30 batters, giving up only five hits, and doubling in the insurance run. He also posted a save of the sixth and final game. After giving up a pinch hit double to Phil Masi, Bearden buckled down and set down the last four batters in order, as the Indians beat the Boston Braves 4 games to 2.

Bearden earned his nickname of The Arkansas Traveler in the next five years as he bounced around four other teams in the American League: Washington, Detroit, St. Louis, and Chicago. Never in great shape, never fully recovering from a leg injury, never bedazzling the batters with his knuckler again, Bearden never came close to his 20–7 season again. In fact, he won only 25 games the rest of the way. His major league career had expired by 1953 and his final record was 45–38.

Jack Banta had his banner year in 1949. That was when he went 10–6 for Brooklyn, winning the last game of the season to give the Dodgers the pennant. The next year he hurt his arm and was out of baseball with a modest four-year record of 14–12.

It sounds like a kid's dream come true, but it happened for outfielder **Ed Sanicki** of the Philadelphia Phillies. "My greatest thrill was hitting a home run in my first time at bat in the big leagues in September 1949 in Pittsburgh." Although he had only 17 at-bats in '49 and '51, he hit three home runs. To give perspective to this, Sanicki's home run percentage for times at bat was 17.6; the leader in this department, Babe Ruth, had an 11.6.

"I had two great moments in my life playing baseball," remembered **Herman "Doc" Horn**, the centerfielder of the Kansas City Monarchs from 1949 to 1954. "Once I hit four home runs in four at-bats. But to me my greatest moment was when I got to hit against the super great Satchel Paige. I was oh-for-fourteen before I got a hit off him. I was twenty; he was sixty."

In 1950, the Pittsburgh Pirates signed 19-year-old, 6 foot 2, 195-pound **Paul Pettit**, to a $100,000 contract that made him the first bonus baby. This youngster was as bright a prospect as they had seen in a long time, pitching six no-hit games in high school, three in a row. But in 1951, Pettit pitched for two and two-thirds innings and gave up two hits and a walk. The next year he was with four different teams in as many leagues. But in 1953, Pettit was back with the Bucs for a short stay, posting a 1–2 record in 28 innings and giving up 33 hits and 20 walks. He did strike out 14, but the Pirates had seen enough.

Bill "Fireball" Beverly, a hard-throwing righthander, began his career as the Negro Leagues were winding down. In Victoria, Texas, in 1950, he was pitching for the Houston Eagles against the Eastern Greyhounds. "My dad hit a home run and I was pitching," wrote Beverly. "He was hitting eighth and I came up behind him and hit a home run. We had hit back-to-back home runs. I danced all the way around that ball park because

I wasn't known for hitting home runs. I was known for stopping people from hitting them. My father was elated and I was elated and we both broke down and cried. It was a moment I will never forget because my father was so happy to see that I was finally coming into my own. I must have been, at that time, sixteen or seventeen years old."

Sam Jethroe is one of the lesser-known African Americans who helped break down the racial barriers of major league baseball. Arriving in Boston to play for the Braves a year after Pumpsie Green started playing for the Red Sox, the 32-year-old Jethroe displayed why his nickname was Jet, leading the league in steals in '50 and '51 with 35 both years. (His age was sometimes listed as 28 when he was a rookie.) How fast was Sam Jethroe? He beat Harrison Dillard in a race in 1948, the same year that Dillard won a gold medal in the 100 meters in the Olympic Games.

It was once said he had a questionable arm, but as Harold Kaese of the *Boston Globe* wrote: "This Jethroe looks so fast and his arm looks so weak that it's even money he can carry the ball in from center field as fast as he can throw it in."

First baseman **Ed Mickelson** played briefly for the Cards in '50, the Browns in '53, and the Cubs in '57. This amounted to only 18 games. (The rest of the time he spent in the Pacific Coast League.) Mickelson drove in the last run to be batted in by a Brownie in the last game of the season that the Browns played in St. Louis. He only had two other RBIs in the majors.

* * *

The date of August 19, 1951 may not go down in the annals of baseball history as a shining moment, but it sure was an unusual one. As usual, the St. Louis Browns were having a losing season—they were taking up residence in the cellar—and general manager Bill Veeck was having a hard time putting fannies in the seats in Sportsman's Park. Veeck, sometimes known as Sportshirt for his loud tops, had tried handing out bats, orchids, and lobsters, and even had the scoreboard rewired to blast Handel's "Messiah" every time the Brownies scored. Alas, that was something that happened all too infrequently. There were midgets in the stands selling midget hot dogs . . . hmmm, there were midgets in the stands. . . . James Thurber had written a story in 1941, "You Could Look It Up," about a midget who was a pinch hitter. Hmmm. . . .

This was an attention-grabber like none other in Veeck's long career. He hired **Eddie Gaedel**, a 26-year-old entertainer who topped out at three feet, seven inches, to pop out of a cake between games of a doubleheader and go into the first inning of the second game to pinch hit for the Browns. In case umpire Ed Hurley objected to this move, manager Zack Taylor took the contract along to show him. After about 15 minutes (during which time the president of the American League, Will Harridge, frantically tried to get hold of Veeck), and after finding the contract to be a real one, Hurley motioned for play to resume.

With Gaedel's exaggerated batting stance, there were about two inches left for Tiger pitcher Bob Cain to fit in a strike. The 65 pounder uttered words like "Let's go" and "Throw it in there, fat, and I'll murder it." If it had not been for his squeaky voice, these words might have had more bite. Bill Veeck had even prepared for the circumstance of Cain's getting one into the strike zone. He had told his little pinch hitter that there was a sniper with a rifle trained on him who would fire if he so much as dared swing. On his first two pitches to catcher Bob Swift, who was down on his knees, Cain tried to hit the tiny strike zone. Not surprisingly, his first two pitches were balls. After a good laugh, Cain just tossed in the last two pitches for ball four. The little guy with the turned-up toes and the number 1/8 on the back of his jersey—he was wearing the uniform of the seven-year-old son of the club's vice president—trotted down to first with a walk. Immediately, Gaedel was taken out of the game for Jim Delsing, a pinch runner. In spite of the ploy, the Brownies lost the game, 6–2.

"Eddie Gaedel's name has appeared in a major-league box score," wrote Arthur Daley, "and he now is an official part of baseball history along with Ty Cobb, Honus Wagner, and Babe Ruth." Two days later, Gaedel was banned by the American League president from ever playing again. "Now that somebody has finally taken a step to help us short guys," said a tongue-in-cheek Gaedel, "Harridge is ruining my baseball career."

Bill Veeck was often criticized for stunts like this one. His reaction remained pure Veeck: "All I have ever said is that you can draw more people with a losing team plus bread and circuses than with a losing team and a long, still silence."

Bob "Sugar" Cain began his baseball career playing Midget League baseball in Salina, Kansas, and ironically, one of his best-known moments was pitching to Eddie Gaedel, the midget that Bill Veeck sent up to pinch hit in 1951. Cain told the story hundreds of times and was appreciative of how this was a part of baseball lore.

"Two of the most exciting things that happened," wrote Cain, who was 37–44 during his 6-year career, "was pitching against the midget [Cain was the only baseball person at Gaedel's funeral in 1961] and also a game against Bob Feller when we both pitched a one-hitter and I beat him 1–0." This was the first time that two opposing pitchers had thrown one-hitters since Three Fingers Brown of the Cubs and Lefty Leifield of the Pirates had done it in 1906.

Eleanor Engle was a twenty-four-year-old shortstop good enough to turn heads and raise interest in her abilities. "She can hit the ball a lot better than some of the fellows on the club," said Howard Gordon, the general manager. Although she had only played softball up to that time, he was willing to take a chance on her. So on June 21, 1952, the Harrisburg Senators gave her a contract to play for them in the Class AA Interstate League in Pennsylvania.

Buck Etchison, the manager, saw things differently. "I won't have a girl playing for me . . . ," he vowed.

"She'll play when hell freezes over." League president George M. Trautman agreed with this sentiment. When he learned of Engle's contract, he voided the document. Organized baseball was not ready for women, except in the stands. Blacks in '47, women in '52, what would be next?

As a coda to this story, Eleanor Engle was slated to try out for Jimmy Foxx's Fort Wayne Daisies in the All-American Girls Professional Baseball League, but it never came about.

Five years after Jackie Robinson had broken the color barrier in Brooklyn, its effects had not yet reached Georgia. There were still black leagues and white leagues. On July 19, 1952, in the all-white Georgia State League, Fitzgerald was taking a hiding from Statesboro, 13–0. By the eighth inning the fans were venting their anger toward their home team. "Kill the umpire" had been replaced by "Put in the bat boy." And that's exactly what Fitzgerald manager Charles Ridgeway asked plate umpire Ed Kubrick if he could do. No objections were raised, so **Joy Relford**, a 12-year-old African American, found himself playing in a minor league game in place of Ray Nichting, the center fielder who was batting .330.

Relford did not whiff in his time at bat; he hit a hard grounder to third and was thrown out at first. He was even more impressive in the field. When a hard line drive was hit his way, the young center fielder snagged it cleanly and fired it back to the infield.

Sending in the bat boy may not have seemed like a

bad idea, but the Georgia State League was not amused. Kubrick was fired; Ridgeway was fined and suspended; Relford was replaced as the bat boy. But what no one could erase was the fact that Relford had been the youngest person ever to play in the minor leagues and the first African American to play in the Georgia State League. And to top it off, Joy Relford had played well.

No-hitters win kudos. Perfect games are like winning Academy Awards. But how about striking out 27 batters in a single game? Moral infallibility? The only person to do this in professional baseball is **Ron Necciai**, a 19-year-old from Monongahela, Pennsylvania.

On May 13, 1952, playing for the Pittsburgh Pirates minor league team and in the Appalachian League, Class D ball, Ron Necciai accomplished this feat. Before 1,853 fans in the ball park in Bristol, Virginia, the young fastballer for the Twins faced the team from Welch, West Virginia. In the first inning, Necciai struck out the side. In the second, he struck out two and got one batter out with a ground ball from short to first. But for the next six innings, from the third to the eighth innings, the fireballer from Bristol struck out the side. Three men had reached first base, one hit with a pitch, another with a walk, and the third on an error, but the Bristol kid had fanned 23 batters. In the ninth inning, Necciai struck out the first three batters, but the catcher, Harry Dunlop, had dropped the third strike of the final strikeout and the batter made it safely to first. The Bristol ace struck out the next batter up, so Ron Necciai had struck out a total of 27 batters and pitched a no-hitter in the bargain, as Bristol beat Welch, 7–0.

Branch Rickey, the Pirates' general manager, sent his son to Bristol to keep an eye on Necciai and two other pitchers worth watching. But it was Rocket Ron who had captured the imagination of the baseball world. The president of the American League, Warren Giles, wired: "I hope it won't be long before you're striking out American League batters in an All-Star Game."

In his next outing, before 5,000 on May 21, Necciai struck out 24 hapless batters on the team from Kingsport, Tennessee. And in his next two starts, against Kingsport and Pulaski, Virginia, Rocket Ron struck out 20 and 19. So, in four complete games, 36 innings, Ron Necciai had struck out a grand total of 90 batters. His complete record at Bristol was 109 strikeouts in 43 innings.

These figures were enough to get the wheels turning. Necciai was promoted to Durham, North Carolina. Even with better competition, Rocket Ron struck out 172 in 126 innings. By year's end, Ron Necciai found himself in a Pittsburgh Pirates uniform.

"There have been only two young pitchers I was certain were destined for greatness . . . ," declared Branch Rickey. "One of those boys was Dizzy Dean. The other is Ron Necciai."

In the majors, Ron Necciai pitched in parts of 12 games, 54 and two-thirds innings, and struck out 31 batters. He won one and lost six. But it wasn't his record that did him in. The Pirates were in a rebuilding phase and were a weak team that year. It was his body. The pressure proved to be too much. Necciai developed a sore arm and ulcers. Ron Necciai hung around in the minors for a while, but the dream of striking out the side in an All-Star Game disappeared like the ball into the catcher's mitt on May 13, 1952.

In 1953, **Frank Verdi** played in his one and only game in the major leagues. Here's how it happened for the onetime Yankee shortstop:

"We're in Boston and we're losing 3–1 in the eighth," recalled Verdi, "and Stengel puts Mize up to hit for Rizzuto. In the bottom of the eighth, Casey says, 'Verdi, you go to short,' and I almost hit my head on the dugout. We get 'em out in the eighth and in the ninth we bat around and go ahead, 5–3, and we have the bases loaded and I'm stepping in the batter's box to hit. All of a sudden, I hear a gravelly voice behind me shout, 'Hey, wait a minute!' and I turn around and there's Bill Renna swinging three bats. I never did get an official at-bat in the big leagues. Three days later, I was back in Syracuse." After his playing days were over, Verdi became a minor league manager.

On May 6, 1953, **Bobo Holloman** took the mound for the St. Louis Browns. It was a lousy night. Rain had kept the crowd to a measly 2,473. But for Holloman this was a night unlike any other. This was his first game ever as a starting pitcher in the major leagues.

Holloman had been with the Chicago Cubs organization, most recently at Syracuse, until the Browns bought out his contract. Owner Bill Veeck was willing to take a chance on him. But even Veeck's optimism was challenged. "He had charm and he had humor and he had unlimited—if sadly misplaced—confidence in himself," Veeck later wrote. "In spring training he was hit harder trying to get the batters out than our batting-practice pitchers who were trying to let them hit." Although this 28-year-old pitcher may have had all the confidence in the world—he was nicknamed after Bobo Newsom, another pitcher oozing with confidence, who had pitched three 20-game winning seasons in a row—Holloman's record for the Brownies in relief amounted to a measly 9.00 ERA. Still, you had to like a guy who stooped down to carve the initials of his wife and child in the dirt outside the foul line before he strode out to the mound. Perhaps it was this and his constant pleas to let him start that led manager Marty Marion to pencil him in.

And what a game it was that night. In the second inning, the Athletics' Gus Zernial hit a booming drive to left that the Browns' Jim Dyck caught against the wall. In the bottom of the second, with catcher Les Moss on second, Holloman came up to the plate and slashed a single. Moss scored and the Browns were out in front 1–0. In the fifth inning the Athletics again threatened. Allie Clark hit a ball that just curved foul before clearing the fence. Zernial hit a grounder that Bobo bobbled. The official scorer ruled an error. In the sixth the Athletics' catcher, Joe Astroth, bunted along the third baseline. Neither third baseman Bob Elliott nor Holloman could get it. Bobo waved the others off and crouched alongside the ball, pleading with it to curve foul. It did. In the seventh Holloman came to the plate with two men on. Again, he hit a single to drive in both runs. The score was now 6–0. In the eighth Joe Astroth hit a ball behind second base that looked like a sure hit. But Billy Hunter somehow got to it and made the throw to first for the out. "When Hunter made that great play," said Holloman, "I knew right then that I was going to pitch a no-hitter." But in the ninth inning, a visibly tired Holloman was having trouble controlling his sinker ball and walked the first two batters, Elmer Valo and Eddie Joost. The Browns' pitching coach, former All-Star Harry Brecheen, told the rookie to slow down and follow through. This time the sinker sank and .303 hitter Dave Philley hit a grounder to second. Bobby Young turned a double play. One out to go, Valo on third, and Eddie Robinson up. On the first pitch Robinson hit a curve over the fence for a long foul. Catcher Les Moss came out to talk to Bobo and told him that Robinson would be expecting a fastball, so pitch another curve. Bobo did and Robinson flied to right fielder Vic Wertz for the last out of the game.

Bobo had not only silenced the bats of the Philadelphia Athletics, but he had also awakened his own. His two hits had accounted for three RBIs as he had blanked the Athletics 6–0. Not only did the Athletics not score, they didn't even get a hit. An auspicious debut as a starter, if ever there was one. (There have been only two others who pitched no-hitters in their major league debuts, Ted Breitenstein of the Cardinals against Louisville on October 4, 1891 and Charlie "Bumpus" Jones for Cincinnati against Pittsburgh on October 15, 1892.)

But it turned out to be a short-lived superstar career. In his next outing he went to the showers before completing two innings. Holloman not only never hurled another no-hitter, he never even pitched a complete game again. Nor did he ever get another hit. Alva Lee Holloman finished his one and only season in the majors with a 3–7 record and a 5.23 ERA.

What a treat it would be to have your dad and mom (and on her birthday, no less) in the stands for your first major league start and you come through with a shutout. Well, that's just what Milwaukee Braves' southpaw **Don Liddle** did in 1953, as he threw a two-hit shutout against the Chicago Cubs in his very first major league outing.

Another of Liddle's high points was being brought in to pitch to Vic Wertz in the eighth inning of the first game of the 1954 World Series. Wertz, who already had three hits in the game, unleashed a 440-foot drive that Willie Mays caught with his back to the plate in that huge 480-foot center field of the Polo Grounds. Who hasn't seen that highlight film? (Interestingly, Mays once said that the hardest part about the play was the throw back in.) Well, Liddle was the pitcher. After Mays's catch, Liddle was taken out and Dusty Rhodes won the game for the Giants in the tenth with a three-run, 260-foot home run over the right field wall. Liddle also started the fourth game and won it 7–4 to complete the Giants' World Series sweep of the Indians. The rest of Liddle's career was much quieter. After four years he departed the scene with a 28–18 record.

* * *

In 1953, **Toni Stone** played second base for the Indianapolis Clowns of the Negro American League. "I come to play ball," she told the skeptics. "Women have got just as much right to play baseball as men." Stone had paid her dues, playing with the San Francisco Sea Lions and the New Orleans Creoles. Still, this was the first time that a woman had ever played in the highest black league. Her reaction? "There's always got to be a first for everything." Appearing in 50 games, the 32-year-old batted .243.

But it was facing Satchel Paige on Easter Sunday of 1953 that gave Toni Stone the most pleasure. (Her real name was Marcenia Lyle; she took on Toni because people used to call her Tomboy; perhaps the last name developed because it showed how strong she had to be to be a woman playing in a men's league.) Taking off from the St. Louis Browns to pitch an exhibition against the Clowns, Paige asked their batters where they wanted it. (This was standard practice for Paige; throughout his career he often liked to give hitters a fighting chance.)

"It doesn't matter," replied Stone. "Just don't hurt me." Stone stood transfixed, watching Paige go through his windup. "I stood there shaking, but I got a hit. Right out over second base. Happiest moment in my life."

In 1954, Stone was traded from the Clowns to the Kansas City Monarchs. (Stone was replaced on the Clowns by 19-year-old Connie Morgan.) Toni Stone later quit because she felt she wasn't playing enough and became a nurse.

* * *

Bill Renna hit .239 during his six-year, 200-game, four-team career from 1953 to 1959. But the day he remembers most was the day in 1953 his son was born. Just before the outfielder took the field his wife called him from the hospital to say he was the father of a son. His first at-bat Renna hit a home run off Ted Gray. On his son's first birthday Renna hit another homer. Unfortunately, dad was on the bench during Burry's second birthday.

Here is a walk-on story par excellence. In the spring of 1954, 21-year-old **Joe Carolan** traveled from Detroit down to Columbus, Georgia, to seek a tryout with the Columbus Cardinals. After paying his way into the ballpark, Carolan went to speak to the Cardinals' manager. The manager let the 230-pounder take batting practice with his team. After hitting three homers, Carolan was offered a contract and played in that day's game against Macon. In the first inning, Carolan got his first at-bat, and what an at-bat it was. Joe Carolan connected for a grand slam. Carolan never made it to the majors.

On July 18, 1954, **Bob Greenwood** was in charge during his very first start in the majors. Pitching for the Phillies, he held a commanding 8–1 lead over the Cardinals in the top of the fifth inning. But darkness was approaching and Cards manager Eddie Stanky knew that the lights could not be turned on in the middle of a game, so if he could only stall long enough, the game might be canceled. In the bottom of the fifth, Stanky put a reliever into the game and after the reliever had taken his warmup pitches, Stanky changed his mind and put in another relief pitcher. After that pitcher had his warmup pitches, Stanky called for the third reliever. At this point umpire Babe Pinelli charged the game as a forfeit. Although Philadelphia was awarded the win, no individual statistics survived, so Greenwood did not get credit for the win. Later that year, he did win a game and lost two. His career ended the following year with no decisions.

Jim Davis had a good rookie year for the Cubs in 1954, when he was 11–7. After that, one of the highlights in his 24–26 career was in 1956, when he struck out four in the sixth inning of a game with the St. Louis Cardinals. After striking out Hal Smith, Jackie Brandt, and Lindy McDaniel, the catcher dropped the ball, allowing McDaniel to go to first and a man on third to score. The next batter up was Don Blasingame. Davis struck out Blasingame for four strikeouts in one inning. It was the first time since 1916 that anyone had done that.

The last week of a season is often a good time to try out a new player. **Karl Spooner** was given a mound start by the Dodgers at the end of the 1954 season and he came through with a shutout of the Giants. Of course, the New Yorkers had clinched the pennant the day before, so the game was meaningless to them, but certainly not to Spooner. To show that this wasn't a fluke, the southpaw then shut out the Pirates. Then again, the Pirates had the worst record in the National League, but so what? Spooner had movement on a terrific fastball. In 18 innings he had given up only 7 hits and 6 bases on balls, while striking out 27. Spoonerism! What a start, no matter what part of the year.

Things looked good for the following year, until Spooner injured his arm in spring training. Oh, he won a respectable eight games while losing six that year, but his arm would never be right again. He even started the sixth game of the World Series that year. In the first inning he gave up two walks, singles to Yogi Berra and Hank Bauer, and a home run to Moose Skowron. Spooner left the game in the first inning after getting out only one batter. Those five runs were all the scoring the Yankees needed that game as they beat the Bums 5–1. It was the last time Karl Spooner ever appeared in a major league uniform.

Forrest Jacobs played 188 games at second base from 1954 to 1956 for the Philadelphia Athletics, the Kansas City A's (yes, they had moved west for the '55 season), and the Pirates (still in Pittsburgh). Jacobs got his nickname Spook because his softly hit balls somehow went past the infielders. In his major league debut, Jacobs got four straight hits. This is the major league record that Delino DeShields tied 36 years later in 1990. Interestingly, Jacobs and DeShields lived 18 miles apart in Delaware.

Freddie Patek was called The Flea and he was five-foot-five and 148 pounds. **Ernie Oravetz** was only five-foot-four and 145 pounds, one of the smallest men ever to play in the major leagues. But he lasted for two years with Washington, '55 and '56, and manager

Charlie Dressen used him as a pinch hitter 49 times the second year, the most appearances of any pinch hitter in the American League. Dressen said that he'd rather have Oravetz up at the plate when it was crunch time than anyone else on the Senators. After all, Dressen had nothing against short people. He was only five-foot-six himself.

Jim Brady signed a contract with the Tigers at nineteen after one year at Notre Dame. The year was 1955. Brady was a bonus baby. He didn't get into any games, but he threw on the sidelines a lot. So much so that he ruined a tendon in his elbow.

In 1956, Brady pitched six innings in six games for Detroit, giving up 15 hits, 11 bases on balls, and striking out three. But his arm never recovered, so Brady altered his direction and earned a B.A., M.A., and PhD, and became the president of Jacksonville University. Jim Brady may not have pitched again, but he had three sons who all became pitchers.

Sometimes softball pitchers are successful against baseball players. That was certainly the case for **Bob Fesler** in 1955 when he struck out 11 major leaguers in a row. It was enough to start Fred Hutchison thinking and to get this manager of Seattle in the Pacific Coast League to give Fesler a chance to start for him in a baseball game.

Watching from the dugout allowed Hutchison time to think about the 45 feet that Fesler was used to throwing versus the 60 feet 6 inches. Fesler lasted only two-thirds of an inning and gave up five runs. Hutch gave him another shot, but it turned out about the same. So, Bob Fesler happily returned to being one of the most dominant softball pitchers of his day. He would no longer ever be tempted to wonder, "What if . . . ?"

Joe Brovia couldn't even wait to graduate from high school to get his baseball career started. But his was a career that stayed locked into the minors. In 1,804 minor league games he batted .311. One of the reasons he stayed in the Pacific Coast League so long was that the PCL wanted to become the third Major League, so they hung onto their good players. In 1955, Brovia was given a chance with Cincinnati (Lefty O'Doul, his first manager in the PCL who had switched him from a pitcher to an outfielder, had paved the way). But by this time the outfielder was 33. The Reds wanted a pinch hitter, but Brovia was the kind of player who needed to play every day in order to hit well. In 18 at-bats he had two singles and four RBIs. Then it was back to the minors.

"When Cincinnati just gave me a short 'how do you do' and the fast 'goodbye,'" remarked Brovia, "I began to hurt all over, mostly right in the pit of my stomach."

After careers with the Homestead Grays and the Kansas City Monarchs, **Bob Thurman** broke in with the Cincinnati Reds in 1955. They thought he was 32, but actually he was 38. One of his biggest games in the majors came in his rookie year, August 18, 1955, against Milwaukee when he hit three home runs and a double. Nicknamed El Murcaro (The Owl), half of Thurman's appearances in games, 178, were as a pinch hitter. In 1957, El Murcaro knocked out four pinch hit home runs. In 334 games over his five-year major league career, this man from Wichita, Kansas, hit .246.

After a mere six games for Cincinnati in 1955, **Bob Hazle** came on like a hurricane for Milwaukee in 1957, replacing the injured Bill Bruton in July and batting .403 in 41 games, to help the Braves win the National League. Hurricane Hazle also had two hits and scored two runs in the World Series as the Braves bested the Yankees in a seven-game series. But like his hurricane namesake of the 1950s disappearing from the radar screen, Hazle went 24 for 114 the next year and was soon out of baseball.

In 1956, **Pat Scantlebury** became the last player to go from the Negro Leagues to the major leagues when he pitched for the Cincinnati Reds. At 38, his best days were over, but the six-foot-one, 180-pound southpaw started two games and pitched 19 innings in all. His record was 0–1.

The first major league game that **Red Murff** ever saw was the one he was in. Opening Day, 1956, Milwaukee County Stadium. Lew Burdette on the mound for the Braves. In the ninth Burdette ran out of gas with men on first and third, one out. Manager Charlie Grimm called for the rookie righthander, so the spectator became a participant. Murff found himself on the mound, staring at Bob Thurman with big Ted Kluszewski on deck. Murff retired the side and got the save. For his two seasons in the majors, Murff only got two more saves, two wins, and two losses.

The youngest player to start a Major League game in the twentieth century is **Jim Derrington**, who was only 16 when he took the mound in 1956 for the Chicago White Sox against the Kansas City Athletics. Pitching six innings, Derrington struck out three and gave up nine hits and six bases on balls. He did better at the plate, rapping out a single in two at-bats.

The next year Derrington started five games, appearing in 20 games in all. In his 37 innings of work he struck out 14 and gave up 29 hits and 29 bases on balls.

On August 1, 1957, **Glen Gorbous**, a one-time Major League ballplayer (Reds and Phillies, '55-'57), threw a baseball 445 feet, 10 inches. He may not have set any records in the majors, but the six-foot-two outfielder sure made an impact that day for Omaha in the American Association. It wasn't in a game, though—the park couldn't have contained it—but rather in a special exhibition beforehand. With a running start of six steps, Gorbous had four attempts to beat Don Grate's 1952 record of 434 feet, one inch. Gorbous did to become the present-day man with a golden arm.

But was "the throw" his biggest thrill? "I guess it was my first Major League homer [against Brooklyn in 1955]. Carl Erskine was the pitcher."

To be outdone but not undone, on August 18, 1957, **Amelia Wershoven** set the record for women when she threw a baseball 252 feet, 4 and a half inches.

* * *

The star of the 1957 World Little League Championship series was **Angel Macias** from Monterrey, Mexico. Angel could play any position and was his team's star pitcher, pitching either right- or lefthanded. In the championship game Angel threw a no-hitter, striking out 11 batters in six innings. The future looked bright for this phenom from south of the border.

There was only one problem and it became bigger as time passed. Angel was the smallest member of his team. And that was something that didn't change. He never really grew to a size where he could be effective. He eventually went from a fantastic prospect to a so-so outfielder in the minors.

After graduating from Lynwood High School near Los Angeles in 1957, **Rod Miller,** a five-foot-ten, 160-pound second baseman signed with the Brooklyn Dodgers. Although he went on to have a mediocre record with Cedar Rapids that summer, batting only .183 and committing 36 errors, Miller was mysteriously called up to spend September with the Dodgers. (Miller later found out he was blind in one eye so didn't have any depth perception.)

On September 28, 1957, in the next-to-last game of the season, Walter Alston sent the 17-year-old to pinch-hit for Randy Jackson in the ninth inning of a game the Dodgers were leading 8–3. Not much was riding on this at-bat; the Dodgers had a lock on third place and Philadelphia was most likely not going to rally to victory.

At first Miller didn't trust his ears. Why would Walter Alston want him? Then Miller couldn't find a bat that suited him—he liked a bat under 34 ounces—so he grabbed one of Duke Snider's. With a bat that weighed over 40 ounces—he had to choke way up— Miller went to the plate to face Jack Meyer. Joe Lonnett, the catcher, told Miller that the pitch was going to be a fastball. Miller watched the pitch. It was a fastball right over the plate for a strike. Lonnett said the next pitch was also going to be a fastball. It was and Miller hit it over the right field fence in foul territory. Although the next two pitches were balls, Lonnett was telling him every pitch. Of course, Miller still had to hit it. The next pitch was over the plate, and Miller swung and missed.

The Dodgers wound up winning 8–4. Miller's strikeout turned out to be his only at-bat in the major leagues. Why would Walter Alston have put him in? The six-time Manager of the Year and Hall of Famer had also had only one at-bat in the majors. Walter Alston had struck out, too.

What rookie pitcher was on the cover of *Sports Illustrated* in 1957 with his pitching brother? **Von McDaniel.** Von couldn't do anything wrong his rookie season with the St. Louis Cardinals. He was but a recent high school graduate when he shut out the Dodgers 2–0. A later outing was a one-hitter versus the Pittsburgh Pirates. For the season Von was 7–5 with a 3.22 ERA.

The next season for Von McDaniel was as discouraging as the previous season had been promising. After two games and a 13.50 ERA with St. Louis, he was released and wound up in the minor leagues. But a hitch in his delivery, arm trouble, and hitters hitting him hard ended a once-bright career.

It's not often that a .225 lifetime hitter will bat for Roger Maris, Ted Williams, and Carl Yastrzemski. In 1958, while with the Indians, **Carroll Hardy** went in to pinch-hit for Maris; and Hardy hit his first major league home run to win the game. In 1960, Hardy continued Williams's turn at bat, the only time anyone ever hit for The Splendid Splinter. (Williams had injured his foot on a foul tip and had to leave the game.) In 1961, Hardy pinch-hit for Yaz when the Boston star was a rookie. It's not often that a .225 lifetime hitter will bat for Maris, Williams, and Yastrzemski, but that's what Carroll Hardy can boast.

On August 11, 1959, a 23-year-old outfielder named **Gil Carter** of the Carlsbad, New Mexico, club was trying to surpass the home run record of 27 in the Sophomore Baseball League. Carter hit a shot, his twenty-eighth homer of the year, that went over the lights that stood 360 feet from home plate and kept on sailing out of sight. It wasn't until later that a builder in a subdivision found the baseball. It had traveled 730 feet. No one else has ever hit a baseball that has actually been measured as traveling that far.

Eli Grba pitched for the New York Yankees (1959–60) and the Los Angeles Angels (1961–63). He was the first expansion player in the draft and won the first game for the first expansion team. His record was 28–33. What Grba remembers most is his first strikeout victim in the majors: it was none other than Ted Williams.

Righthander **Ted Sadowski** was 2–3 in three years of pitching for the Senators and Twins (after the Senators moved to Minnesota). Here is what he had to say about it: "The greatest thrill of my baseball career was that in my first appearance in the big leagues, I struck out Ted Williams and won the game."

One doesn't usually think of Little League games as being dangerous. Nevertheless, on May 18, 1961, in Temple City, California, **Barry Babcock** was at bat. A pitch hit Barry right in the chest and the nine-year-old collapsed at the plate. Before an ambulance could arrive, the youngster died in the arms of the umpire.

Southpaw **Gary Dotter** appeared in seven games for the Minnesota Twins in '61, '63, and '64, but he only wound up with an 0–0 record and a sore arm. His career highlight was in '65 when he was 11–4 for Oklahoma City in the Pacific Coast League. But what stands out more than anything was hitting a home run. "I guess that's just like a pitcher," he wrote, "to remember his only home run."

Craig Anderson was 4–3 with the St. Louis Cardinals in 1961, but it was with the New York Mets that he made his entry in the record books. The righthander started out at 3–1 with the horrible '62 team, but then lost 16 in a row. In '63 he added two losses and topped off the tank with another in '64 to give Craig the major league consecutive loss record of 19. Roger Craig, another Met, threatened to surpass this record, but he managed to win one after 18 straight defeats. His career record of 7–23 disguises a grander futility. (See Roger Craig at 1963.)

Ironically, Anderson did something else that few have ever done. He won both games of a doubleheader. It was on May 12, 1962. He came on as a reliever in the first game against the San Francisco Giants at the old Polo Grounds, and Hobie Landrith won the game on a ninth-inning home run. Then in the nightcap Anderson was relieving again, and this time Gil Hodges won the game with a ninth-inning homer.

Tracy Stallard was not a pitcher for the ages. In 1964, he led the league by losing 20 games with the New York Mets, and his career record is 30–57. But there is one thing that Stallard will be remembered for, and that is serving up home run number 61 to Roger Maris.

Unlike the experience of Mark McGwire and Sammy Sosa chasing a new home run record in 1998, the experience of Maris and Mantle doing this in 1961 was far different. Many people did not want Babe Ruth's record broken. But if it were, it seemed that Mickey Mantle was the player that people wanted to do it. Maris was often regarded as surly and not fit to be mentioned in the same breath as Ruth. As might be imagined, this was at best a bittersweet experience for Maris, even when he hit number 59 off Milt Pappas of Baltimore in his 154th game. For unlike McGwire, Maris had to suffer the indignities of Commissioner Ford Frick maintaining that if Maris were to break the record, an asterisk would need to be placed alongside Maris's record to show he had played in 162 games and not 154 games as Babe Ruth had.

As the countdown continued, Maris tied Ruth with 60 against Jack Fisher in the 158th game. The sour attitude toward Maris continued, as evidenced in this account from the Associated Press: "Roger Maris blasted his sixtieth homer of the season Tuesday night, but it came four official games too late to officially tie Babe Ruth's 34-year-old record in 154 games." With that kind of press and negative reaction to the Yankee slugger, it's small wonder that his hair was beginning to fall out.

On the last regular day of the season, game 162, there were only 23,154 fans at Yankee Stadium as Maris tried to rewrite baseball history. (Compare this to the acclaim that greeted McGwire and Sammy Sosa throughout the later stages of the 1998 season.) On the mound for the Boston Red Sox was Tracy Stallard. In the first inning when Maris came up to bat, he hit an easy fly ball to left field. In the third inning, Maris came to the plate again. The man whom many wished had been Mantle threatening the record only had two or three more at-bats. The first pitch from Tracy Stallard was high. Stallard's second pitch bounced in the dirt. Sensing that Stallard was not going to give Maris a decent pitch to hit, the crowd began to boo. On his next pitch Stallard threw a fastball over the plate. Maris swung and connected on a line drive that went into the right field seats, 360 feet away. Roger Maris had broken Ruth's illustrious record set in 1927. And Tracy Stallard had served up the record-breaking pitch.

ost went unnoticed that he lost the well-pitched
1–0.

en," Stallard said afterward, "he hit a good
was a fastball on the inside part of the plate.
not a control pitcher. I just throw the ball. I put my
best stuff against his best stuff and he hit my best
stuff."

Roger Maris had this to say about Stallard: "He was
man enough to pitch to me and try to get me out."

Unfortunately, breaking the record brought Maris
little joy. "It would have been a helluva lot more fun,"
he admitted a few years later, "if I had never hit those
sixty-one home runs."

Oddly enough, being a part of breaking Ruth's
record seemed to be easier for Tracy Stallard. Once
when asked about the pitcher who would be giving up
the 715th home run to Henry Aaron, thus breaking
Ruth's total home run mark, Tracy Stallard commented: "Personally, I think he should consider it an
honor."

The name **Bo Belinsky** might be synonymous with
playboy for many people. (Paraphrasing Babe Ruth's
roommate, Ping Bodie, Bo's roommate, Albie Pearson
said: "I was just Bo's answering service. I never saw
him at night. I just roomed with his suitcase.") Belinsky was as well known for his dates with Tina Louise,
Ann-Margret, Connie Stevens, and Mamie Van Doren
as he was for his baseball playing. But he was a pitcher
and he did win his first three major league starts for the
Los Angeles Angels in 1962.

Bo (the nickname was probably after the fighter

Bobo Olson because the young Belinsky was always getting knocked down in school) had an odd path to the playing field. He never played high school baseball. As he once put it, "I didn't dig the sis-boom-bah . . . yes-sir, no-sir stuff." What he did do was hang out in pool halls and work in a factory, carrying around material for women stitching together clothing, until he couldn't stand it any longer.

"I can join the Army," thought Belinsky. "That's out. I can be a gambler, maybe. That's risky. So I think of baseball. That's it. I'll be a professional baseball player. Got a nice sound to it."

Bo Belinsky's biggest moment on the field came on May 5, 1962, when he threw the first no-hitter ever on the West Coast. The Angels were playing the Orioles that night and the Birds had a lineup that featured Jim Gentile, Brooks Robinson, and the young Boog Powell.

Sometimes when a pitcher has a no-hitter going, the players will not mention it to him and will even keep away from him on the bench. But things with Bo were often the opposite. Players kept reminding him of it. Belinsky felt his good luck had come from the woman he had been with the night before. "When I lost her," he said of the rest of his career, "I lost my pitching luck." As Felix Torres caught a Dave Nicholson pop-up in foul territory for the final out, Bo seemed more moved by a blonde in the stands than by his accomplishment. He was also put off by how the no-hitter cost him money. "I had to buy drinks for everyone," he said. "It was like a hole-in-one."

Belinsky hung on until 1970 with stints playing for

the Phillies, Astros, Pirates, and Reds. His record was a lackluster 28–51, but Bo himself had no regrets.

"I don't feel sorry for myself," he once said. "I knew sooner or later I'd have to pay the piper. You can't beat the piper, Babe; I never thought I could. But I'll tell you who I do feel sorry for—all those guys who never heard the music."

Tom Cheney may have had a less-than-stellar record, 19-29, for three different teams during eight years in the majors, but along the way he threw eight shutouts. Overshadowing the shutouts was the game Cheney pitched on September 12, 1962.

The 5-11, 170-pound righthander had 147 strikeouts that year, but that night against the Orioles, the 27-year-old Cheney struck out 21 Orioles in a 16-inning game, setting a major league record. Also, the Orioles sent four pitchers into the game to try to stop Cheney. But that was his night to glow with a golden flame as the Senators beat the Birds, 2–1. Cheney was also helped by a player who was in his last of two seasons, Bud Zipfel. Zipfel's two RBIs out of a lifetime total of 39 notched the win.

The major league record for consecutive losses in a single season was set by Jack Nabors of the American League's Philadelphia Athletics back in 1915. Nineteen straight losses. This seemed unapproachable until **Roger Craig** of the hapless New York Mets had 24 total losses in their first year. The next year Craig had tied the National League record of 18 consecutive losses and was one short of Nabors.

On August 9, 1963, Craig faced Paul Toth of the Cubs at the Polo Grounds, one game shy of the record. But Craig wasn't pitching like a man who was going to lose. The Mets righthander and Toth were locked up in a thriller. Bottom of the ninth, Mets up, score tied 3–3.

Frank Thomas hit a fly ball to left field. One out. Joe Hicks knocked a single. Choo Choo Coleman struck out. Al Moran hit a rope into the corner. By the time the left fielder had thrown it back to the infield, there were runners on second and third. Two outs. Craig up. Stengel sent in Tim Harkness to pinch-hit for Craig. Harkness walked. Next up was Jim Hickman. Count three and two. Bases loaded. "Casey at the Bat" stuff. Hickman hit a grand slam. Mets win.

"The Ballad of Roger Craig" greeted the readers of the sports section the next day. "A woeful tale of one of the great right-handed tragic heroes of modern times, came to a glorious end last night as the New York Mets ended his losing streak. . . ."

Craig went on to manage and teach his slick split-fingered fastball to Jack Morris and Mike Scott, who won the Cy Young Award with it in 1986.

Dick Nen had only eight at-bats for the 1963 Brooklyn Dodgers, but he chose well when to connect for his one hit. The scene was September 18 in St. Louis at Sportsman's Park. The Dodgers and the Cardinals were in the throes of a tight race for the National League pennant. It was Nen's homer that kept the Dodgers in the game, a game they later won in 13 innings.

Inspired by Nen's homer, Dem Bums went on to clinch the pennant, then swept the Yanks in four straight. Nen's teammates certainly did not forget who had made the championship possible, as they voted Dick Nen a share of the World Series money. Afterwards Nen's fame fizzled. It was to be two long years before he posted another major league at-bat.

The name of **Steve Dalkowski** may not appear in *The Baseball Encyclopedia*, but he does exist in the memory of many old-timers as being the hardest thrower of all time. One of his catchers in the minor leagues, Cal Ripken Sr., once said, "Nobody else was close." Some outfielders on one of his many minor league teams would agree. One day they had been trying to one-hop the ball to home plate 430 feet away when Dalkowski strolled over and sailed the ball over the backstop. There was a batter who would also cast his vote for him. On an 0–2 pitch, Dalko fired a brushback pitch. The ball cleanly sliced off part of the batter's ear and sent him to the hospital with a concussion. That young ballplayer never played again.

The problem with Dalko was he was wild. There was the time he pitched a no-hitter. Eighteen strikeouts, what a night! However, along with that stellar performance there were also 21 walks. Another time he pitched a one-hitter and lost 9–8. Or the night he struck out 19 but lost 8–3. For his entire nine-year career in the minor leagues Dalko registered 13 strikeouts every nine innings, but he also chalked up about the same number of walks.

Another problem with him was his wildness off the field. During his playing career and most of his life, he was an out-of-control alcoholic. He was practically as legendary as a drinker as he was as a pitcher. After practice he once drank 30 beers. And that had only been a warmup.

Certainly his drinking and low self-esteem didn't help him as a person and as a pitcher, but there were times when the opposing batter felt his bat wasn't of much use either.

What was it like to face Steve Dalkowski?

Joe Pepitone, who later played outfield and first base for the New York Yankees, told of his experience. "He struck me out five times in one game," recalled Pepitone. "He threw harder than anybody who ever lived. The ball started low and rose above your chest. It was ridiculous. The umpire called a strike and I said, 'That's no strike, the ball sounded low.' The ump said, 'It sounded like a strike to me.' I was scared to death. Here I was with a chance to make some progress in the minor leagues and I had to face this guy who could kill me."

There was one time, though, when it all started coming together for Steve Dalkowski. Pitching for Elmira in 1962, in 160 innings he had 192 strikeouts, 114 bases on balls, and a 3.04 ERA. The next summer he posted a 2.79 ERA for Elmira. He had seemingly finally tamed his wildness on the mound and showed the promise that Earl Weaver had been hoping for. So, the next spring training he was invited up to the bigs and down to Florida for a tryout with the Orioles.

"Steve was a good kid at heart," said Baltimore manager Weaver, "but nobody could handle him. I tried to leave him alone as much as I could. In 1962, he was right there, mechanically. He still drank the same, but he always did, whether he was winning or losing."

Big leaguers who had been hearing about this pitcher for years were now finally able to get a look at him up close. One thing they found out was that he wasn't much to look at. Short, skinny, five-o'clock shadow, glasses. (For the record he was five-ten and weighed in at about 185 pounds.) But his fastball was something else. "He'd come right over the top with the ball," explained Weaver, "and it would rise as much as six inches. I honestly believe he was faster than Nolan Ryan." Two times in spring training he struck out the side. One of his victims was baseball great Ted Williams. "Fastest ever," a taciturn Ted said. "I never want to face him again."

Just how fast was he? The speed gun had not been invented yet, but there was a tube that was sometimes used at the Aberdeen Proving Grounds to measure a pitcher's speed. After having pitched the night before, Dalko threw for forty minutes before he finally hit the tube. Still, that pitch, which was not thrown off a pitcher's mound, was clocked at 93.5 miles per hour. (Nolan Ryan made it into *The Guinness Book of World Records* in 1974 with a 100.9 pitch.) But there were many others who said he could throw a lot harder than that. A few claimed 120 was more like it. Harry "The Cat" Brecheen, whose World Series ERA of 0.83 is tops, said Dalkowski had the "best arm in the history of baseball."

Cal Ripken Sr., agreed. "Steve Dalkowski threw harder than anyone in baseball. I saw Nolan Ryan and

Dalkowski from the third-base coaching box, and Nolan Ryan didn't compare with Dalkowski. I caught Steve, too. His ball was light as a feather. He was wild high, not in and out. You never worried about a ball in the dirt with him, only over your head. His ball took off two feet. If he didn't throw it at your shoe tops, you couldn't catch it."

What a success story in the making! An American League Sandy Koufax. ("Later I faced Sandy Koufax," said onetime Yankee manager Gene Michael of his experience playing for Grand Forks and facing Dalko, "but Steve Dalkowski was the hardest thrower I ever saw.")

With seven and two-thirds innings under his belt pitching against major league batters in spring training, Steve Dalkowski had 11 strikeouts, five walks, one hit, and no earned runs. When the Orioles would leave Miami and spring training behind, Dalko was slated to fly north with them.

"I don't know why," Dalko said, "but it was easy to strike out major leaguers."

In his final outing Dalkowski pitched against the Yankees. The first man up, Roger Maris, Dalko set down on three strikes. But later, with a runner on first, pitcher Jim Bouton came up to bat. Bouton bunted to move the runner over to second. Dalkowski charged off the mound, maybe not as catlike as Brecheen, but he fielded the bunt cleanly and threw over to first. And then nada. Nothing. With that toss to first, Steve Dalkowski's arm had gone dead. He couldn't even slow-pitch to the next batter, Bobby Richardson.

"I think a higher power took it away from me when

I had it all together," remarked Dalkowski. "I'm not mad. It was my own fault."

Sure, Dalko kicked around in baseball two more years—Rochester, Elmira again, Stockton, Columbus, Tri-Cities, San Jose. But the fastball had disappeared. Finally, he wound up playing winter ball for Mazatlan in the Mexican League. And in the spring of 1966 they asked him to return. Dalkowski did not want to go back. It was over.

His record for those nine years in Class C and D? Forty-six wins, eighty losses, and a 5.57 ERA. But the most interesting statistics are that in 995 innings, Dalko had struck out 1,396 batters and issued 1,345 walks.

"I truly think," said Cal Ripken Sr., "that Steve Dalkowski, if he had pitched in the big leagues, would have been a legend. He was capable of striking out 21 batters in the big leagues."

One thing is for certain. Ted Williams never had to face him again.

Who was the oldest rookie ever? Some say it was Satchel Paige, but he may have been 42 when he put on a Cleveland Indians uniform. Or it may have been **Diomedes Olivo**, who was definitely 43 when he was a rookie for Pittsburgh in 1962. The southpaw from the Dominican Republic was 5–1 that year with 7 saves and an ERA of 2.77 in 62 games. In 1963 he was 0–5 for St. Louis.

John Paciorek was the oldest brother in a baseball family. His brother Tom played for six different teams over a 15-year career in the major leagues and sported a .282 batting average. His brothers Jim and Mike played minor league ball with Jim spending part of 1987 with the Milwaukee Brewers.

Born in 1945, John Paciorek Jr., played for only one major league team, the Houston Colt .45's, and he played in only one game. However, this right fielder does have bragging rights on a spotless record; and of all the players with a 1.000 major league batting average, John has the most hits. In five appearances at the plate in the final game of the 1963 season, on September 29, against the cellar-dwelling Mets, 18-year-old John rapped three singles and drew two walks. "Every time I came up," said John, the seventh batter in the lineup, "the ball looked like a watermelon." To top matters off, this six-foot-four, 215-pound outfielder also knocked in three runs and scored four himself. "I was hurting the whole time," said John, who was in Houston from his minor league team for the doctors to check his chronic bad back, "but I just didn't let it bother me that game. It was really exciting. I felt great. I was looking forward to more of it."

Declared in the *Houston Press* to be "a cinch to make it as a big leaguer," the next year John received bad news from the doctors. His bad back was a congenital spine problem. After spinal fusion surgery, John Paciorek spent the next few years with seven different minor league teams, but in 1968 he was released for the second time, this time for good. John Paciorek's auspicious major league debut proved also to be his departure.

* * *

In 1964, **Dave Bennett** was a bonus baby for the Phillies. In his only appearance in a major league game, Dave relieved his older brother Dennis Bennett. The younger brother pitched only one inning, giving up two hits and getting one strikeout.

Although neither one got the decision, Dave and Dennis Bennett are the only lefthanded and righthanded pitching brothers ever to appear for the same team in the same major league game.

In 1966, **John Miller** hit a home run for the New York Yankees in his first major league at-bat. In the final at-bat of his two-year major league career, the five-foot-eleven, 195-pounder hit another home run in 1969 for the Los Angeles Dodgers. Miller had a total of only two homers in his 61 at-bats.

"The greatest thrill of my career was the first big league victory that I pitched at the age of 18," recalled **Charlie Vaughan**. "I started the game against the Houston Astros in September 1966. Luckily, I struck out the first batter that I faced and singled my first time at bat. We won the game 12–2. Ha! Easy or what! It's too bad the big leagues aren't that easy all the time." Charlie Vaughan appeared in an Atlanta Braves uniform for one game in 1966 and one game in 1969. The game against the Astros was his only major league victory and his only hit.

St. Louis called **Larry Jaster** up to the Red Birds late in the 1966 season and the rookie responded with three complete game victories in three starts. The next year he totally dominated the Dodgers (and this was a team that would win the pennant) by pitching five straight shutouts on his way to an 11–5 year. There were few fireworks in the rest of his seven-year career, as Jaster wound up with a record of 35–33.

It was one of those situations that a kid might set up while throwing at the garage door. Yankee Stadium. Ninth inning. Two outs. Full count. One batter left who might ruin the perfect game underway.

And that was the situation on April 14, 1967 for **Billy Rohr**. It was Opening Day and the Yankees had veteran Whitey Ford on the mound. Rohr, a 21-year-old, six-foot-three, 170-pound lefthander for the Red Sox, was making his major league debut. Yankee catcher Elston Howard stood between Rohr and history—no one in the twentieth century had ever thrown a perfect game in his first outing. The count went to 3-and-2. On the next pitch, Howard stroked a single to center. You could hear a collective groan in the stadium. Retiring the next batter, Rohr had to settle for a 3–0 shutout.

Rohr hooked up with the Yankees again in his second start and beat them 6–1. There would be no more wins in 1967, however, only three losses. The next year found him in Cleveland, where he won only one game. And that was it. Three wins. Three losses. Two complete games out of eight started. Appearances in 27 games. Pitched 60 and two-thirds innings. Gave up 61 hits and 32 bases on balls while registering 21 strikeouts.

After such an auspicious beginning, Rohr was out of the majors. Another collective groan would be in order.

Gene Stone had six hits (no home runs) in 28 at-bats for the 1969 Philadelphia Phillies. So it stands to reason that he might look back longingly on a time he hit a homer. "I think my biggest thrill in baseball was in 1967 when I played Class A ball with Bakersfield in the California League," recalled Stone. "Against Lodi in June I hit grand slam homers in consecutive times at bat. The third time up I was drilled in the back with a fastball. I was kinda expecting it."

On April 8, 1969, pitcher **Dan McGinn** of the Montreal Expos hit his one and only career home run for the first home run ever hit by a member of the expansion team. Later that same month, in the first major league game ever played in Canada, McGinn singled home the run that gave him the victory. He only had 14 more victories to go with his 30 defeats.

In July 1971, 12-year-old **Sharon Poole** played on the Little League's Haverhill (Massachusetts) Indians. The Little League organization cut her from the team and got rid of her coach, Donald Scuto. In 1972, 12-year-old **Maria Pepe** became a member of the Hoboken, New Jersey, Young Democrats team, and Little League pressured her off the team. In June 1973, another 12-year-old, **Carolyn King**, made the Ypsilanti (Michigan) Orioles, and Little League told the team it would be kicked out of Little League. The families of all three girls went to court. On September 7, 1974, Little League agreed to admit girls.

If you want to play baseball, it might not be easy to have a younger brother like Hall of Famer Robin Yount. But **Larry Yount** also had his big chance. He was called up from the minors to the Houston Astros and on September 15, 1971, Yount the Elder was sent into the game in the ninth inning to pitch to the Atlanta Braves, who were ahead. As Yount put his foot on the rubber and went into his windup for his first warmup pitch, he hurt his shoulder. After that it was back to the minors for him. He never got back to the bigs again.

On August 10, 1974, a record was set that no one leafing through a fat book of baseball statistics would know about. It was on that date that the youngest person ever to have signed a contract played in a game of organized baseball.

Jorge Lebron had been playing shortstop in a game in Puerto Rico when he was spotted by a scout for the Phillies. The 14-year-old was signed and sent to the Phillies' farm team in Auburn, New York, a member of the New York–Penn League. (Joe Nuxhall had been fifteen when he was signed by the Cincinnati Reds.) The newest member of the ball club was so young that the Auburn general manager had to be appointed as his legal guardian.

Lebron's debut took place on a Sunday in a game with Batavia. To comply with the New York child labor laws (no one under sixteen can work past seven o'clock), the game was moved up from its usual starting time of seven-thirty to six o'clock. On the first pitch of the game, the ball was smacked up the middle. Lebron moved to his left, fielded the ball cleanly, and fired to first. One out. In the rookie's first time at-bat he drew a walk. Before leaving in the third inning, Lebron had a putout and another assist at shortstop.

The next game was with Newark. Lebron's presence in the lineup was certainly not hurting attendance. There were 3,642 fans squeezed into the 3,500-seat stadium in Auburn. In this game the five-foot-ten, 150-pounder made two sparkling plays in the field— snagging a line drive and catching up with a blooper before it fell in for a hit. At the plate he was hitless in four tries.

All in all, the experiment with the youngest rookie had been a success. It came to an end, however, after Lebron's second game. Jorge Lebron had to hustle back to Puerto Rico for the start of the school year. Perhaps at his junior high school the excuse of "But I had to play professional baseball" ranked alongside "But the dog ate my homework." Jorge Lebron never rose above the minors.

Who appeared in 104 games in the 1974–75 seasons but picked up neither a bat nor a glove? **Herb Washington.** It would take a Charles Finley to sign this world-class sprinter to serve as a "designated runner" for the Oakland Athletics. Washington's world indoor record speed in the 50- and 60-yard dashes (5.0 and 5.8) paved the way to his 30 steals. But it is the second game of the 1974 World Series with the Dodgers that stands out in memory. Sent in as a pinch runner for the heavy-footed Joe Rudi, Washington was picked off second by the mustachioed Mike Marshall.

The wonderful 1975 World Series between the Cincinnati Reds and the Boston Red Sox went right down to the seventh game. With the score tied 3–3 in the bottom of the eighth, two outs, no one on base, Red Sox manager Darrell Johnson pulled out his hot relief pitcher, Jim Willoughby, for a pinch hitter. With the score still tied in the top of the ninth, Johnson put in rookie pitcher **Jim Burton**, who had only 53 innings in the majors. To go with his 1–2 record, Burton had 19 bases on balls, 39 strikeouts, and 58 hits. After getting two outs on the Reds, Burton gave up a single to Joe Morgan that scored Ken Griffey. In the bottom of the ninth, Boston failed to score. After falling behind, three games to none, Cincinnati had come back to take the Series.

The next year Burton pitched only two and two-thirds innings, giving up one base on balls, two hits, and three strikeouts. That was the last he was heard of in the big leagues.

Mark Fidrych had more than 15 minutes of fame, but it all amounted to the same thing. It was too s-h-o-r-t.

On April 6, 1976, the Bird was told he was going to fly north with the Tigers after spring training. He had made the team. What a rush. What excitement.

At the first game he pitched at Tigers Stadium, the Bird showed how he had gained his nickname. (His coach back in Bristol was the one who named him because he thought Mark looked like Big Bird on *Sesame*

Street. Plus, Fidrych was too difficult to pronounce.) The rookie scratched around on the mound. He fluttered his elbows like a chicken. He squawked at the ball. Well, not really.

"I never did talk to the ball," he said. "I ain't sayin', 'Hey c'mon ball, c'mon ball.' I'm saying, 'C'mon, Mark, you gotta throw a strike.' "

In any case, with his antics and frizzy hair and zest for baseball, Mark took the baseball world by storm. He was a happening. There was even a dance modeled after him called The Fried Egg, in which people would lie on their backs and scootch around the floor.

Fidrych even got the nod to start for the American League in the All-Star Game on July 13, 1976. By year's end, he had won 19 while losing nine and had a league-leading 2.34 ERA. He won the American League Rookie of the Year honors in a walk.

But all of this came to a sad ending the next spring. For a reason known best to the Bird, or maybe it was just to save a half-minute, Mark climbed over a fence and jumped down on the other side on the way to the clubhouse. He hurt his knee, and then reinjured it the next day shagging a fly. Eventually he had surgery, then when he came back he injured his shoulder. Five years later he was out of baseball. He had won only 10 more games and wound up with as many losses, 19, as he had racked up wins in his rookie year.

Glenn Burke played in 225 games for the Dodgers and then the A's from 1976 to 1979. It may be stretching the definition of hero, but Burke did make an important personal stand by declaring his homosexuality in a 1982 issue of *Inside Sports*. In 1995, at the age of 42, Glenn Burke died of complications from AIDS.

Al Autry gave up the idea of going to college on a baseball scholarship to go directly into baseball in 1969. That way, he thought, he would get to the big leagues faster. He had a hopping fastball, even though he displayed little control. That was okay when he was 17. There was still time. But as the years rolled by and he still didn't have much control, things began to look a lot less certain about his making it.

Then in 1976 in Richmond, everything seemed to come together. Autry pitched eight complete games, had a 2.85 ERA, and beat such future greats as Ron Guidry and Dennis Martinez. Atlanta noticed and put him on the roster for the last part of the season.

Autry got his chance on September 15, 1976. He was to start the second game of a doubleheader against Houston. But it was one of those moments when you get your opportunity and realize that you don't have the stuff that got you there in the first place. Nothing much was working for him except pride. Autry gave up homers to Cesar Cedeno and Jose Cruz and two other hits, walked three, struck out three, and allowed three runs. Still it was good enough. When Autry left after five innings, the Braves were ahead 4–3. It was a score that would remain the same, giving Al Autry his first win in the majors. The next year he was back in Richmond, then he was traded, and then he was out of baseball. Perhaps it was a combination of bad luck and a lack of desire, but it was to be his only win in the major leagues.

* * *

Brian Doyle wasn't much to shout about during his four years in the majors from 1978–81. In 199 at-bats, he had only 32 hits for a dismal .161 batting average. But in the 1978 World Series he replaced the injured Willie Randolph at second base for the Yankees and it all came together. Doyle had a splendid series, connecting for 7 hits in 16 at-bats, scoring 4 runs, and knocking in 2 runs.

In 1979, **Crystal Fields** won the annual Pitch, Hit, and Run contest before the Major League Baseball All-Star Game, which was held in Seattle. The 11-year-old girl from Cumberland, Maryland, beat a field of boys to win.

From a good baseball town, Texarkana, Texas, **Terry Felton** pitched for the Minnesota Twins from 1979 to 1982. He started 10 games, appeared in 55, but his won-loss record, 0–16, is the worst in all of baseball.

Joe Charboneau passed through the majors like a comet. In 1980, Super Joe batted .289 with 23 homers and 87 RBI. That was enough to garner American League Rookie of the Year honors for this outfielder-designated hitter. The big guy was celebrated with a book about him, a song, and a fan club 500 strong.

But as it turned out, Charboneau could have been nicknamed Super Joe for what he did off the field. He dyed his hair different colors, chomped on lighted cigarettes, snuffled beer up his nose after opening the bottle with his eye socket, swallowed eggs whole, pulled out a rotten tooth or two. Before he entered baseball, he used to box bare knuckled in boxcars for some extra dough. The guy was a tough flake.

By 1981 the magic had vanished and Charboneau was sent down to the minors after batting a disappointing .210 and hitting only four more home runs. From there things got worse. He had two back operations and by 1982 could only muster a .214 batting average for the Indians. The last indignity was when he flipped the bird to the Cleveland fans. It was to be his swan song.

On April 18, 1981, the Pawtucket Red Sox had played the Rochester Red Wings to a 2–2 tie in 32 innings when the game was called at 4:07 in the morning. Only 20 fans out of the 1,470 fans who had been there for this International League game at eight o'clock were still awake. The game was to be completed on the next swing of Rochester into Pawtucket, but that didn't take place until June 23. This time the stadium overflowed with 5,756 fans, as well as TV, radio, and newspaper coverage from as far away as England and Japan. (The longest professional baseball game before this one was a 29-inning game between Miami and St. Petersburg in 1966 in the Florida State League.) But this time the game seemed to be played in quick time. In the top of the thirty-third, Bob Ojeda set the Red Wings down in order; in the bottom of the thirty-third, the Red Sox loaded the bases and **Dave Koza** singled Marty Barrett in for the 3–2 victory. Koza never made it to the major leagues.

After eight years in the minors and going 1–2 for Atlanta in 1982, **Joe Cowley** made it to the Yankees, where he was 9–2 in 1984. In 1985, with a 12–6 record, he was traded to the White Sox. On May 28, 1986, Cowley struck out the first seven Texas Ranger batters he faced to set an American League record. And on September 19, 1986, Cowley threw a no-hitter against the Angels. (He also had seven walks and won 7–1.) But that was it. He never won again. He was traded to the Phillies, was 0–4, then he was sent back to the minors. Joe Cowley is the only player to post a no-hitter as his last victory in the big leagues.

Julie Croteau played baseball from the age of six: T-ball, Little League, Major League, Babe Ruth League. She had less success with her high school baseball team, however, the Osbourn Park Yellow Jackets. Finally, when she was cut from the team again her senior year, her parents sued. As a sympathetic observer, the baseball coach at Catholic University, Ross Natolli said: "I'm seeing seventy to eighty high school games a year, and she has enough ability to make most high school teams." But the district court judge stated that Title IX did not apply to her case. One of the reporters in the courtroom, Mike Zitz, was also a baseball coach and offered her a tryout on his team, the Fredericksburg Giants of the Virginia Baseball League. Croteau made the team in 1987 and played with them for years.

In 1988, Croteau enrolled at St. Mary's College of Maryland. The Division III school assured her they would not prevent her from playing baseball. She made the team and in March 1989 played her first game at first base. It was a big story at the time: a woman playing in an NCAA baseball game. She fielded six grounders and didn't strike out, though she didn't get a hit either. The Seahawks lost 4–1 to Spring Garden College of Philadelphia.

The next year Croteau started in two-thirds of the games at first and hit .250. She quit before her senior year because women were still regarded as second-class citizens in mainstream sports.

"What happened is that for some reason I was this hero and everyone accepted it and the media covered it and the media and school were telling everyone it was a great thing," said Croteau. "When the media went away, so did the message."

In 1994, Croteau played a season for the Maui Stingrays in the Hawaii Winter League and for the Colorado Silver Bullets. She played in 29 games and was outstanding defensively. She made only two errors and was a part of 21 double plays. At the plate she walked more than she struck out (13 versus 9), but she had only 4 hits in 51 at-bats. In 1995, Julie Croteau became the first woman assistant coach for a men's college baseball team at the University of Massachusetts at Amherst (Division I).

On August 23, 1989, **Victoria Brucker** played in the Little League World Series. But by no means was she a token girl who just got in the record book because she was a girl. Victoria Brucker was a starting pitcher and batted cleanup. In the quarterfinals against Tampa Bay, Brucker scored three runs—the first girl ever to get a hit and score a run—as her team from San Pedro, California, defeated the Little Leaguers from Florida, 12 to 5.

* * *

The name **Ila Borders** seems to beg a dot-com after it, but this five-foot-ten, 150-pound woman has been in the vanguard of women in baseball. It began her senior year at Whittier Christian High School in La Mirada, California, where she posted 52 strikeouts in 42 innings, a 4–2 record, and a 2.42 ERA. This earned Borders the baseball MVP award from the high school, the all-league first team honors, and a scholarship to Southern California College (NAIA Division II) in Costa Mesa—the first woman ever to receive a scholarship to play men's baseball. In 1995, Borders became the first woman to win a college baseball game. She not only pitched a complete game but she also allowed only five hits as Whittier beat Claremont-Mudd, 12–1. In her second start, Borders didn't allow an earned run in a 10–1 victory over Concordia. All of this pointed the way to the dream that she had held since the age of ten, to play professional baseball. "This has nothing to do with women's rights," said Borders. "I love the game, nothing else."

Paying her way to the St. Paul Saints' training camp, the 22-year-old lefthander struggled to make the team. Her first big moment came on May 22, 1997, in a practice game before a sellout crowd of 6,329 at Midway Stadium. Coming into the game in the seventh, the first batter Borders faced was Jeff Jensen. Running the count to 2 and 2, Jensen dug in and Borders looked down from the mound, got her sign, and pitched a swinging strike three.

"She painted the outside corner and came back with a good change-up," said Jensen. "I tip my hat to her."

The rest of the inning was a walk and two ground

outs. Coming off the mound Borders got a standing ovation.

The next inning was as bad as the seventh had been good. But it wasn't all Borders's doing. A bobbled ball turned into a double, an error let in a run as Borders lost the game in relief.

"Her velocity is short," said Saints manager Marty Scott of her 82-mile-per-hour fastball, "but her work ethic is as good as anyone I have been around." It was her attitude that made people want to take a chance on her.

On May 31, in her first game in relief in a regular season game in the Northern League, Borders faced the Sioux Falls Canaries. On her first pitch she hit a batter in the back. She balked and a runner came home. She made a throwing error. Before she left the game without getting anyone out, three runs had scored on two singles and three errors.

In her next outing on June 1, also against Sioux Falls, Ila and everyone else knew that her future was then and there. After giving up a single, Borders went on to strike out the side. It was a sweet moment. "What's the most fun?" Borders once said. "The competition. Going out there and knowing that I'm laying everything on the line and all the hard work I've done to that point will either pay off, or will teach me a lesson."

But there were too many relievers on the St. Paul staff and Borders was expendable. "I truly enjoyed having Ila here but the fact is that we have four left-handed relievers on our staff and that is simply too many," reasoned Marty Scott. On June 25, Borders was traded to the Duluth-Superior Dukes. Ila Borders ended the year with 22 innings pitched over 15 games. She had an ERA of 7.53; she had allowed 16 runs, walked 9, and struck out 12.

On July 9, 1998, Borders achieved another first. She became the first woman to start a professional baseball game, going five innings, giving up three runs, five hits, walking two, and striking out two, before being relieved after five innings, trailing Sioux Falls, 3–2.

On July 24, 1998, Borders beat Sioux Falls, 3–1. It was the first time a woman had won a regular season game in men's professional baseball.

On August 29, 1998, the team from Toms River, New Jersey, met the team from Kashima, Japan, for the Little League Championship of the World. Kashima took the early lead, 3–0, but in the fourth, Scott Fisher and Casey Gaynor hit home runs for Toms River. And in the fifth, **Chris Cardone** came off the bench to pinch-hit.

Chris had been in a series slump, having gone only 1 for 10. "No matter how hard it gets," reasoned Chris, "you got to keep going, you can't give up. I was planning to make every moment I get into my moment." And he certainly did. Chris hit a homer to give the team from New Jersey an 8–4 lead.

No one in the crowd of 41,200 in Williamsport, Pennsylvania, could have been more surprised than Cardone when he connected for a round-tripper. Chris Cardone had never been a home-run hitter. His fifth-inning blast was his first homer of the team's 28-game season. "I thought that if [manager Mike Gaynor] put me in that I would do something," Cardone said later.

"I just wanted to help the team. I really didn't think I was going to do what I did today."

But that was only a preview of what was to come in his next at-bat. In the sixth inning, the 4-foot-10, 98-pound Cardone ripped another homer. This time his two-run home run broke the 8–8 tie and put Toms River in the lead for good. With two swings of the bat Chris Cardone had gone from warming the bench to being the boy of the moment. "I got lucky," he admitted. The team near the Jersey coast went on to win the Little League World Series. The final score was Toms River 12, Kashima 9.

The whole area turned out for the welcoming celebration: fire trucks from 12 local towns, acres of cars, thousands of fans. "Marry Me Chris Cardone" pleaded the large sign of seven-year-old Alexa Manforti.

"He's an inspiration to me on how to handle things," declared Chris's proud father, a grade-school principal. "He taught me patience."

That's a good thing to know whether you're a Little Leaguer, a big leaguer, or a parent.

Jim Morris had always dreamed of making it to the major leagues, but instead, at 35 found himself a science teacher and baseball coach at Reagan County High School in Big Lake, Texas. One day while challenging his team to attempt greater heights, the catcher asked Morris why he didn't pursue his own dreams. Joel DeLaGarza knew how hard their coach threw batting practice and guessed the rest. Morris had once pursued a dream of being a big league pitcher but had given up 10 years earlier after three arm operations. A bargain was struck with the team. If the Owls won their first district championship ever, Morris had to attend a major league tryout camp. In the district championship game, Big Lake surprised both Van Horn High School, 10–3, and Jim Morris.

Morris heard that Tampa Bay was holding a tryout in Brownwood on June 19, 1999, for players between the ages of 18 and 24. Although he was at first mistaken for the father of one of the 70 prospects, when it was Morris's turn, he threw what turned out to be his first of 50 pitches. Another radar gun was sent for. Before long, everyone was standing near the catcher. Morris was consistently clocking 98 mph fastballs.

By the time Morris got back home, the phone was ringing. The Devil Rays wanted him. The next day, however, they asked to see him throw again. Morris understood more than they realized. Again he threw 50 pitches. Again, it was all smoke, all the time. Not one was under 96 mph. After saying goodbye to his wife Lorri and three kids, it was off to the Tampa Bay Devil Rays' compound in St. Petersburg, where he worked to get in shape. It wasn't a fluke. Morris was still pitching in the 90s.

Morris was sent to join double-A Orlando. In the seventh inning Morris went in the game and balked. But then he got the next hitter on a grounder and struck out the next batter to end the inning. Two nights later he got a save. Morris was soon on his way to the triple-A Durham Bulls. Three games later Morris was on the mound in relief. The first batter hit a home run, but then Morris settled down and got the next six batters out. His slider and 98-mph fastball did the trick. He finished the season at Durham and thought that just might be it. But after the last game Morris was called into the office and told he was going up to the majors for the last two weeks of the season. He joined the Devil Rays in Arlington on September 18 for a game with the Texas Rangers.

Morris had pitched in the final two games for Durham and had had only one hour of sleep the night before, and though family and friends were in the stadium he didn't figure he would get in the game, until the phone rang for him in the bullpen. It was put-up-or-shut-up time for the 35-year-old rookie.

The batter was Royce Clayton. Morris threw a fastball. Strike one. Morris threw another fastball. Strike two. Morris threw another fastball. Clayton got a piece of it for a foul toward first. All of the pitches had been low and away and 98 mph. John Flaherty, the catcher, signaled for another fastball up high. Clayton tried to check his swing but had come around far enough for strike three. Morris had made it from Big Lake to the Big Show.

For the rest of 1999 and 2000 Jim Morris appeared in 21 games and pitched 15 innings. He struck out 13 and allowed 13 hits (2 of them homers), 9 bases on balls, and 8 earned runs, before arm trouble forced him out of baseball. Jim Morris retired with an 0–0 won-loss record, no saves, and an ERA of 4.80. But it's not the statistics that tell the story. It's the story—a story that has led to a book, *The Oldest Rookie*, and a feature film, *The Rookie*, starring Dennis Quaid.

Basketball

*"The only difference between a good shot
and a bad shot is if it goes in or not."*
—Charles Barkley

On February 25, 1924, **Marie Boyd** set a new standard for personal dominance of a basketball game by pouring in 156 points as Central High School of Lonaconing, Maryland, defeated Ursuline Academy by the whopping score of 163–3. Ms. Boyd had accounted for all but 10 of the game's 166 points.

Even the occasional basketball fan took notice of what happened in girls' basketball on January 10, 1931. **Louise Hicks** pumped in 69 points and **Ruby Selph** added 53, as the Magnolia A&M School in Monticello, Arkansas, overpowered Jonesboro Baptist, 143–1. During a five-game span, Magnolia outscored their adversaries, 455 to 29.

Have you ever watched pros miss free throw shots and wondered why it wasn't more of an automatic than an adventure?

One of the best free throw shooters ever was five-foot-four **Harold "Bunny" Levitt**. On April 6, 1935, Levitt stood at the foul line of the Von Steuben gym in Chicago. There were 30 baskets set up for all the shooters. The National Amateur Athletic Association rules were that you shot until you missed twice. With 4,000 people watching, Levitt walked up to the line at precisely 7 P.M. and lofted the first of his underhanded free throws. He usually shot 100 free throws in an hour, but tonight he was taking his time. "After the first 100 throws," he often told himself, "try not to try too hard; or else the concentration will cramp your muscles and mind, and tire you out." Another thing he did was to spin the ball until he found the exact center and the same seam before shooting. He also sanded his fingertips to increase his sensitivity to the ball and focused on the front lip of the rim. Five hours later Levitt missed one. But he had hit 499 straight. After that the crowd thinned out, but Levitt continued to shoot his underhanded free throws. It was almost two-thirty in the morning and Levitt had hit another 371 in a row before the gym had to be closed for the night.

That night was only the beginning for Levitt, as he was to travel with the Harlem Globetrotters, staging free-throw contests. The challenge was that anyone who could beat him would win $1,000. There were 400 challengers, but no one ever did. Levitt's worst performance was 96 in a row, but his average was 98. The closest anyone ever came was 86.

In 1948, Bunny Levitt performed in another official free-throwing contest. Would you believe that he again netted 499 before missing one?

* * *

Sometimes players seem to win singlehandedly for their teams. Think of Michael Jordan and many of his exploits during his long career. But at the other end of the skill spectrum, there was once a high school game when it was literally true. On May 16, 1937, in a game between the seniors and sophomores at St. Peter's High School in Fairmont, Virginia, **Pat McGee** found himself alone on the floor for his team with the score tied at 32–32. All of his teammates had fouled out. But not to be undone, McGee made up in enthusiasm what he lacked in numbers. He scored a basket, sank a free throw, and prevented the other five players from scoring for four long minutes as his "team" two-stepped to a 35–32 victory.

The first game of the National Invitation Tournament in 1946 featured the University of Rhode Island and Bowling Green State University. With Bowling Green on top 74–72 and time fading from the clock, the Falcons decided to foul Rhode Island. Only three seconds were left. Back in the '40s, a nonshooting foul was always worth only one shot, so the Falcons thought they would be getting the ball back. No such luck, however. One could also choose to take the ball out of bounds, and that's just what the Rams did. **Ernie Caverley** got the ball near the midcourt stripe and lofted a 55-foot shot that just made it and sent the game into overtime. Rhode Island eventually won by the score of 82–79.

"I consider two accomplishments most rewarding," wrote All-American **Gerald Tucker**, who was also a singer with his college quartet and choir. "As a player at the University of Oklahoma, reaching the NCAA finals in 1947 was one of the highlights. Our team that year was composed mainly of veterans just returned from service in World War II. Our coach, Bruce Drake, pulled us veterans and younger fellows together to form an excellent team. We won the Big Six Conference, and during the season, beat several teams that won their respective conferences. Although we were defeated in the NCAA finals by Holy Cross, it was a thrill to do as well as we did, and for my part, to be associated with a fine group of men.

"My highlight as a coach of the Phillips 66ers was being selected as coach of the 1956 United States Olympic basketball team. We had players with outstanding talent selected from across the US and they banded together, unselfishly, to be a fine team. We won the Olympics at Melbourne, Australia, without a loss. Our closest game was with Russia, whom we beat by thirty points. I was proud of our men and honored to compete as a representative of good old USA."

In 1948, **Joe Richey** scored a record-setting 41 points in the Arizona state tournament. At BYU in 1953, his senior year, he averaged 17.6 points. Richey was also known for his ability to steal the ball from opponents.

"It was a great moment when we won the NIT at Madison Square Garden in 1951," he wrote. "In those days the 'Garden' was the ultimate arena for basketball.

"My most exciting time was in a game against the University of Utah. At the end of the game with one minute to go, I scored six points in thirty-four seconds to bring us up within one point. We lost but the arena was in a frenzy for that last minute."

In 1952, the coach of Notre Dame, Johnny Jordan, found himself shorthanded as he prepared for a game with NYU at Madison Square Garden. So Coach Jordan brought along **Johnny Lattner** to help out, even though Lattner was a football player rather than a varsity basketball player. As it turned out, Lattner was needed. He only played a total of 26 seconds, but with nine seconds left in the game, Lattner scored the winning basket as Notre Dame upset NYU, 75–74.

Johnny O'Brien was short for a basketball player. Five-foot-nine. So short he wasn't able to make his high school basketball team until his junior year, and even then he was more comfortable on a baseball diamond. It was at a baseball tournament in Kansas, in fact, that Johnny and his twin brother Eddie were recruited by Al Brightman to go to Seattle University to play basketball. Both brothers were the same height and both played guard.

During Johnny's sophomore year, Coach Brightman was frustrated with his team's play in the first half of a game and told Johnny to play center for the first five minutes of the second half. Johnny did so well that he played center for the Chieftains from then on. He played center on offense, that is; on defense he moved back to guard. Their tallest player, the six-foot-three Wayne Sanford, played center on defense.

Teams in those days played mostly zone defenses

and didn't move around as much as they do today. This gave Johnny room to operate. He was a good leaper and had an array of shots: lefthanded hook, righthanded hook, jump shot, push shot, two-handed set shot. Not knowing what he was going to do next, the other team was kept flat-footed. In his junior year, the '51–'52 season, the Mighty Mite became the first player to break the 1,000-point barrier in a season by scoring 1,051. (This did not count as a record because some of their opponents were junior colleges.) He did set a record by making 361 free throws. That was also the year that Seattle played the Harlem Globetrotters. Forced to play a straight basketball game, the Globetrotters lost to the Chieftains, 84–81. Johnny had scored 43 points. "That O'Brien ain't no little man," admitted Goose Tatum. "He's a giant."

Johnny's senior year he set records with 884 points for a season and 2,537 for a career. The Mighty Mite had averaged over 28 points per game both his junior and senior years. Johnny won All-American honors that year, the shortest All-American center in history. He won more votes than Bevo Francis, Tom Gola, Bob Pettit, and Frank Selvy. Only Walter Dukes had more. In the NCAA Far West Tournament, Johnny scored 42 as the Chieftains beat Idaho State, 88–77. In their semifinal game, the Washington Huskies beat the Chieftains, 90–72. Johnny had scored 24. Seattle won its consolation game against Wyoming. Johnny had scored 30, his last points on a basketball court. There was no time either to be consoled or to celebrate. Johnny and Eddie both signed with the Pittsburgh Pirates the following day and on the day after that were off to Cuba for spring training.

Johnny's fame came next in a Pirates baseball uniform. He played six years, primarily at second, but he even pitched. His batting average was .250 and his pitching record was 1–3. Eddie was mostly a shortstop for five years, with a batting average of .236. Like his brother, he was also a pitcher in '56, '57, and '58 and was 1–0.

In the old days there was no 24-second clock. That allowed teams to stall the ball, to go for long periods without shooting. That's what happened on the night of February 21, 1953, in a game between Niagara University and Siena College. **Niagara University** was heavily favored but Siena College played them to a 54–54 deadlock at the end of regulation play. At the end of the first overtime they were 61–61. After the second overtime they were 63–63. Third overtime found them equal. Fourth the same. Fifth, too. In the sixth overtime, Larry Costello scored six points before fouling out and Niagara University hung on for an 88–81 victory.

February 2, 1954, is a very special date in the NAIA (National Association of Intercollegiate Athletics) record books, for that is the date that **Clarence "Bevo" Francis** set his individual single game records. (His father had started calling his son Beeve, after a popular soft drink of the day; the nickname gradually changed into Bevo.)

Bevo's college, Rio Grande College (with only 96 students) in Rio Grande, Ohio (pronounced rye-o), had beaten their opponent that night, the Hillsdale Redmen from Michigan, 82–45, earlier that year. Tonight's outcome wasn't expected to be much different. Again, Hillsdale would try to slow things down; Rio Grande would try to speed the game up. Except for one thing. Tonight there would be the added incentive that Coach Newt Oliver was going to let his center, the six-foot-nine Bevo Francis, go for the record.

Bevo had scored 116 points the year before, but it was disallowed because the opponent, Ashland Junior College of Kentucky, was not a four-year college. Ironically, the record of 87 was set by Paul Arizin of Villanova against a junior college. But tonight was going to make up for all that.

Hillsdale abandoned the idea of slowing the game down when Rio Grande jumped out ahead. Before the half was over, Bevo had 43 points, the same number he netted for the whole game during their previous meeting. At the end of the third quarter, Bevo had poured in 74 points. Bevo and everyone else in the gymnasium realized that the record was within reach. Bevo's goal was to hit 100. He overshot it by 13 points. Rio Grande won the game, 134–91. Bevo Francis had scored the most points in a game, 113, scored the most field goals, 38, and the most free throws, 37. (To show what a good free-throw shooter he was, he only attempted 42 that night.)

Bevo and Rio Grande went on to a 21–7 record his sophomore year. (Some of the opponents they beat were Providence, Wake Forest, Creighton, and Arizona

State; some they lost to were Adelphi, North Carolina State, and Villanova.) Bevo's other records from that year are a 46.5 point average; most field goals attempted, 71; most free throws attempted, 45; most free throws attempted during a season, 510; and most points over 50 for a season, eight. His record for both his years was most games over 50 points for a career, 14.

After his sophomore year Bevo left college. He played for the team that toured with the Globetrotters and then spent some time knocking around in the minors before disappearing from the basketball scene.

In 1954, Milan High School had a 19–2 record before the Indiana state tournament began. Then the Indians won three games in the sectional playoff, two in the regional, and traveled to Indianapolis to win two more games to put Milan into the final four. Finally, Milan beat Terre Haute Gerstmeyer, 60–48, to reach the finals.

At that time in Indiana, there were no different divisions. The smallest school could meet the largest for the state championship. And that was about the size of it. The Milan High School Indians, with an enrollment of only 161 students, was meeting powerhouse Muncie Central for the state championship of Indiana.

In the closing minutes of this low-scoring game, the Indians' **Bob Plump** hit two free throws to make the score, Milan 30, Muncie Central, 28. Then Gene Flower of Muncie hit a long shot to tie the score again. Milan was playing for the last shot.

With eighteen seconds left, Milan called a time-out.

Coach Marvin Wood had four of the players lined up on one side to isolate Bob Plump, who could either drive to the basket for a layup or shoot a jumper. Plump did both. He started to drive, then when the Muncie players backed up, Plump stopped and pumped in a jumper. It fell in at the buzzer. As has since been chronicled in the popular film *Hoosiers*, one of the smallest schools in Indiana had won the state championship. Small or not, over 40,000 people lined the streets of Milan for their favorite sons' victory parade.

The University of Alabama was playing the University of North Carolina at Foster Auditorium in Montgomery on January 4, 1955. With the first half about to expire, North Carolina's Lennie Rosenbluth tried a shot that missed, the tip-in was off, and six-foot-four junior **George Linn** of the Crimson Tide came down with the rebound. Standing near the out-of-bounds line and hearing the hometown fans yelling for him to shoot, Linn did just that. He flung the ball the length of the court. (The court was the maximum length of 94 feet; backboards are set in four feet from the out-of-bounds lines). Linn's shot went in. North Carolina's Frank McGuire went out and placed his foot where Linn had been standing. A crew from Alabama measured the shot at 84 feet, 11 inches. This stands as the longest basket ever made in a college basketball game.

What was **Tommy Kearns**, the star five-foot-nine playmaker, doing jumping center against Wilt Chamberlain to start the 1957 NCAA championship game? The coach of North Carolina, Dean Smith, was making a statement about how confident his Tar Heels were against the favored Jayhawks of Kansas. Naturally, Kearns lost the opening tip-off to Chamberlain, but North Carolina went on to win the championship in triple overtime. From there this third-string All-American was drafted by the Syracuse Nationals for the 1958–59 NBA season. Kearns played only seven minutes of one game against Cincinnati. He took only one shot—from what would be three-point range today—and the basket was good. The next day Kearns was cut because the coach, Paul Seymour, wanted to be a player-coach and there were only ten spots on the roster. Tommy Kearns departed the NBA with a 1.000 shooting percentage.

"I think the top thrill was being selected to the All-American five following the 1955 High School North-South Game," wrote **Joe Ruklick**. "It was a moment when basketball thrills were still a relatively new experience (I was only sixteen years of age) and the sense of achievement against 'national' competition was something I didn't experience again until the East-West college All-Star game. However, you know how it is when you are in college: You are supposed to be cool and sophisticated and the thrill of success in the East-West game was nothing compared to the feeling I had when I was a high school kid."

Joe Ruklick went on to become a cool six-foot-nine, 220-pound center for Northwestern whose specialty was the hook shot. As a professional from 1960 to 1962, he averaged 3.5 points per game.

"For your trivia collection," Ruklick wrote, "my

greatest offbeat thrill was getting the assist on the basket that gave Wilt Chamberlain his ninety-ninth and one hundredth points in a game against the Knickerbockers. All I got for that, however, was a notation in the box score and Wilt's assurance that I should have been credited with two assists!"

For anyone who believes in the power of names, here is one for the record books. The high-school scoring record for boys belongs to **Danny Heater** of Burnsville High School. Straight out of Central Casting, right? A story conference couldn't have hammered out a better account either.

It happened on January 26, 1960, in Burnsville, West Virginia. Heater, the star of the team, was a senior guard. His poor coal-mining family needed help if he were ever going to attend college.

At 6 feet and 140 pounds, Heater was not an imposing figure on the basketball court. But could he ever jump. He played center on defense and could dunk the ball on offense, long before this became a standard part of the game.

The best way his coach, Jack Stalnaker, could attract the attention of colleges was to let Heater score a lot of points. The West Virginia record was 79.

On the night of January 26, Heater and Burnsville put their 18-game win streak up against Widen. Burnsville was heavily favored; few schools in the area could keep pace with a high school that averaged almost 100 points a game.

Almost two minutes had gone by before Heater took a shot. He ended the evening with seven assists, but that wasn't what would win him a scholarship. Then Heater opened up. With his teammates feeding him the ball at every opportunity, Heater scored on jumpers, dunks, and even hook shots. Widen was overpowered, so Stalnaker had the reserves in with Heater. Before the third quarter had ended, Heater had the state record. With ten minutes to go, Stalnaker pulled Heater from the game.

But coach, reasoned some of the team members, the national record of 120, recently set by a high-school player in Pennsylvania, was within reach. Why not let Danny try to break that, too?

Back into the game went Heater. In the final ten minutes Heater was tough on defense and unstoppable on offense, scoring 55 more points. His stats for the game were 53 of 70 from the field, 29 of 41 from the free-throw line for a total of 135 points. His teammates had added another 38 for a total of 173.

Danny Heater had scored more points in a shorter period of time—32 minutes—than Wilt Chamberlain and Bevo Francis. It took Chamberlain 48 minutes to set the pro record of 100; it took Francis 40 minutes to set the college record of 113.

Coach Stalnaker and Danny Heater got the desired result. Heater won a scholarship to the University of Richmond. Unfortunately, this story does not have a happy ending. Before the next installment could be written, Danny Heater was injured in an automobile accident and never played college basketball.

Ordinarily, **Jay Roberts** wouldn't have expected to play much in the 1962 Big Eight Holiday Tournament in Kansas City. For Roberts was primarily a football player at the University of Kansas. But there was nothing ordinary about their title game with Kansas State. As the Jayhawks moved into the fourth overtime with the Wildcats, the bench was wearing thin. Roberts had already played long enough to get four points, but it was his turnaround jumper at the buzzer that clinched a 90–88 win for the Jayhawks from Kansas.

Although **Walter Garrett** of Birmingham, Alabama, may have scored fewer points than Danny Heater, he has his own claim to fame. Garrett scored all of his team's points as he singlehandedly led West End High School in a 1963 victory over Glen Vocational High School, 97–54.

One of the legends of the playgrounds of Harlem is **Earl "The Goat" Manigault**. There are eyewitnesses who recall the many exploits of this ballplayer, but there was one in particular that took place in 1965 that left more than a few people shaking their heads in amazement. After hitting five soft jumpers in a row in a semipro game, Manigault received a pass from a teammate and found a defender determined to prevent jumper number six stationed between him and the basket. Although he was only six-foot-one, The Goat took a long upward stride, planted his foot on the man's forehead, and continued to the basket for a slam dunk.

Another time he amazed New York basketball greats Lew Alcindor (Later Kareem Abdul-Jabbar) and Connie Hawkins by going over both of them and their outstretched arms for a dunk.

One trick that even Manigault couldn't perfect was to dunk the ball and then sit on the rim. He came close several times, but he wrenched his back trying to do it and had to give it up. He also hurt himself by diving deep into the world of heroin addiction. By the age of 22, Earl Manigault had faded into a mere afterglow of his onetime brilliance.

The game between the Dallas Chaparrals and Indiana Pacers on November 13, 1967, had more last-second heroics than you might get to see in a season. With the game tied 116–116, the Chaparrals got the ball to John Beasley, who sank a jump shot with only one second left on the clock. With arms and smiles upstretched, the Chaparrals congratulated Beasley and each other for their hard-won victory. Even their coach, Larry Staverman, was moving toward the locker room. But underneath the goal and out of bounds, Oliver Darden threw the ball in to his Pacer teammate, **Jerry Harkness**.

Harkness was an interesting case. He had played briefly in 1963 for the New York Knicks, but they had cut him because of his poor outside shooting. Harkness was only six-foot-two, so this drawback seemed a fatal flaw. But when the American Basketball Association sprang up, Harkness was ready to given pro ball one last try.

Instinctively, Harkness heaved the ball up court. Perhaps a teammate could catch the ball and be fouled. Well, that didn't happen. The ball was in the air; the buzzer had sounded; the ball fell through the basket. The Pacers had won the game, 119–118. (The ABA had instituted the three-point shot years before the

NBA.) The court was only 94 feet long. The point from where Harkness was standing to the basket was measured at 92 feet.

Although Jerry Harkness had once been on a championship Loyola team, this was his finest moment in basketball. In a short time Harkness had vanished a second time from professional basketball, this time for good.

At a time when most have already ended their playing careers, **Doug Williams** was just beginning his. First he had had some living to do: six years in the Air Force, a wife and four kids. When he finally got around to entering St. Mary's University in San Antonio, Texas, Williams was 28 years old. He went out for the team and scored 511 points his freshman year. The next year he put in 643 points; his junior year 605. His senior year, Williams scored fewer points, 487, but he was a more complete ballplayer. He did most of the rebounding and kept the team moving. For his skills Doug Williams was selected to the 1970 NAIA first team.

It is hard to score a basket longer than 92 feet, but that's just what **Steve Meyers** did on January 16, 1970. Playing for Pacific Lutheran University, Meyers made a desperation shot from the far end of the court that went through the hoop. Only problem was he had been standing out of bounds. But sometimes minor considerations like that are overlooked. The officials allowed the basket, a 92-foot, 3-and-a-half-inch swisher.

* * *

The Rucker League final in 1970 pitted the best of the Harlem players versus the pros. On Milbank were Eric Cobb, **Joe Hammond**, and Pee Wee Kirkland (see 1974); on the Westsiders were Julius Erving, Charlie Scott, and Brian Taylor. The game began at one; the shooting star of Milbank, Jumpin' Joe Hammond, was late. In fact, it wasn't until two o'clock that he stepped out of a limousine near the Rucker Playground in Harlem. (Hammond made so much money dealing drugs that he later turned down a $50,000 offer from the Lakers because that was just walking around money for him.)

Hammond had missed the whole first half and the Westsiders, led by Erving, were out to a double-digit lead. The second half began with Charlie Scott guarding the six-foot-five Hammond. The first time down the court, Hammond hit a jumper. The second time another jumper. The third was a dunk. Next, Brian Taylor tried his luck; he couldn't stop Hammond either. Now, it was time for Doctor J. This was what everyone had come to see. The best against the best. What a show the best of Harlem and the ABA put on. But if truth be told, Joe Hammond was putting moves on the Doctor that Erving hadn't seen on a hardwood court. By the end of the game, Milbank had closed the gap but not enough. However, what really stood out in people's minds was that Doctor J had scored 39 points in the game, and Jumpin' Joe Hammond had scored 50 in only one half.

"It was all offense," said Hammond. "We slammed in each other's faces, we hit J's, we hit pull-ups—we were both just sizzling. But anybody will tell you I got the better of him."

* * *

In 1971, 24-year-old **Mike Janofski**, a sportswriter for the *Baltimore Evening Sun*, went to the training camp of the Baltimore Bullets. The idea was to keep a record of what it was like to be a rookie trying out with the pros.

On September 25, the Bullets played an exhibition game with the Carolina Cougars of the American Basketball Association. Janofski sat on the bench until 1:21 was remaining in the game. It was at that point that Coach Gene Shue sent Janofski into the game. Quickly, Janofski got into the action, fouling Larry Miller. Then he fouled Gene Littles intentionally. Not much of a showing thus far.

But after a time-out, Mike Janofski got the ball. Having once been a guard at the University of Maryland, Janofski had obviously not lost his touch, connecting with a 20-foot jumper over Carolina's Littles. Mike Janofski had made the one and only shot he was ever to take in the pro leagues.

When someone is in a groove, it is almost as if the ball has eyes. Just such an occasion was in a demonstration on May 18, 1972, at a high school in Park Ridge, Illinois. A blindfolded **John T. Sebastian** hit 63 free throws in a row.

Sometimes there are games between a ragtag of alumni and the varsity squad at college reunions, perhaps even a bit of half-court basketball. But the **Rio Grand College** alumni game in 1973 blew the lid off what is usually done. They staged a game that lasted 125 hours. For anyone interested in putting on their own marathon, each team had fifteen players and each player was out on the court for four-hour tours of duty. For the record, the White team dumped in 10,752 points; the Red team came up short with 10,734.

Essex Community College was coasting along to a 17–3 record while averaging 108 points a game during the 1973–74 season. But could they double that number of points in a game? That's what this small college in New Jersey was attempting on a night in January 1974 in their bandbox of a gym against Englewood Cliffs College.

Essex not only had Englewood outmanned, they also had them confused. When they were expecting a man-to-man defense, they were playing a zone, and vice versa. This allowed Essex to steal the ball and fast break their opponents to death. The Wolverines ran up the first 26 points and by the intermission were leading 110–29. But could they double that?

Englewood Cliffs was tired; Essex kept putting in fresh troops to keep the pressure up on both ends of the court. And the shots kept falling. By game's end, the Wolverines had made 97 of 129 shots from the field and 16 for 22 from the free-throw line for 212 points. Englewood Cliffs in their last season of existence not only as a team but also as a college, had only 67.

How many of you have shot baskets alone to see how many you can hit in a row? Or to see how many you can hit in five or ten minutes? But how about 24 hours? For most people that isn't even something contemplated. But that is just what **Fred L. Newman** of San Jose, California, did.

Beginning on May 31,1975, Newman shot a basketball at the basket for an entire day. In that 24-hour span of time, Newman sank 12,874 baskets. That's a basket every six seconds. His efficiency was just as amazing. Newman missed only 242 times. There must have been many moments in the middle of the night when Newman's arms became tired or his mind wandered and it became a major challenge to sink a shot. Even if unguarded under the basket that's a fantastic .982 shooting percentage.

But wait, there's more. Newman could also shoot free throws even when blindfolded. Three years later, on February 5, 1978, at the Central YMCA in San Jose, California, the blindfolded Newman sank 88 free throws in a row. He wasn't so blind he couldn't hit the side of a barn door.

But then Newman went up against himself. And isn't that the biggest challenge? Ourselves? From September 29–30, 1990, Fred Newman shot free throws at Caltech in Pasadena, California. During this 24-hour stretch, Newman shot a total of 22,049 free throws. And even more amazing, he hit 20,371 of them. That's a fabulous 92 percent from the line. When is the last time you heard of a pro hitting with that consistency?

Ted St. Martin is another player with a knack for hitting free throws. On February 28, 1975, he made 1,704 in a row, but that was only a warmup for what came two years later. On June 25, 1977, he sank 2,036 consecutive free throws.

Then on May 16, 1988, during the halftime of a basketball game in Jacksonville, Florida, St. Martin established a different mark for free throw consistency and difficulty by tossing in 169 in 10 minutes, missing only six. The kicker for his second record is that there was only one ball and one rebounder.

And, are you ready for this? On April 28, 1996, also in Jacksonville, Ted St. Martin beat his own record by sinking 5,221 free throws in a row. Now there's a record to beat!

Bill Wanstrath did not have a breakaway game, that moment of transcendence, of suspension in midair before a reverberating slam-dunk. This six-foot-seven, 200-pound senior was steady, game in, game out, for the Batesville High School basketball team during the 1978–79 season. His end-of-year statistics were not off the page: 8.8 points, eight blocked shots, 12.2 rebounds. But his spirit was. He was the 1979 recipient of the United States Basketball Writers Association's "Most Courageous Award." For you see, Bill Wanstrath only has one arm.

Ann Meyers had many firsts in her basketball career (first high school student on the national team, first woman with a full scholarship to UCLA, member of the first US women's Olympic basketball team), but it was the first she achieved in 1979 that really stands out. Ann Meyers was the first woman ever to try out for a team in the NBA. The Indiana Pacers were serious enough to give her $50,000; if she didn't make the team, she could work in some other capacity for the organization.

Not everyone was pleased about her trying out for a men's team in the NBA, Red Auerbach for one. "Annie's a nice girl," said the longtime coach and general manager of the Boston Celtics, "but this is reminiscent of Bill Veeck signing that midget." (See **Eddie Gaedel** under Baseball.)

Bobby Leonard, the Pacers coach, treated her as he did any other player. "She's just another athlete to me," he said. Meyer's main drawback was her size. She was only five-foot-nine and 135 pounds. "From a fundamentals standpoint," observed Leonard, "Ann is excellent. Some of the guys had better thank God that she doesn't have about six more inches and forty more pounds."

Meyers enjoyed every moment. "It's something I'll cherish for the rest of my life," she said. "It was the chance of a lifetime, to be first at something." After two months in the announcer's booth, Ann Meyers packed her gym bag and went back to the Women's Basketball League. Playing for the New Jersey Gems, Meyers was the MVP during her first season in the WBL.

On December 23, 1982, the University of Virginia Cavaliers were in Hawaii to play the **Chaminade Silverswords**, a small college of 900. Virginia had already beaten Georgetown that year—the Cavaliers' Ralph Sampson keeping the Hoyas' Patrick Ewing in check—and were just returning from Japan, where they had won a tournament. In other words Virginia was having a banner year: they were undefeated and ranked number one in the nation.

Although Chaminade was a team that you might not expect to find on Virginia's schedule, the Silverswords had beaten the University of Seattle and the University of Hawaii. But then again they had lost to Wayland Baptist and they were fourth in the NAIA. Some might have considered the game to be a breather for Virginia, a mismatch, something to do while the plane was being refueled, but Chaminade's coach, Merv Lopes, certainly didn't think of it that way.

"You have nothing to lose," Lopes reminded his team before they took the court, "so just go out there and play. It's an honor to be able to play a team like Virginia, but let's be sure we make them believe that we aren't just showing up to be beaten."

Chaminade certainly wasn't, as they scored the first seven points. Even when Virginia caught up, they couldn't keep the lead. The teams went into the locker rooms at halftime tied 43–43.

In the second half it looked like things were going to turn. Virginia started scoring and held a 56–49 lead midway through the second half. But Tony Randolph was still doing a great job containing Ralph Sampson, and the Silverswords came back and again tied the score. Moving into the stretch run Chaminade moved ahead 70–68 with 1:37 left in the game. Chaminade sank some key free throws and the game ended with the little school in Hawaii beating number one Virginia, 77–72. Tony Randolph wound up with a game high 19; Ralph Sampson had only 12.

Although Sampson had been shaking off the flu, he

didn't blame the loss on bad health. "They're a good team and they won," said the seven-foot-four center. "That's the story."

Playing for the State University of New York at Purchase on January 22, 1984, **Annette Kennedy** scored 70 points (hitting 35 field goals in 43 attempts) versus Pratt Institute.

On October 7, 1985, **Lynette Woodard** got rid of another thing that women can't do when the former University of Kansas great (a four-time All-American and a gold-medal member of the 1964 Olympic squad) signed a contract to play for the Harlem Globetrotters. "I always say, playing with the Globetrotters is like playing jazz," she said. "You get to be as creative as you want to be." Woodard played jazz with the 'Trotters for two years.

Spud Webb (a shortened form of Sputnikhead, a nickname given to him at birth by a friend of the family's who thought the newborn's head looked like the Russian satellite *Sputnik*) played point guard for two years at North Carolina State and 12 years in the NBA. What is unusual about that is Spud Webb is only five-foot-seven inches tall. "I don't play small," said Webb. "You have to go out and play with what you have. I admit I used to want to be tall."

Why Spud Webb is especially remembered, however, is not for a short man having a long basketball career but for his winning the 1986 slam dunk contest. When Webb slammed down two perfect scores to beat the six-foot-seven Dominique Wilkins, the arena in Dallas erupted. "It was the highlight of my career and everybody recognizes me from the slam dunk contest."

No one figured the **Arizona Wildcats** would go anywhere in the 1997 NCAA Tournament. After all they were no better than fifth place in the Pac-10 Conference. But they pulled off upset after upset. To get to the finals, Arizona beat Kansas—the team favored to win the tournament—in the Mideast Regional Final, and North Carolina in the national semifinal. That led to the national finals with Kentucky, the defending champion.

"I think we went to the Final Four with an advantage," said junior Miles Simon. "We didn't have a care in the world. We weren't nervous out there."

The game seesawed back and forth; the score was tied twenty times. Arizona was ahead as the game drew to a close, until Kentucky tied it for the last time. In the overtime, Arizona hit free throw after free throw—10 in all. Simon hit 4 in the final 41 seconds and ended the game with 30 points. The final score was 84–79.

Bicycling

A bicycle does get you there and more . . .
And there is always the thin edge of danger
to keep you alert and comfortably apprehensive.
Dogs become dogs again and snap at your raincoat;
potholes become personal. And getting there is all the fun."
—Bill Emerson

On April 22, 1884, **Thomas Stevens** set off on a most ambitious quest: to become the first person to ride around the world on his high wheeler (that curious contraption with a large front wheel and small back wheel). By August he was in Boston and soon after he was on board a ship bound for Europe. Europe was comparatively easy cycling and there were many places to repair the five-foot front wheel. But Persia was another story. "Arrayed in a summer suit with sun helmet, cycling stockings and gear, I had to ford through snow drifts, when the cold was sufficient to form icicles on eyelashes and transform the mustache into a cake of ice," Stevens wrote to *Outing*, the magazine that was sharing his journey with its readers. Not surprisingly, China was difficult, too. Foreigners were not particularly welcome, especially one atop a high wheeler. When Stevens debarked the ship in San Francisco on January 4, 1887, he found a hero's welcome waiting for him.

* * *

When **Frank G. Lenz** resigned his position as a book-keeper in May 1892 "to travel around the world with wheel and camera," he caught the attention of many Americans. Perhaps it was the Walter Mitty in him and others that accounted for the crowds.

So many turned out for his departure in New York City "that I found it impossible to mount my wheel, much less make the start. The police, seeing my predicament, cleared the way for my escorts and myself, and amid the cheers from thousands of throats, I mounted precisely at three o'clock and . . . rode up busy Broadway."

Not that he had always been behind a desk—Lenz had been making long-distance cycling trips for years—but the bravura of this undertaking was something special. So much so that he would be posting the account of his adventures back to *Outing* magazine.

The trek to the West Coast was uneventful, unless you take into consideration the number of dinners he attended. On October 20, 1892, Lenz arrived in San Francisco and departed five days later aboard the *Oceanic* for Yokohama, Japan.

In January Lenz was bicycling in China and his experience was the opposite of being feted by the locals. He looked down on them as opium eaters and they shook their fists at him as if he were the devil incarnate. Things improved as he cycled across Asia from Burma to Persia, although the 15 months on the road was beginning to wear on him. "I must confess," he wrote to *Outing*, "to a feeling of homesickness. I am tired, very tired of being a stranger. I long for the day which will see me again on my native hearthstone and my wanderings at an end."

But that was not to be. On May 2, 1894, Frank Lenz wrote his last letter back to the States. "I leave today on my way to Constantinople, now only nine hundred miles distant." Lenz then rode into the Delibaba Pass between Persia and Turkey, a place that was notorious for wandering bands of desperadoes. There was a story circulating in those parts that there had been someone seen riding a newfangled contraption who must be the devil. Sometime later a body, apparently Lenz's, was found floating in a river.

In the Gay Nineties there were dance marathons, pedestrian marathons, and bicycle marathons. The first six-day bike marathon for women took place on January 6 through 11, 1896 at New York's Madison Square Garden. The winner was **Frankie Nelson**, who rode 418 miles.

Humans set barriers. Until 1954 there was the four-minute mile. Back in 1899 there was the one-minute mile on bicycle. **Charles Murphy** felt he could crack that barrier, and he found a sympathetic ear at the Long Island Railroad. A three-mile stretch of wooden track was built between the rails. On June 30, 1899, riding behind a special open car pulled by a train that increased its speed until it was traveling at 60 miles per hour, Murphy was timed in 57 and 4/5 seconds for the mile. From that moment on, this bicyclist was known as Mile-a-Minute Murphy.

* * *

Sometimes competition can lift everyone's expectations and performance. Just such a thing happened as the 1800s drew to a close when three women pushed each other to new heights on the bicycle. By that point bicyclists were no longer using the high wheelers but something more akin to today's same-sized wheel bike. But still they were a far cry from the geared and alloy-crafted bikes of today.

The first to set the pace on the flat roads of Long Island was **Irene Bush**, who clocked 400 miles in 48 hours. Next up was **Jane Yatman**, who covered 500 miles in 58 hours. Completing the trio was **Jane Lindsay**, who rode 600 miles in 72 hours.

But it didn't end there. Jane Yatman got back on her bike in September of 1899 with a goal of 700 miles. Reported the *New York Times:* "On the smooth macadam roads of Long Island a little woman . . . bent on accomplishing a task which the average woman, or the average man, for that matter, would no more undertake than she or he would attempt to fly." Sometimes riding as fast as 14 miles per hour and not resting for more than two hours, Yatman rode on and on, even through a blinding rainstorm at the end. But she made it. Seven hundred miles in 81 hours and 5 minutes.

Not to be outdone, Jane Lindsay set her sights on 800. Borrowing a pair of her husband's pants and putting a light on her bike, Lindsay rode through Long Island day and night, stopping only for food and massages. By the end of her ride she was hallucinating, but Lindsay had logged 800 miles in 91 hours and 48 minutes.

*   *   *

The first ever US bicycling championship for women was held on September 4, 1937, in Buffalo, New York. Sponsored by the National Amateur Bicycling Association, the one-mile event was won by **Doris Kopsky** of Belleville, New Jersey, in the time of 4 minutes and 22.4 seconds. Bikes have gotten a lot better since those days.

Eugene McPherson, a 22-year-old student at Ohio University, completed a bike trip on September 21, 1949, from Santa Monica, California, to New York, New York. McPherson had spent fewer days than his age, 20 days to be exact. It was the first time anyone had ever bicycled across the country in less than 21 days.

If speed is your thing, on August 25, 1973, **Dr. Allan Abbott** rode a bicycle over Utah's Bonneville Salt Flats at a record 140.5 miles per hour. But of course, records are set to be broken. John Howard pedaled his bicycle 152.284 miles per hour at the Bonneville Salt Flats in 1985, and Fred Rompelberg established the new record of 166.9 miles per hour in 1995.

Bowling

In 1908 in Hartford, Connecticut, **Frank Griffith** and **J. F. Upson** bowled 100 games in 13 hours.

That 1908 record was the one that **Darrell Hamlet** took aim at in January 1915 at Elk Point, South Dakota. It only took him nine hours and 56 minutes to bowl a century of games. His average? A very respectable 183 pins per game.

A week earlier at Sioux City, Iowa, Hamlet had bowled 194 games over 36 straight hours. His best game was 256.

On March 10, 1913, **William Knox** from Philadelphia became the first person to bowl a perfect 300 game in a tournament sanctioned by the American Bowling Congress.

On March 5, 1924, **Frank Caruana** of Buffalo, New York, bowled not one but two perfect games in a row.

In his third game he had five more strikes before missing. His 29 strikes in a row is still a record.

Floretta McCutcheon had only been bowling a few years when Jimmy Smith, one of the greatest bowling exhibition champions, blew into Pueblo, Colorado, in December 1927. Smith consented to bowl one of the locals and the 39-year-old McCutcheon was chosen. Although Smith put together a three-game total of 686 points, the Pueblo housewife's total was a cooler 704. "She'll become one of the greatest bowlers in the world," Smith predicted.

During the next 15 years, "Little Lady Mac" bowled 8,076 games in tournaments and exhibitions. Ten times she bowled a perfect 300 game and her highest total for a three-game match was 832. She also bowled 10 other three-game series over 800 and more than 100 three-game series over 700. Her career average was 201 per game.

McCutcheon, as much as anyone, is responsible for the popularity of bowling in America. The Mrs. McCutcheon Schools of Bowling taught millions of men and women how to bowl.

Some say the first woman to bowl a 300 game was **Rose Jacobs** in 1929 in Schenectady, New York, or Jennie Kelleher of Wisconsin on February 12, 1930.

Others say it was **Emma Fahning**, who bowled a perfect game on March 4, 1930. Fahning let loose her perfect game while bowling for the Germain Cleaning Team in Buffalo, New York.

In any case, it must be something about those long snowy upper New York State winters.

Barney Koralewski was a regular in the Guiness Business House League in Buffalo, New York. But what happened on March 22, 1934 was anything but regular. Koralewski bowled strike after strike and seemed on a collision course with a perfect game. After eight strikes teammates, friends, and spectators were crowded around his alley. Just then an electrical storm threw the bowling alley into darkness. There would be no more bowling that night.

A week passed until the next time the league would bowl. It was a long time to think and worry about the chances of rolling four more strikes. Finally, on March 29, Barney stepped up to the line again to resume his quest for a perfect game. Strike. Strike. Strike. Strike. Barney Koralewski had withstood the seventh game of the Series, bases loaded, two outs, bottom of the ninth, three-and-two count, and you're at bat kind of pressure to get his perfect game.

In 1957, the eyes of Conroe, Texas were on **Bill Dillon**, who bowled 440 games nonstop. It took the 37-year-old 73 hours and 55 minutes. His average score? A respectable 144.

Don Newport bowled 1,000 games over four days in Fort Lauderdale in 1960. Newport's highest game was 212, his total number of pins 123,205.

* * *

In 1961, **Frank Mazzei** knocked down 120,209 pins over a period of 110 hours and 30 minutes in a bowling alley in Roslindale, Massachusetts. An ambidextrous bowler, Mazzei had 115 strikes and 2,903 spares en route to an average of 119 per game. He also shed 20 pounds.

On August 19, 1971, **Matt Throne** of Millbrae, California, became the first 12-year-old to roll a perfect game in official league play.

Helen Duval is the oldest woman ever to bowl a perfect game. She was one proud 65-year-old.

Richard Dewey, 46, of Omaha, Nebraska, bowled 1,472 games in a row over a period of 114 and a half hours. Bowling with either his left or right hand, Dewey racked up an average of 126.

On June 3, 1972, the 75-year-old **Wing Wong** did something he had never done before. He bowled a 300 game. Normally a 154 bowler with a previous high of 268 in 1967, the five-foot, 110-pound bowler was participating in the Schenectady (New York) Press Tournament. After bowling a 157 and a 181, Wong started throwing one strike after another.

"I wasn't nervous at all," said Wong. "At my age, there isn't too much to get nervous about, and you don't expect to bowl 300 games."

"This frail old man kept getting strikes," said Chuck Clayton, one of the tournament directors, "and nobody in the place expected him to keep going, but he did.

The cheers grew louder and louder. He looked calmer than a pro at the end, and when he got the last one, a girl bowling nearby came over and kissed him, and that seemed to shake him up more than the 300."

And how did Mr. Wong react to his newfound fame?

"My phone didn't stop ringing for a week," he said. "I got my name in the newspapers and everybody treated me like a hero."

During 1975, **Jerry** and **Norma Hill** both bowled perfect games. Jerry's came on February 13, and Norma matched his score on August 4, the ninth time that a husband and wife had accomplished that feat. What made an even bigger splash was that on October 4, 1976, their son **Mark** also bowled a 300 game. According to the American Bowling Congress, this was the first time for a mother-father-son split.

Sometimes a bowler will wish there was one more game or even one more frame. There was one time **Bob Atheney** of St. Petersburg, Florida, certainly did not feel that way. Starting on November 9, 1975, Atheney bowled the year and one for good measure— 1,976 straight games. It took 265 hours to complete his marathon madness.

In 1984, **Jim Webb** kept bowling for 195 straight hours. He was sleepless in Gosford at the Gosford City Bowl in Australia.

Fourteen-year-old **Chrissy Wolking** of Riva, Maryland, bowled a total of 173 games in 18 hours on

November 29, 1987. This works out to almost 10 games per hour.

The six-man team of **Tim Graham**, **Steve Hopkins**, **Mike Hudson**, **Tony Lanning**, **Kent Scott**, and **Terry Webb** knocked down a total of 176,702 pins during a 24-hour period. Their marathon demolished the previous record by over 50,000 pins and took place on January 14–15, 1989, at the Oakwood Bowl in Enid, Oklahoma.

On March 26, 2001, **Barry Thomas** of Nashville, 12 days shy of turning 88, became the oldest person to bowl a 300 game. "When I got to the twelfth ball I got a little nervous," admitted Thomas, who first began bowling in 1939, "but I made it all right. My son has had a few three hundreds and I was hoping to get one before I quit bowling."

Boxing

*"If one guy has one fight left in him,
he seems to save it for me."*
—Floyd Patterson, heavyweight champion

The **Earl of Lonsdale** was an English gentleman who could not resist a bet or a sporting challenge. During his colorful life (1857–1944) he won many, but the one that stands out was when he whipped the heavyweight champion of the world. When Lonsdale heard John L. Sullivan proclaim, "I'll fight anyone except pigs, dogs, and niggers," the Englishman was ready to take him on.

Lonsdale was not a novice. As a boy he had been trained by the English champion Jem Mace. So he knew a thing or two about fisticuffs. But the Boston Strong Boy? Lonsdale was fearless and sailed for New York in the early 1880s.

After the end of his reign as heavyweight champion in 1879, Sullivan toured the country giving exhibitions. But this was still during the champion's prime. You could have sold tickets to this bout, but this wasn't for money.

The fight took place with only the handlers for each boxer present at a riding stable, the Central Park Academy. For the first two rounds, Sullivan and Lonsdale felt each other out—the heavyweight champion checking for weaknesses, the challenger searching for possibilities. In the third round Sullivan opened up with a withering blow to Lonsdale's ribs. It shook the Englishman to the core. "I thought I was done for," he admitted later. "It took all the wind out of me and sent me staggering against the ropes." But Lonsdale hung on. By the fifth with his left eye closing and his ribs battered and sore, the underdog still managed to get off "several good stingers." In the sixth round Lonsdale made his move. He reached back into those inner resources that a boxer needs to be capable of and hit the champion a blow to the solar plexus. The Great John L. was down for the count. The Earl of Lonsdale had won.

May 30, 1880 was the date of the first professional bout for **Paddy Ryan** and he beat Joe Goss at Collier Station, West Vancouver, for the American Championship. The one-hour, 24-minute bout lasted 87 rounds. (A round ended when one of the fighters went down.) Ryan lost to John L. Sullivan in the ninth round (after ten and a half minutes) in Mississippi City on February 7, 1882. The two staged a return bout on January 19, 1885. Ryan lost in only 50 seconds.

John L. Sullivan, the Boston Strong Boy, had a standing challenge that no one could survive four three-minute rounds with him. **Tug Wilson** rose to the occasion with his head rather than with his fighting prowess. Every time The Great John L. as much as touched him, Wilson went down to the mat for a nine-count. To be sure, Wilson's 1882 bout was a strange victory.

On April 6, 1893, **Andy Bowen** and **Jack Burke** met in New Orleans, Louisiana, to fight for the lightweight championship that Jack McAuliffe had abandoned undefeated. (He only defended the title six times in 10 years.) The ground rules were that Bowen and Burke were to use boxing gloves and fight three-minute rounds until someone won. The winner would receive $2,500.

The fight began at nine o'clock at the Olympic Club. Both fighters began quickly because neither one wanted the bout to go on too long. Round after furious round they fought. After 50 rounds, there had been no knockdowns. If it was tedious for the fight fans, no one let on. If someone had to go somewhere the next day, they quietly slipped out, but most stayed through the long night of boxing. Round after round after round. When the bell sounded for round 111, neither fighter budged. Both Bowen and Burke refused to continue. They had been fighting for seven hours and nineteen minutes. How would it come out? The referee strode to the middle of the ring. "No contest," he declared. Both fighters had lost.

This long, unhappy night was the last fight for Jack Burke. Andy Bowen next fought George "Kid" Lavigne and was knocked out in the eighteenth. He died soon afterward.

Aaron Lister Brown, AKA **Dixie Kid**, was from Fulton, Missouri, and one tough fighter. He took pride in his

willingness to fight anyone, anytime, and anywhere—
no matter what the weight class. On April 28, 1904, in
San Francisco, he fought Joe Walcott, the world welterweight champion. For most of the fight Walcott had
the upper hand. But there was one constant problem.
Walcott was landing punches to the kidneys on breaks.
He was warned, but he continued to do it. In the eighteenth round, Walcott fought so well, it wasn't certain
if Dixie Kid would be able to come out for the next
round. But he did and when the Barbados Demon
fouled again in the twentieth round, referee "Duck"
Sullivan awarded the fight to Dixie Kid. Walcott's
manager, Tim O'Rourke and one of the promoters,
Alex Greggains, were so irate that they attacked Sullivan in the ring. The referee suffered more damage than
the fighters had, losing two front teeth. Dixie Kid never
defended his title. He spent the later years of his career
fighting mostly in England.

In 1905, James J. Jeffries was no longer interested in
being heavyweight champion, so he retired and chose
Jack Root, the onetime light heavyweight champion,
and **Marvin Hart**, a tough fighter from Kentucky, to
fight for his crown. On July 3 the two met in Reno,
Nevada, with none other than Jeffries as the referee.
After Hart went down in a surprise punch, he was back
on his feet to pummel the lighter Root until the twelfth,
when he registered his own knockdown and knockout.

On February 23, 1906, in his first defense of the
crown, Hart was outpointed by Tommy Burns, a
French Canadian (his real name was Noah Brusso)
with superior boxing skills. Hart continued to box for

another 11 fights, but he never had another brush with the championship.

After his death in 1931, the secret about Hart was finally revealed. Marvin Hart was blind in his right eye. The big Kentuckian had been all heart.

In 1913, **Preston Brown**, a 125-pound phenom, made an unusual announcement to those assembled at the Broadway Athletic Club in Philadelphia. Brown would take on any and all fighters there that night, one at a time. Six fighters answered the call. Brown floored the first five for the count and won a decision over the last fighter. Either the sixth boxer was the best or Brown should have been happy there wasn't a seventh.

Harry Wills was a fine contender in the 1920s who was never given a title shot because he was black. Still the public clamored for this bout. Finally, promoter Tex Richard signed "The Black Panther" for a title fight with Jack Dempsey. There was even a clause built into the contract that if the fight did not go through as planned, Wills would be awarded $50,000. Both fighters were hard at work in their training camps when the governor of New York called off the bout. Wills got his money, but he never got the championship fight he deserved.

This boxer out of Perth Amboy, New Jersey, began his boxing career while in the US Navy. After leaving the service and turning pro, **Johnny Buff** fought for more than two years before stepping into the ring to battle Abe Goldstein for the American flyweight championship. Buff registered a knockout in the second round. Six months later, on September 23, 1921, Johnny Buff was in the ring to challenge Pete Herman for the world bantamweight championship. Herman had enjoyed a reign from 1916 to 1921 and was acknowledged to be one of the all-time true masters of bantam boxing. But Buff caught him at the end of his career and outpointed Herman to win the championship. (Herman retired soon afterward because of eye trouble.) Next was Jack Sharkey on November 10, 1921. Buff won in 15 rounds. On July 10, 1922, Buff lost his bantamweight title to Joe Lynch by a knockout in the fourteenth round. Next, Buff challenged Pancho Villa for the world flyweight crown, but Buff was knocked out in the eleventh. Johnny Buff continued to box for four more years before going full circle and reenlisting in the Navy.

The life of Louis Phal reads like a potboiler. Discovered by a German ballerina in West Africa, this Senegalese was brought back to Paris. Adopted by a French family, he learned languages and learned to box. During World War I he became a war hero and a winner of the Croix de Guerre and Medaille Militaire by destroying a machine gun nest all by himself. As a boxer, by this time he had changed his name to **Battling Siki**; he was all offense with very little defense. But he was often exciting to watch and became a favorite of the French fans.

The toast of the Parisian fight world was Georges Carpentier, the "Orchid Man." He was also a World War I hero, having won both the Croix de Guerre and the Legion d'Honneur as a pilot. He needed a fight and his plan was to film it with the climax of a thundering knockout. On September 24, 1922, in Paris, of course, the 28-year-old Georges Carpentier met the 25-year-old Battling Siki for the light heavyweight championship. In the early going, Siki was falling over his own feet, but by the sixth he had found his footing and his range. He unleashed a terrific barrage and hurt the champion. Carpentier's cornermen could barely get him back. One of his cornermen threw in the towel. But the referee still disqualified Siki for tripping. That decision did not sit well with the 40,000 fans in attendance. They knew who should have won the fight. So did Carpentier's corner. The referee reversed himself and Battling Siki was the new light heavyweight champion.

Siki enjoyed *le beau monde*. Strolling around the boulevards with a leashed lion, he indulged in Champagne dinners and the Parisian nightlife: the sorts of pursuits that eat up your money. Siki needed another fight. What he came up with was going to Dublin to take on the Irish-American Mike McTigue for the championship. Siki was only getting $10,000 for his gamble. And gamble it was. Imagine fighting an Irishman in Dublin on St. Patrick's Day before 50,000 partisan fans for a world championship! That's just what Siki did. It may come as no surprise that the referee awarded the victory to McTigue. This time there was no need for the referee to reverse himself.

Two years later, Siki journeyed to New York City to try to get his boxing career back on track and fight for another world championship. Before he could do that, on December 14, 1925, he was shot in the back and died on the street. It is a murder mystery that has never been solved.

What is the shortest reign for a world championship? Would you believe three hours?

After Mike McTigue's decision over Battling Siki for the light heavyweight championship in March of 1923 and two non-decisions against Tommy Loughran, McTigue's manager Joe Jacobs arranged for a fight in Georgia in order to cash in on McTigue's newfound status. The fight was with a local boxer, 17-year-old **Willie Stribling**. No one had ever heard of this fighter, so no one in McTigue's camp had any reason to expect much of a fight. But once down in Georgia, Jacobs realized his man was not going to be stepping into the ring with a sacrificial lamb. Young Stribling was the real McCoy.

Jacobs tried to cancel the fight, but the preparations had progressed too far and pulling out of the match would be impossible. Next, Jacobs wanted to have the fight not sanctioned as a title fight. But it was too late for that, too. As a last resort, Jacobs imported his own referee, one Harry Ertle, who had instructions to make sure that the challenger would remain just that.

On October 4, 1923, the bout for the light heavyweight championship of the world was held in Columbus, Georgia. The partisan crowd was delighted with their local challenger. He fought with a finesse and toughness that were far beyond his 17 years. Thirty-one-year-old Mike McTigue was in the middle of what he had not wanted—a real fight. Although there were no knockdowns by either boxer, there was little doubt that Willie Stribling deserved to be the winner by decision. But the fix was in.

Harry Ertle went to announce the winner. The partisan crowd swelled in anticipation of the verdict. Ertle must have seen the ropes as little restraint against irate fight fans, so he asked the fight promoter, John Paul Jones, to announce the winner. "If that's your decision," snarled Jones, "get back out there and tell it to the folks." Ertle didn't dare. Walking back to the fighters, he raised young Stribling's arm as the winner. The crowd erupted in jubilation, as Joe Jacobs and his fighter stormed out of the ring. Later, Joe Jacobs cornered the referee and forced Ertle to announce the fight as a draw. Young Stribling was stripped of the title he had held for only three hours.

Eight long years later, on July 3, 1931, Stribling was coming off a record of 18 knockouts in a row and was given another shot for a world championship. This time his opponent was Max Schmeling. Before 35,000 fans at the new Municipal Stadium in Cleveland, Stribling did well for the first four rounds. Then Schmeling took the upper hand. He blocked everything Stribling threw and worked in his right hand to open up cuts over both eyes. Stribling continued until the fifteenth round, when a Schmeling right hand put him on the canvas. The man from Georgia was up before the count of 10, but Schmeling put him down for good with only 14 seconds remaining in the fight.

Heroes don't always win. Sometimes they just stand up for what they believe in, whatever the consequences.

This was true in the case of **Joe Salas**, a featherweight from California.

Joe Salas and Jackie Fields were boxers and best friends. They always trained together and supported each other in all their fights. They seemed to be of equal ability, too. That's what disturbed Salas so much when he and not Fields was chosen for the 1924 Olympic squad.

No way, said Salas. Fields has got to go, too. He wrote letters, cajoled officials, buttonholed anyone who would listen. If Fields doesn't go, then I don't go either. Finally, the US Olympic officials relented. Perhaps they believed Salas, or perhaps they just got tired of the barrage of words.

In Paris, Salas and Fields won every bout all the way to the finals. It was now time to fight for the gold and these two young men from the Golden State were slated to fight each other. Leaving their friendship alongside their robes, they fought like bitter enemies. At the end it was Jackie Fields who wore the gold medal around his neck. Joe Salas had been right all along.

A veteran of 59 fights, **Al Singer** from the Lower East Side in New York City had proven himself and was given a shot at the world lightweight championship. Some even said Singer was the new Benny Leonard, another boxer from the Lower East Side and one of the all-time top lightweights. In a bout at Madison Square Garden on July 17, 1930, Singer kayoed the lightweight champion, Sammy Mandell, in only one minute and 46 seconds of the very first round. This established a new record for the fastest knockout in a lightweight championship fight. In his next outing, a non-title fight with Jimmy McLarnin, a boxer who later went on to become the lightweight champion, Singer was down and counted out in the third round. This did not bode well for Singer's first title defense. And sure enough, Singer did not last as long as Mandell had. On November 14, 1930, Singer was knocked out by Tony Canzoneri in only one minute and six seconds of the first round—a new record for a lightweight title fight. Singer would fight six more times in 1931 and then had a hiatus until 1935. It was apparent to all that the future for this 26-year-old was long behind him.

So, who both won and lost a world championship in the first round? Al Singer is a good name for any boxing buff to remember.

After a series of elimination bouts for the vacant NBA world light heavyweight title, **George Nichols** defeated Dave Maier in 1932 for the title. But that seemed to be enough for Nichols, the boxer from Sandusky, Ohio. Although he continued to fight for another seven years, he never defended his title. Interestingly, in a non-title fight in 1936, Nichols battled John Henry Lewis, the light heavyweight champion, to a draw.

Tony Marino, a 23-year-old club fighter from California, had a most unusual brush with fame. When Baltazar Sangchili of Spain, the world bantamweight champion, came to the United States in 1935, he needed a tune-up fight. Marino was selected, and they met at the Dyckman Oval in Brooklyn.

Everything was running true to form, when suddenly in the fourteenth round there was something very wrong with the Spaniard, and he was unable to continue. Tony Marino was now the proud wearer of the world bantamweight champion's belt.

The new champion's reign was short-lived. Just two months later Marino was in the ring with NBA bantam champion Sixto Escobar, who relentlessly pursued Marino until he knocked him out for good in the thirteenth round.

Tony Marino fought five more fights before meeting Indian Quintana on January 30, 1937. A battered Marino lost the fight on points, and two days later lost his life from a cerebral hemorrhage.

Tony "(Two Ton)" Galento's moment in the sun came on June 28, 1939. Lightly regarded as another of Joe Louis's Bum of the Month Club fighters, the five-foot-nine, 233-pound Galento stunned the fight world and Louis when he knocked down the Brown Bomber in the third round. Louis bounced back and beat Galento senseless in the fourth.

There were only two times that Louis felt antipathy for his opponent. One was Max Schmeling and the other was Galento, because of his racist remarks.

On January 6, 1947, **Harold Dade** was presented a gift when he was only 22, a bout with Manuel Ortiz. From Puerto Rico, Ortiz was the great bantamweight champion who had held the crown since 1942. From Chicago, Dade fought a smart fight, lasted the 15 rounds, and won the championship on points. In their return bout on March 11, 1947, Ortiz outpointed Dade to take the bantamweight championship back. Dade never had another shot at a title, but his brush with glory made him a good draw until he hung up his gloves in 1952.

Palmerston, New Zealand, was the site of one of the shortest fights in boxing history. On July 8, 1952, **Ross Cleverly** knocked down D. Emerson with his first punch. The referee stopped the fight at seven seconds of the first round.

In 1975 **Chuck Wepner** was offered the chance of a lifetime: to step into the ring with the heavyweight champion of the world, Muhammad Ali. Rebounding from the 1974 slugfest with George Foreman in Zaire, Ali just wanted a breather, and that's what the match with this liquor salesman from Bayonne, New Jersey, represented. Ranked number 11, Wepner had been knocked out by some formidable opponents—Buster Mathis, George Foreman, Sonny Liston, Joe Bugner— and Ali figured he would add his name to the list. After this March 24 fight in Cleveland, Ali would be ready for the rematch with Foreman, who was taking on the seventh-ranked heavyweight, Oscar Bonavena. "This sucker is a cinch," declared Ali.

Although Ali was in control of the fight from the opening bell, the Bayonne Bleeder was a gamer and still around in the ninth when referee Tony Perez ruled Ali had been knocked down. Thinking he'd been tripped and pushed, Ali came back in a punching fury, but Wepner was not going down. In the fifteenth round

Ali had beaten Wepner all but senseless into the ropes, but the man from New Jersey was still not going down. With only 19 seconds remaining Perez stopped the fight. "There's not another human being in the world that can go 15 rounds like that," said an amazed and admiring Mahammad Ali afterward.

After watching the fight in a theater in California that night, Sylvester Stallone was also amazed and admiring of Wepner. Four days later Stallone had come up with the first *Rocky* script featuring the Rocky Balboa character, a hard-nosed fighter based on Chuck Wepner.

At the age most boxers have long hung up their gloves was when **Dr. Herbert Odom** of Chicago turned professional. Having boxed as an amateur, Odom was no stranger to the ring, but that had been 23 years earlier. So now on July 20, 1979, at the ripe age of 46, Odom was once again stepping into the ring. His opponent, Eddie Partee, was a mere 19. In the boxing world, a difference of 27 years could be measured in light years. But none of this stopped old man Odom. In fact, Odom stopped Partee in the second round. The oldest person ever to turn pro in boxing had won the bout.

Heather Poyner was not really in shape to fight, but it was for a good cause: to get women's amateur boxing on the map. So, on October 30, 1993, Poyner stepped into the ring for a welterweight bout with a better-conditioned **Dallas Malloy**, at Edmonds Community College in Seattle. Poyner studied martial arts; Malloy had been training at a boxing gym.

After receiving a pummeling for three rounds, Heather Poyner in defeat couldn't let it slide by unnoticed that the two boxers on Malloy's trophy were both male. As this was only the second fully sanctioned women's amateur boxing match in the United States (the first was won by Claire Buckner in St. Paul, Minnesota, in 1978), it took a while to update the trophies. Their landmark bout turned out to be the last fight for both boxers.

Coaches and Officials

"Now I know what it's like to have people coming at me, ready to tear me apart. There were twenty thousand people screaming for my blood. They hated my guts. How can so many people hate so much?"
—Red Storey, hockey referee

Here's a story about a man who had all kinds of fame in one field, then took the afternoon off to oversee another. It was none other than **Wild Bill Hickok**, an inveterate baseball fan, who was contacted in 1872 by the town fathers in Kansas City, Kansas, to umpire a ball game between the Antelopes and the Pomeroys. The previous meeting of these two semipro teams had ended in a riot. Afraid that their next game would escalate beyond the injury of players and fans, Hickok was behind the plate wearing his six-shooters. It worked. No fights broke out, no one was hurt, there wasn't even a serious rhubarb. For his assistance in this matter Wild Bill asked to be paid with a new carriage and two white horses. They complied and Wild Bill Hickok rode out of town, pistols by his side, in style.

In June 1911, there was a convicted murderer, **Patrick Casey**, who was slated to be hanged the next day at the Nevada State Penitentiary in Carson City. As in the movies, the condemned prisoner was granted a last wish. Casey had a love for baseball and had umpired some games earlier in his life.

"Before I die, I'd like to umpire a ball game," Casey told the warden. "Could you have a game tomorrow and let me umpire it?"

"Play ball!" Patrick got his wish and not one of the cantankerous convicts questioned any of his calls.

The next day Casey swung.

The NFL championship game on December 9, 1934, between the unbeaten Chicago Bears and the New York Giants was held under miserable playing conditions at the Polo Grounds. The footing was treacherous for both teams on the icy field and that was probably why the Giants were only behind 10–3 at the half. Giants coach Steve Owen remembered a comment before the game by end Ray Flaherty about how his college team had once played in sneakers on an icy field. Owen told trainer **Gus Maunch**, who ran off with the clubhouse attendant, **Abe Cohen**, in search of footwear. When they returned after the third quarter, the Bears were leading 13–3. As soon as the Giant players discarded their cleats and put on sneakers, the Giants turned the game around. In the final ten minutes, they scored 27 points—Ken Strong had touchdowns from 42 and 11 yards out—to upset the Bears, 30–13. As guard Jules Carlson of the Bears put it, "We should have won in '34, but the field was frozen. The Giants put tennis shoes on and went wild."

Belle Martell of Van Nuys, California, became the first woman boxing referee when she received her license from the state of California on April 30, 1940. Her first and last time in the ring was the eight fights she refereed in San Bernardino on May 2. Martell retired in June when she was assigned to Los Angeles.

The Dartmouth-Cornell football game is always a big game, but the one on November 16, 1940, was bigger than usual. Riding a 19-game winning streak, Cornell was behind 3–0 but threatening to score. With only one minute showing on the clock, Cornell had driven to Dartmouth's six-yard line. The Big Red had four downs to push the ball into the end zone.

Back Mort Landsberg ran for three yards. On the next play quarterback Walt Scholl ran the ball to the one. Third down and Landsberg was stopped for no gain. With only 10 seconds remaining, Cornell ran in a substitute with the play. However, Cornell had already used all their time-outs, so they were penalized five yards. (Nowadays, of course, you don't need to use a time-out to substitute players.) Back on the six-yard line once again, Cornell's Walt Scholl passed into the end zone, but the ball was batted away by Dartmouth's Ray Hall.

Referee **"Red" Friesell** marched the ball out to the 20, where it would be Dartmouth's ball, first and 10. The game seemed all but over. Head linesman Joe McKenney informed Friesell that Cornell had been offside, but that wouldn't make any difference. Dartmouth would simply refuse the penalty. In a moment of confusion, Friesell took the ball back to the six-yard line and indicated that it was fourth down for Cornell. A stunned stadium of 30,000 spectators watched as

Cornell lined up and Walt Scholl hit Bill Murphy in the end zone. The extra point was good; Cornell had won 7–3.

But it didn't take long for the truth to surface. Everyone, including "Red" Friesell, knew that Cornell had been given a fifth down.

On Monday Friesell wrote to the commissioner of the Eastern Intercollegiate Athletic Association. The last paragraph of Friesell's report to Asa Bushnell read:

> This mistake was entirely mine as the game's referee and not shared in or contributed to by any of the three other officials. I realize of course, that my jurisdiction ceased at the close of the game and that the football rules give me no authority to change even an incorrect decision such as the one I described; but I do want to acknowledge my mistake to you as Commissioner of the Eastern Intercollegiate Football Association and, if you see fit, to the football public as well.

But it did not end there. When word of Friesell's report reached Cornell, James Lynah, the director of athletics at Cornell, and Carl Snavely, the Cornell coach, reacted immediately. They informed Dartmouth: "In view of the conclusions reached by the officials that the Cornell touchdown was scored on a fifth down, Cornell relinquishes claim to the victory and extends congratulations to Dartmouth."

"If we hadn't made that decision, we'd have been explaining that game as long as football has a place in intercollegiate athletics," explained Edmund Ezra Day, the president of Cornell.

So, Dartmouth went down in the record books as the winner 3–0 and Cornell had its unbeaten streak stopped at 19. What today's coaches, athletes, and athletic programs could learn from such a surprising and honorable outcome.

Edna "(Tiny)" Tarbutton is not a name that has much name recognition except in certain basketball circles. But Tarbutton was a coach who ran up the most consecutive victories of anyone. Beginning in 1947, Tarbutton's practices with her teams of girls at Baskin High School in Louisiana (there were only 70 or so girls in the school) lasted only an hour, but they were long enough to instill in her charges the importance of fundamentals and using their heads. That year her girls' team went 38–0. And it was similar year after year. The average size of their wins was 54–23, and Baskin didn't even have to come from behind until their 190th victory. It wasn't until 1953 that they lost a game. Along the way Baskin High won 218 straight and nine state championships, including eight in a row from 1948–55.

Sometimes baseball owners will try anything. That was certainly the case with the DeWitts, Bill and Charlie, owners of the St. Louis Browns, who were seeking ways to improve on their previous records. So in 1950, they hired a psychologist, **David Tracy**, to hypnotize the players. Whatever works, they figured.

Manager Zack Taylor would have nothing to do with it and didn't even allow Tracy in the dugout. After hearing that Tracy was trying to help the Browns' pitching staff "keep the ball away from Joe DiMaggio," sportswriter Bob Cooke noted, "Sometimes, they keep it 400 feet away from him."

On June 7, after Tracy tried to get them out of their deep sleep, the Browns lost to the Red Sox, 20–4. The next day, the Browns were beaten by the Sox again, this time 29–4. Tracy was through and so were the Browns. They ended the year with 58 wins and 96 losses, and a firm grip on seventh place.

Not to be outdone, the New York Rangers also thought they'd try **David Tracy** to get out of their 12-game losing string in the winter of 1950. Tracy hypnotized the players in the locker room before a game with the Bruins. It certainly didn't hurt as New York was locked in a 3–3 tie with Boston with a minute left. But then the Bruins broke away and scored a last goal to win.

"Next time I'll concentrate more on the Ranger goaltender, Chuck Rayner," Tracy said. But there was no next time. The front office didn't fall under the spell that this was the way to help the Broadway Blues out of their doldrums.

Russ Ahearn began coaching basketball at Alden-Hebron High School in 1948. With only 92 students it was one of the smallest high schools in Illinois, but that didn't stop Ahearn from building the Giants into a powerhouse. Four years later he was ready to make his move. He knew he had the kids—Paul and Phil Judson (six-foot-one twins), Bill Schultz (six-foot-eleven), Ken Spooner and Don Willbrandt (both five-foot-eleven)—they just needed the opponents. Ahearn had scheduled games with larger schools and in their larger gyms. (Alden-Hebron played on the stage in their auditorium.)

The Giants got off to a great start in the '51–'52 season. Their man-to-man defense forced turnovers and held opponents to low scores; their fast break offense turned almost every mistake and advantage into a score. Ahearn's team rose as high as ninth in the state. (Illinois did not have divisions then.) But they had beaten the eighth-place team by 25 points. By season's end Alden-Hebron sported a 24–1 record. The only time they had been defeated was a 71–68 loss to Crystal Lake. That was also the only time a school had scored more than 60 points against them.

It was time for the state tournament. Ahearn told his team they only needed to win 11 times. Methodically they worked their way through the district and regional playoffs. One of their victims was Crystal Lake. Now it was on to the final 16 in Champaign. The three favorites were Champaign, Quincy, and Rock Island—all high schools of over 1,000 students. This was heady stuff for the boys from Hebron, a town of 600 near the border with Wisconsin.

The first team they played was Champaign. Playing a big school in the state tournament in their hometown wasn't easy, but Ahearn's team won by 10. Ten was the magic number for Alden-Hebron's next win, too. In the semifinals they went up against Rock Island. Ahearn's belief in his boys paid off on the court. The third quarter closed with the Giants behind by three points. In the fourth they ran off 15 straight points and wound up beating the larger school by 12. The finals pitted the boys from Hebron against Quincy. Russ Ahearn had made believers of his team and everyone else outside of Quincy. They seemed destined, but it wasn't without a fight. Quincy didn't score more than 60, but neither did Alden-Hebron. At the end of the game the score was tied 59–59. Ahearn's confidence was contagious. In the overtime the Giants scored five points and played a tenacious man-to-man that didn't allow Quincy to score even once.

The boys from Hebron all won basketball scholarships: Paul and Phil Judson went to Illinois, Schultz and Spooner went to Northwestern, Willbrandt went to Valparaiso. But it was Russ Ahearn that the players and the townspeople often talked about when they recalled that championship season.

In July 1974, **Carol Polis** received her license from the New York State Athletic Commission to be a judge of boxing matches. Polis was the first woman to become a boxing judge in the United States.

In 1975, **Lanny Moss** took over the reins as general manager of the Portland Mavericks of the Class A Northwest League. Moss was the first woman to run a club in professional baseball.

Fans

*"How would you like it in your job if every time
you made a mistake, a red light went on over
your desk and fifteen thousand people
stood up and yelled at you?"*
—Jacques Plante, Hall of Fame goalie

At one time the ballpark was a rough place, not the
sort of place where you would want to take the family. (This is sometimes true today in the upper decks of
Yankee Stadium for a game with the Red Sox.) To
counter this frontier mentality, Ladies' Days were begun around 1876. One of the cleverest uses of Ladies'
Day was by Cincinnati owner **Aaron Stern**. Noticing
that there were more women in the stands whenever
his handsome star Tony Mullane pitched—he wasn't
called The Apollo of the Box for nothing—Stern
started using Mullane against the weaker teams when
the attendance sagged and designated these starts
Ladies' Days.

In the 1880s in Boston there was a wealthy fan named
Arthur Dixwell who attended most Red Stocking home
games and even made some road trips with the team.
This fan soon became known as **Hi Hi Dixwell** because he shouted, "Hi Hi," whenever he got excited.
He was liked by the Boston ballplayers not only for his

enthusiasm ("He lives for baseball," reported *The Sporting News*) but also because he handed out cash prizes for good plays.

Fans will often discuss the merits of players in bars, but in one bar in Boston the bartender served up more than drinks from the 1890s to the 1910s. **Mike McGreevey** was the self-appointed authority on the merits of Boston baseball. His nickname "Nuff Ced" spoke reams.

But McGreevey was more than just talk. When his group of like-minded Bostonians, the Royal Rooters, changed the lyrics of a popular song to "Honus, why do you hit so badly?" one of Wagner's teammates attributed the songbirds as being responsible for Wagner's disappointing .222 average in the 1903 World Series. And when the Royal Rooters were not given tickets to the seventh game of the 1912 World Series between the Boston Red Sox and the New York Giants, McGreevey led his troops to storm the gates and marched in protest around the infield.

(A point of interest: this World Series was not settled in the seventh game; the two teams played eight because the second game was called on account of darkness in the eleventh with the score tied 6–6. The Bosox eventually won the series, 4 games to 3.)

Lou Proctor was a telegraph operator who slipped his own name into the stats for a game on May 13, 1912, between the Boston Red Sox and the St. Louis Browns. It's not like he portrayed himself as hitting a grand slam in the bottom of the ninth. He modestly inserted himself as a pinch-hitter who went hitless in one at-bat.

Happy Felsch was a good outfielder on the Chicago White Sox, but like many a player, he was always seeking an edge. One day in 1919 he warmly greeted one of their faithful fans, **Eddie Bennett**, and rubbed the short man's back playfully. For Mr. Bennett, you see, was a hunchback. It did not go unnoticed by the superstitious Felsch that the White Sox won that day. Nor did it go unnoticed the next day when he did the same thing and the Sox won again. By the third day, Eddie Bennett was sitting in the dugout. The White Sox won again. From then on Eddie Bennett was both mascot and batboy. Superstitious or not, it didn't hurt Chicago that season. The White Sox had a glorious year, capturing the American League pennant before losing the World Series in the infamous Black Sox scandal.

The White Sox weren't the only ones to believe in luck. The Brooklyn Robins had Bennett's services when they won the pennant in 1920. And not to be denied, the Yankees had him for their great pennant-winning teams in 1921, '22, '23, '26, '27, and '28.

In the 1920s the Baltimore Orioles had a policy that could win 15 minutes of fame among his buddies for most any kid. During batting practice you could stand outside the ballpark behind home plate and fetch foul balls. As there were no batting cages and the stadium was only a single tier behind home, there were usually a lot of foul balls bouncing around. For every ball turned in to the ticket window, you received a free ticket. "Some of my friends used to hawk four or five balls before the game," remembers **Michael Kawecki**, "and get the whole neighborhood in free."

Hage Rawlings, a former halfback for Navy, was seriously injured while on active duty in 1925. From his bed he became one of Navy's biggest rooters. After the Middies lost the 1925 Army–Navy game, 10–3, Rawlings had a double prediction: "They will do it next year," he said, "and I'll fight to live to see it."

The next year Navy went unbeaten. Even when it was predicted that they would lose to Michigan, they won. Hage Rawlings was not as fortunate. He lost. His last wishes for a victory in the Army–Navy game on November 27, 1926, were conveyed to the Middies in the locker room. The two teams fought to a 21–21 deadlock in what has been referred to as "The Classic Tie."

There were two fans at Shibe Park in Philadelphia who were relentless hecklers. Brothers **Bull** and **Eddie Kessler** would station themselves across the infield from each other to achieve maximum impact and distraction for the players. Their chief target was a fellow Philadelphian, Jimmy Dykes, who enjoyed a long career—22 years in all—but certainly did not enjoy their choice words for him. It got so bad for Dykes that Connie Mack finally traded him in 1933 to the White Sox.

On July 25, 1930, the Kansas City Monarchs were playing the Homestead Grays at Pittsburgh's Forbes

Field. The game was being played under the lights (the first game with lights in the majors was in 1935 at Crosley Field in Cincinnati) and things fell apart for the Grays when Smokey Joe Williams and catcher Buck Ewing got fouled up on their signals because of the poor lighting. Smokey Joe blazed a fastball that split open an unsuspecting Ewing's hand. In the stands that night was sitting a 19-year-old semi-pro player whom the Gray's manager, Judy Johnson, knew about.

"I called time," said Johnson, "and Josh was sitting up there in the stands and I asked him if he wanted to catch and he said 'yes sir,' so we had to hold up the game while he went and put Buck Ewing's uniform on. We signed him the next day."

Josh Gibson went from fan to a fantastic career with the Homestead Grays and the Pittsburgh Crawfords and in 1972 to the Baseball Hall of Fame.

Years before George Plimpton's reportage from the hockey crease or the football huddle, **Paul Gallico** got into the ring to find out what it was like to face Jack Dempsey in a boxing match. Gallico found out soon enough and was knocked out. It was quite a risky way to begin his career as a sportswriter for the *New York Daily News*, but it successfully launched him. So when he writes that Dempsey was "the greatest and most beloved sports hero the country had ever known," he is not just sharing a cup of tea with him at Dempsey's restaurant.

Few fans have ever been as devoted to one player as Brooklyn restaurateur **Jack Pierce** was to third baseman Cookie Lavagetto. From the moment Lavagetto stepped in as a Dodger (after three years in Pittsburgh), Pierce was ensconced in his 10 box seats behind the visitor's dugout. After draping his blue-and-gray COOKIE sign over the roof of the dugout, Pierce busied himself with blowing up balloons, a hundred in all, and screaming "Cookie" before he popped each one. Whenever Cookie got a hit, Pierce would let go one of the helium-filled balloons that had been delivered by a cab driver to his seat. Even after Lavagetto went off to the war after the 1941 season, "Fierce" Jack Pierce continued his rite for another year.

In the 1940s and 1950s there was a particular fan at practically every game at Ebbets Field in Brooklyn named **Hilda Chester**. This matronly woman made her presence so well known that she acquired nicknames, "Howling Hilda" for all her noise and commotion (she was particularly scornful of the traitorous **Joe Tepsic** in 1947) and the "Queen of the Bleachers" for her steady presence. With her cowbells (one of which is enshrined in Cooperstown) and her carryings-on to congratulate or criticize the action on the playing field, it was hard for the players on either side to ignore her. Sometimes they would even wave to her, and other times she would send notes to Leo Durocher via center fielder Pete Reiser. One time Reiser picked up a note she dropped and stopped to talk to Larry MacPhail on the way to the dugout. When Durocher read the note he thought it was from MacPhail. "Get Casey up," the note read, "Wyatt's losing it." Well, Leo did just that, even though Wyatt had been doing well and Casey got hit hard. But usually she was just the most conspicuous fan in the ballpark. As her sign in the upper center field bleachers spelled out: "Hilda is here," everyone in the ballpark was usually aware that she was.

Due to travel restrictions because of the war, the Army–Navy game could not be played in Philadelphia. The rivalry in 1942 was held at Annapolis on November 28 and only 12,000 showed up. Half of the 3,200 **midshipmen** were designated as Army fans. There were even Army songs and cheers for the midshipmen to learn led by two Army cheerleaders and half of Navy's cheerleaders.

"Everyone told us later we acted like we meant it when we led Army's cheers, and I guess we did," said Navy cheerleader Daniel Webster Herlong. "I certainly felt good about the job we did, but I felt better about Navy winning."

Navy won the game, 14–0.

On November 27, 1943, the situation was reversed. The game was held at West Point; half the Corps of Cadets wore white cap covers and cheered for the mid-dies. As Glenn Stewart, one of the Navy cheerleaders who led the white-capped cadets, they "did it in good spirit, almost as if they didn't know the difference nor did they really care who they cheered for, though there was a considerable difference in volume from the cadets who cheered for Army."

Everything was reversed except for the score. Navy won again, this time, 13–0.

* * *

In 1945, **William Sianis** showed up at Wrigley Field
for a World Series game with his goat and wasn't allowed entry. Sianis, owner of the Billy Goat Tavern,
was so furious he threw a hex on the Cubs. The Cubs
lost the Series in seven games and haven't been in one
since.

It was 1946 and time once again for the annual classic,
the Army–Navy football game. Army was sporting its
magnificent team featuring Mr. Inside and Mr. Outside, Felix "Doc" Blanchard and Glenn Davis, and en-
joying an unbeaten season. Navy, on the other hand,
had dropped its last seven games.

In the first half, Blanchard ran for one touchdown,
Davis for another, and Davis had passed to Blanchard
for a third. The half had ended with the score 21–6. But
that proved to be the end of the scoring for Army. As
the second half ground on, Navy scored in the third
quarter and again in the fourth. Unfortunately for the
middies, they had been unable to convert any of their
points after touchdowns, so the score stood at 21–18.

But with 90 seconds remaining Navy was again
threatening and had pushed the ball all the way to the
Army three-yard line. In the meantime the cadets had
come out of the stands and were standing around the
end zone. It was almost as if they were trying to bolster
their battered team to prevent the Navy team from scoring. The first two plays from scrimmage went for no
gain. Navy sent in a specially designed play that took
so long to explain to the team that they were penalized
for delay of game. By this time the crush of cadets was
spilling onto the field. Third down for Navy and they

ran the ball wide right into the sea of spectators. Was the ball carrier out of bounds or not? If he was, time would be stopped and Navy would have another play from scrimmage. No one knew, no one found out, confusion reigned, and the game ended in a whimper. The **Army fans'** goal-line stand had stopped Navy.

The Cleveland Indians won the World Series in 1948, but 1949 was a different story. So upset was **Charley Lupica**, a druggist, about his seventh-place Indians that on May 29, 1949, he climbed up a 20-foot flagpole, saying he would not return to terra firma until the Indians had returned to first place. Well, Charley stayed on his four-foot-wide platform for 117 days; the Indians were not in first, but they had moved up to fourth. Bill Veeck, the owner, was so impressed with Lupica's perseverance that he presented him with a new car.

The tradition of a dead octopus on the ice for a Detroit Red Wing playoff game started on April 15, 1952. That was when **Jerry** and **Pete Cusimano**, who went straight from work in their father's poultry and fish business, came up with the idea.

"Why don't we throw an octopus on the ice for good luck?" Jerry had asked earlier. "It's got eight legs and that might be a good omen for eight straight wins."

The Red Wings grabbed not only their eighth straight win but also the Stanley Cup that year. A tradition was born.

Tradition or not, this was often tough on the referees. Red Storey once told how he would always be on the alert for an octopus during the first five minutes of the game. Consequently, he rarely called any infractions early in the game. "I was on octopus watch," he said.

At the 1952 Olympic Games in Helsinki, Jean Boiteux of France was cruising to victory in the 400-meter freestyle when Ford Konno of the United States made his move. Boiteux held off the challenger to win the exciting race in the Olympic record time of 4:30.7, over 10 seconds faster than the previous record four years earlier. After the winner touched the wall, a fully dressed middle-aged man in a beret jumped into the pool to hug the winner. Everyone poolside wondered who this man was, but the man himself soon answered the question. The man raised his arms and cried in an emotional voice, **"Papa!"**

As the 1954–1955 season was winding down, Maurice "Rocket" Richard was in the lead in a scoring race with his Canadien teammate Bernie "Boom Boom" Geof-frion. But that was before Clarence Campbell sus-pended Richard for the final three games of the season—and the entire playoffs—for attacking Bruin Hal Laycoe and hitting linesman Cliff Thompson. (Ge-offrion went on to win; each had 38 goals, but Boom Boom had 75 points to Rocket's 74.)

When Campbell showed up at the Montreal Forum on March 17 for a game between the Canadiens and the Detroit Red Wings, many fans exploded in rage, throwing everything that wasn't nailed down. A tear-gas bomb was set off on the ice and the fans streamed toward the exits. The game was forfeited to the Red Wings.

Then the riot moved to the streets. A mob of 10,000 roamed the streets of Montreal, breaking windows, looting, and battling the police in what is known as **The Richard Riot** or **The St. Patrick's Day Riot**. By the raw light of day on March 18, the count was 70 people arrested and $100,000 worth of property damage.

The forfeit cost the Canadiens two points, and when they lost the final game to the Red Wings, Detroit won the league by two points. This cost Montreal the home ice advantage when they met Detroit for the Stanley Cup that year. The series went seven games, each game won by the home team.

A new tradition started with the Melbourne Olympic Games. There had always been the opening ceremonies of teams marching behind the flags of their countries. But something new was added in 1956. It all came about because of a letter to Sir Wilfred Kent Hughes, the director of the Melbourne Olympic Organizing Committee, from a young Australian with Chinese parents.

Dear Friends,
I am a Chinese boy and have just turned 17 years of age.
    Before the Games I thought everything would be in a muddle. [It was the time of the Hungarian Revolution.] However, I am quite wrong. It is the most successful Games ever staged. . . . Mr. Hughes, I believe it has been suggested a march be put on during the closing ceremonies and you said it couldn't be done. I think it can be done . . .

the march I have in mind is different than the one during the Opening Ceremony. . . . During the march there will be only one nation . . . what more could anybody want if the whole world could be made as one nation. . . .

John Ian Wing

Back in the days of the American Football League, the Dallas Texans (now the Kansas City Chiefs) were playing the Patriots in Boston on November 3, 1961. Behind 28–21 in the closing seconds, Texan quarterback Cotton Davidson unleashed a 70-yard pass to Chris Burford, who went up in a crowd of defenders to catch the ball and was pulled down at the three-yard line. Mistakenly thinking the game was over, the Patriot fans streamed onto the field. However, there was time for one more play, so the fans were signaled out of the end zone. Again, Cotton Davidson threw to Chris Burford, but this time a hand reached up and deflected the pass. Only this time it wasn't one of the Patriots. **A spectator** had batted the ball away. Cotton Davidson protested, but seemingly no one else had seen it, so the game was over; the Patriots had won. It wasn't until the game film was later developed that the truth came out. By then it was too late.

An unidentified fan from the gallery so exuberantly shook Gary Player's hand after he had tied with Arnold Palmer for the 1962 Masters tournament that Player's hand was severely sprained. Playing the next day with a bandaged hand, Player lost to Palmer by three strokes.

*   *   *

Hank Aguirre was a notoriously poor hitting pitcher. In 16 seasons he had only 33 hits for an .085 batting average. But there was one season, 1963, when he went on a tear and collected ten hits. What had happened? It was almost magical how it came about.

In Detroit's 1963 spring training camp at Lakeland, Florida, **an older gentleman** came up to Aguirre and slipped a check for $10,000 in his hand, telling him he could cash it after getting his tenth hit that season. Well, this was unusual for a couple of reasons. One of them was that Aguirre had a total of only eight hits in his previous seven seasons.

But things were different that year for the six-foot-four southpaw, and by August Aguirre had collected his tenth hit. Aguirre called the bank in Lakeland to confirm the validity of the check. There was no one there with an account under the name of Santa Claus.

Morganna Roberts Cottrell, aka "The Kissing Bandit," was an exotic dancer who added a little spice to baseball games for more than 20 years before retiring in 1999. She interrupted games to kiss the cheeks of George Brett (at the 1986 All-Star Game), John Candelaria, Fred Lynn, Pete Rose (he was the first), Nolan Ryan, Mike Schmidt, Dickie Thon, and many other major and minor league players. Sixteen times she was arrested.

At one of her court appearances, her attorney offered this defense: "This woman, with a 112-pound body and a 15-pound chest, leaned over the rail to see a foul ball. Gravity took its toll, she fell out on the field, and the rest is history."

One night at a nightclub where Ms. Cottrell was performing, George Brett got her back. In the middle of her act, this 1999 inductee into the Hall of Fame ran onstage and kissed her.

It was the third period in a game between the Miami Dolphins and the Baltimore Colts in December of 1971 when a man in the crowd, **Donald Ellis**, put himself into the action by leaping down to the field and grabbing the ball.

"My friends didn't think I would do it," said a groggy Ellis later. "I didn't know I would do it either. But suddenly I was out there."

Most of the players ignored Ellis but not Mike Curtis, the Colt linebacker. Curtis chased Ellis until he caught him and then hit him with a shot that put Ellis into the hospital.

"I believe in law and order," said Curtis. "That fellow had no right on the field. I felt it was in line to make him aware of his wrongdoing."

In the dead of winter in 1982, a nine-year-old boy was walking to his home in Calgary when he was knocked over and stabbed repeatedly. Besides the assault to his body, **Cory Gurnsey** was upset because his Guy Lafleur jersey was ruined in the attack. Upon getting wind of this, Lafleur sent one of his jerseys to the boy's hospital room. He also called Cory and told him he was going to score a goal for him in an upcoming game. And that's what he did. Lafleur signed the puck and sent it to the boy. Then when Cory was well enough to travel, he was flown to Montreal to watch his favorite player in action. And sure enough, Guy Lafleur scored another goal for his favorite fan.

One of the last major league teams to have a mascot was the San Francisco Giants, so in 1984 they adopted the **Crazy Crab**. It wasn't cuddly, it wasn't funny, it apparently was just annoying. Whenever it appeared the fans would boo and even hurl beer. A grass roots anti-crab campaign appeared on T-shirts. The Giants got the message and gave the crab its unconditional release.

Derek Redmond was one of the finest 400-meter runners at the 1988 Olympic Games in Seoul. He might have won a medal, but he had to drop out because of an injury to his Achilles tendon. Injuries, it seemed, had plagued his track career. One time they didn't was in 1991, when he ran on the 4×400 British relay team that upset the US entry at the 1991 World Championships in Tokyo. He also seemed healthy for the 1992 Olympics in Barcelona. On August 3, 1992, he was ready to run the semifinals and hopefully do well two days later in the finals.

"I saw him on the morning of the race," said his father, **Jim Redmond**. "He was in marvelous shape, in good spirits. He was full of confidence and seemed to be the man they would have to beat."

In lane five, Derek Redmond got off to a good start. He couldn't see the winner of the Olympic 400 in Seoul, Steve Lewis of the US in lane three, but he was making up the stagger on the men in the outside lanes. "I couldn't believe I was going so fast," Derek would say later. "I was running so easily it didn't appear to me I was going that fast."

In the old days, the 400 was a sprint and then a relaxed run and a sprint at the end. Nowadays, it is a sprint the whole way.

"I was getting ready to make my turn around the bend when suddenly I heard a funny 'pop,'" remembered Derek.

For all athletes this is a sickening sound. It is the snapping of the hamstring. Needless to say, the pain is crippling.

"I couldn't believe it," recalled his father. "I knew it was Derek, but I didn't want to believe it."

Derek was stranded on the track. The other runners finished and Derek, with a grimace that could wrench anyone's heartstrings, was trying to continue, hopping on one leg.

Jim Redmond went down on the track to help his son. The love of a parent for his child transcends sport. He had to get to his boy.

"The first thing Dad said as he put his arms around me was, 'Look, you don't have to do this.' And I told him, 'Yes, I do.' And he said, 'Well, if you're going to finish this race, we'll finish it together.'"

For those who saw this on television, it can bring tears to the eyes just remembering the sight of the father in ball cap, T-shirt, blue shorts, sneakers, and white socks, holding his son's right wrist with his left hand; his beloved son in a paisley runner's shirt and blue biker pants, his left arm around his dad's shoulders—the two of them hobbling together toward the finish line.

* * *

Some people have their 15 minutes of fame without ever putting on a uniform. Just such a case is **Jeffrey Maier**, the 12-year-old boy who became the toast of New York in 1996.

In game one of the American League Championship Series, Derek Jeter of the Yankees hit a long fly ball to right field. Tony Tarasco, the right fielder of the Orioles, was waiting with outstretched glove when suddenly a fan in the stands snatched it before Tarasco could catch it. Instead of calling fan interference, the umpire ruled it a home run. What may well have been a Yankee defeat turned into a Yankee victory as they went on to win 5–4 in the eleventh inning.

Maier became an instant hero to some. Yes, mention of "Mantle, Munson, and Maier" was heard muttered in Da Bronx. The boy was feted on talk shows and even featured on *Late Night with David Letterman*.

A different fate could well have been in store for this young fan. Another umpire might have seen things differently and ruled the ball an out (the ball most likely would have been caught if it hadn't been for the fan interference) and Maier booted out of the stadium. By a turn of the screw, Maier would have been regarded a spoilsport rather than a hero, a blight on the House of Ruth rather than an "Angel in the Outfield."

Football

*"For about 15 minutes, Doug Flutie was the toast
of New York—not just the toast but the challah and
the pita and the croissants, too."*
—George Vecsey, sportswriter

At one time the official football field was 110 yards long. That was the case on November 5, 1884, in a game between Wesleyan and Yale universities. Yale took over the ball on their own goal line. **Wyllys Terry** of Yale received the ball five yards deep in his own end zone and followed his blockers all the way to the Wesleyan goal line—a touchdown run of 110 yards.

Has there ever been a time when a woman coached a major college football team for a whole season? The knee-jerk response is no. But there was one time. It happened in 1888 at Yale University when Walter Camp became too ill to go out to the practice field and to the stadium, so his wife, **Ellen Camp**, went in his place.

In the late 1800s there was no three-year (now four-year) rule for college eligibility. So between 1888 and 1894, **Andrew Wyant** played center in 98 games for Bucknell University and the University of Chicago. To top it off, he did not miss so much as a single minute of playing time.

On October 31, 1897, a tragic death occurred in a game between the University of Georgia and the University of Virginia that might have ended football in the South. The captain and star of the Georgia team, Richard Vonalbade Gammon, was knocked unconscious and had to be helped off the field. Later that night he died.

The response to ban football quickly took root. A bill to outlaw football in Georgia passed in the legislature and was awaiting the governor's signature. A similar bill passed in Virginia and was making the rounds in other states when the mother of the dead footballer, **Rosalind Burns Gammon**, pleaded with the governor not to sign the bill. Her son had loved the game and would not have wanted it banned. The governor did not sign the bill and the anti-football sentiment dissolved.

Sewanee was a small school of 97 students that fielded a small team of only 12 players. But that's where the smallness stopped. In November, 1899, Sewanee played and won five games in six days. Their opponents and their winning scores were University of Texas, 12–0; Texas A & M, 32–0; Tulane University, 23–0; Louisiana State, 34–0; and Mississippi State, 12–0.

The first black professional football player was **Charles Follis**. He played for the Blues from Shelby,

Ohio, from 1902–1906. Follis also played baseball professionally.

In 1905, the University of Michigan was playing the University of Chicago. Chicago had a football team in those days and Michigan took its football as seriously as it does today. The game was scoreless when **Denny Clark** of Michigan was back to receive a punt from Chicago. In an effort to break away, he ran back toward the end zone and behind the goal line, where he was pulled down by Chicago. Unfortunately for Michigan and Clark, that was all the scoring done that day. The aftermath was merciless for the hapless footballer both on campus and off. The headline of a local newspaper summed up how Clark must have felt: "Clark 2, Michigan 0." It all proved too much for Denny Clark. He not only dropped out of school a week later, but left for parts unknown in the north country, where he lived the life of a hermit for several years.

On November 11, 1911, Princeton University became the number one college team in the country. Here's how it happened.

In their do-or-die game against Dartmouth, each team had played three quarters to a scoreless tie. In the fourth quarter, **Hobey Baker** (of hockey fame) fell on a fumble on the 35-yard line of Dartmouth. Princeton tried to move the ball but could only pick up four yards. On their third (and in those days final) down, the Princeton kicker, named DeWitt, moved back to the 45-yard line for the snap from center. DeWitt drop-kicked the ball, a ball that had good distance but was too low. The ball struck a Dartmouth player, bounced off the ground, and then over the crossbar and through the up-rights.

Was it good? Most of the crowd of 10,000 hoped so but had to sit while the referee, a man named Langford, studied the rulebook. There was nothing written there that prohibited this play from being good. Princeton had won the game by the score of 3–0.

On October 7, 1916, **Everett Strupper** ran for eight touchdowns and kicked an extra points to rack up 49 points for Georgia Tech. He rushed for 165 yards on eight carries for six touchdowns and ran both his punt returns back for touchdowns. But Georgia Tech as a team was even more impressive. Playing hapless Cumberland College (it had been Cumberland's idea to play), the Ramblin' Wreck scored all 32 times they had the ball. The score was 63–0 at the quarter, 126–0 at the half, 180–0 after three quarters, and by the time the two coaches agreed to call it quits, the final score was a record 222–0.

St. Victor College in Indiana is not a team too many people have heard about, but they played a game in 1916, when a **Leo Schlick** accomplished something truly amazing. He scored a total of 12 touchdowns on the way to racking up a record 100 points.

Sometimes the player would just as soon not have stumbled into the spotlight. Just such a case was **Roy Riegels**. In the 1929 Rose Bowl game between California and Georgia Tech, Riegels grabbed a fumble and saw daylight all the way to the goal line. The roar of the partisan crowd and the footsteps behind him only encouraged Riegels to run faster. The California lineman sprinted 60 yards ("What's wrong with me? Am I crazy?" exclaimed radio announcer Graham Mc-Namee) to the three-yard line of the Golden Bears before one of his teammates, Benny Lom, could catch up to him and turn him around. Roy Riegels had run the wrong way. The Yellow Jackets swarmed over him and Riegels was pulled down on the one. On the next play California tried to punt their way out of trouble, but Georgia Tech blocked the punt, knocking it out of the end zone for a safety. This turned out to be the crucial play of the day as the Ramblin' Wreck went on to an 8–7 victory.

"Centers aren't supposed to be the fastest of runners," reported the *Chicago Tribune*. "But Riegels was grasping at the stuff of which heroes are made. He sprinted like one possessed."

The newspaper story also told how Riegels tried to depart from the stadium, but his teammates stopped him. "Eventually, the captain-elect yielded to their entreaties, and when the whistle blew for the start of the second half, California's greatest goat was in there battling for all his life was worth."

When later asked about that afternoon, the man who became known as Wrong Way Riegels had this to say: "I just got a bit confused because the teams had just changed ends after the first quarter. I'm not ashamed of the mistake—at least I was trying."

* * *

Raymond "Snooks" Dowd was another runner who became confused. In a 1934 game with Lafayette, Lehigh University back Dowd got turned around and ran all the way to his goal line. When he realized what he had done, he reversed his course and ran all the way to the other end zone, covering over 200 yards in his jaunt.

The name of **Beattie Feathers** may not ring a bell, but in 1934 this running back averaged 8.4 yards per carry to become the first ball carrier in the NFL to rush for 1,000 yards in a season. That was this All-American from Tennessee's rookie year; after that it was all downhill. Although he stayed in the game until 1940, Feathers only added 976 more yards to his total.

Edwin "Alabama" Pitts became famous for being an outstanding player on Sing Sing Prison's team. When he was paroled in 1935, the Philadelphia Eagles signed Pitts to a contract. But as some convicts have trouble making it on the outside, Pitts had trouble making it with the Eagles. He was released after just three games.

Left end **Leo F. Paquin** played left end on the line known as the Seven Blocks of Granite at Fordham University in 1936. But he later coached football at Xavier High School in New York City. In 1970, Paquin wrote that his greatest pleasure and pride was in seeing what his players went on to become: 85 doctors, 125 lawyers, 150 priests, and 72 engineers.

* * *

In 1939, quarterback **Johnny Pingel** had a glorious first season with the Detroit Lions. Pingel picked up 301 yards on the ground, made good on 56 percent of his passes, and averaged 43 yards a punt over nine games. Wow! It was all that this Michigan State All-American could have dreamed might happen. But then, Pingel disappeared. Vanished. He never played another game in the NFL.

In September 1943, in a game between New Castle High School and Morton Memorial of Knightstown, both schools in Indiana, a 16-year-old woman went in to kick the point after touchdown. **Agnes Risner** missed on her first attempt and later on her second. But a barrier was broken. Her team, New Castle, could spare the points, winning 25–0.

In 1947, **Frankie Groves** played in a game for Stinnett High against Groom High School deep in the heart of Texas. It was the first time a young woman had played in a football game in that football-loving state. What makes it all the more remarkable is that the 16-year-old did not have the role of kicking or holding the PAT. Groves played tackle. Coach Truman Johnson had nothing but praise for her, and Groves herself summed up the experience with "It was great fun." She must have been thinking of the play in which she knocked down two Groom High linesmen on the same block.

Fred Gehrke was a halfback for the Los Angeles Rams, but what really put him on the map was in 1948, when he took a long hard look at the uniform in his locker.

"Over the years I felt the uniform needed sparking up," Gehrke said. "And the leather headgear was the worst part."

This one-time art major at the University of Utah painted his helmet blue. Then in a moment of inspiration he added red ram's horns. Over the rest of the year he painted the helmets of his teammates.

Needless to say, Gehrke's idea caught on with the other teams as well. "I guess this was the forerunner of the modern idea among players and fans that an athlete should look sharp."

In 1953, a graduate of Michigan State named **Willie Thrower** became the first black professional quarterback. But even with a name straight out of central casting, Thrower could not overcome the common perception that quarterback was a whites-only position. During his one-season career with the Chicago Bears, Willie Thrower took only a handful of snaps in games and then vanished from the league.

(It would be 15 more years before Marlin Briscoe of the Denver Broncos would become the first regular black quarterback in professional football. But he, too, only lasted a year. Briscoe was then converted to a wide receiver.)

The 1954 Cotton Bowl featured the favored Alabama versus Rice. On Rice's first play from scrimmage, the handoff went to halfback Dicky Maegle, who sliced through the entire Alabama team on his way to a 79-

yard touchdown. The kick was good and the score stood at Rice 7, Alabama 6.

In the second quarter, Alabama quarterback Bart Starr fumbled on the five-yard line, so it was Rice's ball, 95 yards from the goal line. On the first play, the ball went to Maegle. It was the same play he had scored on in the first quarter. Again, Maegle was free. The closest Alabama defender was 20 yards away. Suddenly, at Alabama's 38-yard line Maegle was down. After running 57 yards, after eluding all the Crimson Tide tacklers, Maegle was on the ground. Seventy-five thousand people in the stadium stood up to see what had happened. For a while few knew.

"One minute I was sitting on the bench just thinking what I would do the next time I got into the game," said **Tommy Lewis**, the fullback who had scored Alabama's only touchdown, "and the next minute I was off the bench and racing at him. I hit him a hard tackle and he was down. I'm too emotional. I guess I'm just too full of Alabama. . . ."

Dicky Maegle hadn't seen him. "If I had," said the Rice halfback, "I would have stiff-armed him or side-stepped him or something. I was looking straight ahead at the goal and glancing sideways at the one guy who had a shot at me. He was still 20 yards from me as I crossed midfield. I knew that I was going all the way again. No one could lay a hand on me. The next thing I knew, I was on my back and gasping for breath."

The head referee, Cliff Shaw, went into a huddle with the other officials, the two head coaches, and their assistants. Then Shaw took the ball and ran downfield over the Alabama goal line and raised his two arms, signaling a touchdown for Rice. Dicky Maegle was in the record books with a 95-yard run. There was no penalty on the play. With the point after touchdown, the score stood at Rice 14, Alabama 6.

Rice scored twice more in the game, one a touchdown by Maegle, to give Rice a convincing 28–6 victory.

But it was Lewis's twelfth-man tackle of Maegle (rather than Maegle's 264 yards and MVP selection) that would stick in the minds of many of the 25 million viewers. He was even feted on the *Ed Sullivan Show*.

"I just looked at Maegle on the ground," remembered Lewis, "and I kept telling myself I didn't do it, I didn't do it, and I knew it wasn't so. I knew I did."

On November 23, 1957, **Dick Christy** had one of those once-in-a-lifetime games. Not only had he scored four touchdowns (on three runs from one yard and the fourth from two yards), but he had also kicked two extra points to account for all of North Carolina State's 26 points. But it still wasn't enough, as the Wolfpack was tied 26–26 with South Carolina. With barely enough time for one last play, Dick Christy was attempting his very first field goal in a college game. The ball was snapped, it was down, Christy hit it just right, and the ball sailed 36 yards through the uprights for a 29–26 victory.

It had been five years since they had won when the College All-Stars took the field against the Green Bay Packers, the champions of the NFL, on August 2, 1963, at Soldier Field in Chicago. With the All-Stars ahead 13–10 in the fourth quarter, quarterback **Ron VanderKelen** hurled a 74-yard touchdown pass to former Wisconsin teammate Pat Richter. Jim Taylor of the Bears scored his second touchdown of the game, but the All-Stars hung on for a thrilling 20–17 victory. The All-Stars never won again in this pro-college series. VanderKelen, too, never captured the luster during his pro career that he achieved in his last fling as a collegian.

Joe Don Looney was a heralded back from the University of Oklahoma. A superb athlete with movie-star looks, he could bench press 450 pounds and run 100 yards in 9.5 seconds, so it came as no surprise that Looney was the number-one draft pick by the New York Giants in 1963. But he quickly deteriorated to trade status when he refused to learn the plays in training camp. He had no use for learning where he was supposed to run because of his belief that "a good back makes his own holes."

At Baltimore things were better for a while. He scored on a 58-yard touchdown run against the Chicago Bears, but he did not do much else on the field. Off the field, he was just as unruly as he had been in New York, so he was traded to Detroit. His last straw there was not running in a play. "If you want a messenger," he told Coach Harry Gilmer, "call Western Union." Looney's next stop was Washington, and after his release in 1967, he spent nine months in Vietnam. Then it was one last go-round with football and the New Orleans Saints, until a knee injury forced an end to his quixotic career.

So what was next? A trip to India to be with Swami

Baba Muktananda. He also lived a quiet, meditative life on his hardscrabble ranch in west Texas. Looney followed this guru for much of the rest of his life.

"I like eating regular meals. Everything here is taken care of. The place is clean. The food is on time. It's a matter of getting free. Sure, I like the wind in my face. Athletes are spontaneous people. I don't know what it's like now with all the bucks and the popularity contests, but I did it because I loved to cut loose. That was my payoff."

In 1988, at the age of 45, Joe Don Looney died in a motorcycle accident.

In a game between University of Texas at El Paso and the University of New Mexico, UTEP quarterback **Brooks Dawson** started inconspicuously enough. In the first quarter he threw three incompletions. Then Dawson's next six passes were six completions for six touchdowns. He hit Bob Wallace on a 25-yard pass; Larry McHenry on a 10-yard pass; Volley Murphy on a 74-yarder—all in the first quarter. In the second quarter Dawson threw an 83-yard TD to Paul White and an 86-yarder to Murphy. Finally, he hit Murphy again in the third quarter for a 52-yard score. Dawson had three more complete passes that day, October 27, 1967, for 376 yards and an average of 41.8 yards per completed pass, as UTEP brought down the Lobos, 75–12.

John Amos had a checkered career, but it was not for lack of trying. After playing fullback in high school in East Orange, New Jersey, he tried to catch on with three college football teams: at Long Beach City College (dropped for an attitude problem), Colorado State University (couldn't get off the third team), and the University of Denver (the school dropped football).

Then Amos tried it as a walk-on with the pros. The Denver Broncos gave him a look, until he pulled his hamstring. The Canton Bulldogs in the United Football League also gave him a look and turned their heads. But things were different for one game with the Joliet Explorers of the UFL. For the first time since high school, he grabbed some headlines, gaining 142 yards and scoring three touchdowns. Oh, that felt good as he celebrated in the end zone.

"Now I'm twenty-four or something, I still got the dream. I know I can go all the way, man. So I call Hank Stram." Coach Stram helped him out, but before the first exhibition game, Amos pulled his hamstring. Then he was let go by the Norfolk (Virginia) Neptunes. Wheeling cut him when he injured his ankle. Finally, he was dropped by the Toronto Rifles, the Brooklyn Dodgers, the Victoria (British Columbia) Steelers, and the Vancouver Lions. Enough already.

Next the erstwhile footballer turns to acting and his bad times become *Good Times*, the long-running sitcom of the 1970s. He later landed a part in a Walt Disney production, *The World's Greatest Athlete*. But John Amos now knew better than to try out for the athlete again. This time he played the coach.

Why don't you ever see a woman playing professional football? Well, before you answer that, a woman has. On August 15, 1970, **Patricia Barzi**

Palinkas of Tampa, Florida, was sent into a game between the Orlando Panthers and the Bridgeport Jets in the Atlantic Coast League. Entering the game for the Orlando Panthers just before the first half ended, Mrs. Palinkas got into position to hold the football while Steve Palinkas, her husband, kicked the point after touchdown. The center's snap was off target, so Pat picked up the bouncing ball and started to run with it. Before getting very far, the 122-pound ball carrier encountered a 235-pound lineman, Wally Florence of the Jets, blocking her path. And that's one reason why you don't see women playing professional football. Even so, the Palinkas were successful on their two point after touchdown attempts in the second half.

Rudy. Even the name sounds less than stellar. So-so, second-rate, an also-ran. It was exactly what **Daniel E. "Rudy" Ruettiger** had fought against all his life. From his childhood, when he was relegated to hiking the ball for both sides, to not making good grades in high school, Rudy was not encouraged. Even his father told him he was not good enough. Not good enough. It almost became a mantra. And Rudy bought into it and went to work in the nearby steel mill. But he still burned with the desire to play football at Notre Dame. The turning point was when his best friend was killed in an accident at the mill. Then Rudy knew it was then or never. He took the bus to South Bend and attended a junior college in the hopes that he could do well enough to get accepted to Notre Dame. Finally, after two years his dream was starting to come true.

He was accepted. Now it was time to act on the second part of his dream. Coach Ara Parseghian had a policy that a few players could be walk-ons to join in the task of running the next week's team's plays as well as serving on the defense for the first team to run their plays against. Rudy was small, but he had a big heart and he made the team. But as game after game went by, the problem was that his family back home couldn't see him on TV standing on the sidelines. Rudy told Coach Parseghian about his dilemma and the coach promised he would let him play in one game the following year. But when Parseghian quit, where did that leave the promise to Rudy? Would Dan Devine, the coach newly arrived from the Green Bay Packers, honor the promise? By the last game of the season, the starting team took on Rudy's case. They each turned in their jersey to have Rudy play in their place. Rudy finally got to dress for the 1976 game with Georgia Tech. With his parents in the stands, Rudy led the team onto the field. But Devine wouldn't put him into the game, even when the game was out of reach. With Notre Dame ahead 24–3 and seconds left in the fourth quarter, and seemingly everyone on the sidelines and in the stands chanting "Rudy," the little linebacker was finally sent into the game. After running downfield on the kickoff team, he stayed on the field for the last play from scrimmage. He broke into the backfield and sacked the quarterback. Rudy was carried off the field on the shoulders of his teammates. No other player since, not even Joe Montana, has been accorded such an honor.

* * *

It was in 1977 at a football game between East Carolina State and William and Mary, East Carolina up 17–14, that an unlikely twelfth man plunged himself into the thick of things. **Jim Johnson** had been a spectator on the sidelines when William and Mary quarterback Tom Rozantz had turned the corner on a bootleg and was sprinting toward the goal line. Johnson, a Carolina partisan, found himself entertaining an odd thought.

"I was wondering what I would do if the play came my way," said Johnson. "Then I was standing near the five and here he comes. I had to make a quick decision."

Johnson ran out onto the field and made a clean tackle on Rozantz.

"It was a good hit," said the quarterback, as masterful in understatement as he had been on the rollout. "He read the play perfectly and I never saw him coming."

Yes, that's quite understandable. Nevertheless, the young man won the collision with the older man, as the quarterback carried both the ball and his tackler into the end zone for the score.

"I'm getting too old for this," said the 65-year-old Johnson. One could only hope so.

There were only four seconds left in the game between Stanford and the University of California at Berkeley on November 20, 1982. The Cardinal was kicking off after a successful field goal that had given them a 20–19 lead. The kick was a bouncer that Stanford had hoped to recover. Instead it was picked up by Kevin Moen of the Golden Bears on their own 43-yard line. He ran to the 43 of the Cardinal and lateraled to Richard Rodgers, who ran a few yards and lateraled to

Dwight Garner, who immediately lateraled it back to Rodgers, who lateraled to Mariet Ford, who got it all the way to the 25 of Stanford before flipping the ball over his shoulder to Moen, who snared it while running into a whole cadre of people in maroon and white. It was **the Stanford band**. Having come onto the field before the game was over, they were unwittingly blocking out their own team from getting to the ball carrier, so that the only thing between Moen and pay dirt was trombone player Gary Tyrell. California won 25–20.

This is a story that takes place at George Washington High School in New York City in 1984. George Washington is a school primarily of immigrants, especially from the Dominican Republic.

There was not much in their past that spelled football, but there was not much that spelled anything. It was tough to be in a new country with a new language, a new everything. The percentage for success was not particularly high.

Stepping into this mix was a football coach named **Jim Walsh**. Walsh was a compassionate disciplinarian. Compassionate because his parents immigrated from Ireland. A disciplinarian because he knew from years of experience nothing gets done without it. But if his players worked hard for him on the field and in the classroom, Walsh was the kind of guy who would work hard for them and try to get them into a college.

There was one major drawback to all this. George Washington was in the A League of the Public School Athletic League (PSAL), even though it was much smaller than schools like DeWitt Clinton and John F.

Kennedy. Most of their opponents had more (and bigger) players, more coaches, more money, more everything. The bottom line was that Walsh's players were at risk of serious injury. Indeed, a year before one had suffered a broken neck.

No one seemed to hear the pleas of the coach and the principal, so Walsh took the ball into his own hands. Before their first game of the season, Coach Walsh took the game ball to the referee and read the following speech:

> Excuse me, Mr. Referee, but by the authority invested in me by the City and State of New York, I declare this game a mismatch and a forfeit and I do so to dramatize the plight of students who cannot speak for themselves and who are forced, against their will, to compete against numerical, physical and financial resources overwhelmingly greater than their own to the detriment of their physical safety and morale. This condition was created by an indifferent and incompetent Public School Athletic League.

The PSAL removed Walsh as coach and tried to have a new coach take over the football program at George Washington. But the players signed a letter stating that they would not play for anyone else. Mayor Ed Koch appointed a committee, headed by former Governor Hugh Carey, to investigate the situation. The committee found in Walsh's favor. George Washington would be allowed to play in the B League and Jim Walsh would be allowed to remain as coach. After three weeks of inactivity George Washington took to the field and won 14–6.

Jerry Kretchmer, a local politician, summed up the feelings of many when he said: "That is one of the worst, one of the ugliest bureaucracies in the city. It is supposed to do one thing—look out for the welfare of kids—and it does exactly the opposite. He is my hero for the month."

Larry Brown, a twelfth-round draft pick out of Texas Christian, was hardly a highly touted member of a Dallas Cowboy team that featured Troy Aikman, Michael Irvin, Deion Sanders, and Emmitt Smith. But it was Brown as much as any of his heralded teammates who brought victory to Dallas in Super Bowl XXX.

Brown had already intercepted a Neil O'Donnell pass that Smith converted into a touchdown with a short burst into the end zone. But it was later that Brown really made his presence felt in the Cowboy secondary and in the game. Pittsburgh was behind by only three points, 20–17. The momentum had seemingly swung to the Steelers.

But all that was stopped when Brown stepped in front of another O'Donnell pass to make his second interception of the day. Soon there was another short run by Smith and another Dallas score. The Pittsburgh threat had been successfully squelched. The Cowboys won the 1996 world championship by a convincing 27–17 score. And Brown was named MVP, over all the other star players on his team.

Golf

"An attempt to place a small little sphere . . .
in a slightly larger hole . . . with utensils
totally unsuited to the task."
—President Woodrow Wilson

In November of 1895, **Mrs. Charles S. Brown** won the first US amateur golf championship for women. (It is interesting to note that she was identified as a wife in the newspaper accounts of that day.) Brown finished the 18 holes in 132 strokes.

In 1900, **Margaret Abbott** won an Olympic gold medal in golf, the first and last woman ever to do so. The odd thing was that she didn't even realize she was playing in the Olympics. Here's how it happened.

Abbott was an American in Paris studying art. She arrived at the Paul Golf Club for what she thought was the French amateur championship. To her amusement, "all the French girls apparently misunderstood the nature of the game scheduled for that day and turned up to play in high heels and tight skirts." Abbott won by scoring a 47 for the nine holes on the par 38 course. (**Pauline Whittier**, another American, was second with 49.)

As it turned out, this medal was unofficial. The first

official women's event was held in 1912. This was also the last time golf was played at the Olympics.

In 1913, the names of Harry Vardon and Ted Ray could add a luster to any US Open. And that's just what these two professionals from Great Britain did. Heavily favored, Vardon and Ray found themselves tied with each other at 304 at the end of 72 holes. But they were also tied with a young unknown named **Francis Ouimet**. Who was Francis Ouimet?

He was a 20-year-old who had been a caddy since the age of 11 at the site of the US Open, The Country Club in Brookline, Massachusetts. He was a golfer who was not going to play because he had already taken time off from his job to play in the US Amateurs. He wasn't going to play until his supervisor told him, "As long as you're entered, you'd better plan to play."

But Francis Ouimet did not wilt under the glare of scrutiny. In the 18-hole playoff, Ouimet shot a 72 to win. Vardon came in with a 77 and Ray had a 78.

Golf moved from the sports page to the front page. The country was captured by the mixture of David and Goliath, the Horatio Alger aspect of this story. Herbert Warren Wind got the tenor of the story this way:

"Here was a person all of America, not just golfing America, could understand—the boy from 'the wrong side' of the street, the ex-caddie, the kind who worked during his summer vacations from high school—America's idea of the American hero."

Ouimet went on to win 11 amateur championships and was elected to the PGA Hall of Fame, but he never matched the meteoric fame he enjoyed as an unknown 20-year-old.

Jerome Travers was a natural golfer. It came to him easily, so that he didn't have to work hard in order to win four US amateur tournaments. But it was what he did in 1915 that really set him apart. That was the year he played in his one and only US Open.

The 1915 US Open took place at the Baltusrol Golf Club in New Jersey. That was good for Travers because he wouldn't have to travel far from his tony home in Upper Montclair, New Jersey. The less effort, the better. Travers played the course like he owned it, scoring a one under par for the final six holes, and besting professional Tom McNamara by a single stroke.

The next year the US Open was held at the Minikahda Country Club in Minneapolis. Travers didn't even show up. (He is the only winner of the US Open not to defend his title.) But it wasn't just the US Open that he stayed away from. Travers never entered another big-time tournament the rest of his life.

Joe Kirkwood held a slight lead in the last round of the 1924 Texas Open played at the Brackenridge Golf Club. Off the tenth tee he hit a drive that landed in between a grove of trees and a brook. He couldn't afford a penalty stroke because his lead was in jeopardy.

At this point it helps to know something about this golfer. Born in Australia, Kirkwood first worked on a ranch where the owner had put in three golf holes. It was there after work that Kirkwood discovered his feel for the game. Perhaps it was only having three holes and he had to make things challenging to hold his interest, but in any case, Kirkwood developed an arsenal of trick shots. He not only was able to use thin watches for tees, but he could also hit two balls with a seven iron and at their apogee have one ball hook and one ball slice.

Back on the tenth, Kirkwood pulled a three iron from his bag and hit a shot that sailed forward, then hooked around the trees at practically a right angle. It continued toward the flag and bounced onto the green. It was a shot that was so astonishing to the assembled spectators that day that a monument was later erected between the trees and the brook to commemorate Kirkwood's shot.

The last-second field goal, the buzzer-beating jump shot, the bottom of the ninth homer is witnessed more often than the out-of-nowhere golf shot on the eighteenth hole to win the tournament. But that's what happened in 1953.

Lew Worsham from Washington was not exactly a household name, but he was a fine golfer. (His previous fireworks had been sneaking by Sam Snead in a playoff round to win the 1947 US Open.) Playing the eighteenth hole at the World Championship at the Tam O'Shanter golf course in Chicago, Worsham hit a 140-yard wedge shot that not only hit the green but also bounced three times before disappearing into the cup. It would be an improbable shot to make while practicing alone, but to hit it for a come-from-behind win at a major tournament with a gallery that had formed a horseshoe around the green and before the first national TV audience, was phenomenal.

"It was the luckiest shot I ever had in my life," admitted Worsham.

"Goddamn!" was all radio announcer Jimmy Demaret could say.

Jackie Pung was a 235-pound 35-year-old who won the US Women's Golf Championship in 1957. Or did she? Even though her total round of 72 was correctly registered, her partner had marked the fourth hole of the final round with a five instead of a six on the scorecard Pung had signed, disqualifying her.

Walter Danecki, a postal worker from Milwaukee, Wisconsin, looked forward to his English vacation in July, 1965. For fun he sent in an application to the British Open. Apparently, the people who reviewed his application thought they just hadn't heard of this newcomer. So there he was, a weekend golfer who might break a hundred on a good day, in one of the most prestigious golfing tournaments on the planet.

Danecki arrived at the Hillside Golf Course in Southport, England, and teed off at the appointed time. But it wasn't long before it became apparent that this golfer would not make the cut, and it was also a question of how long it was going to take him to get through the 36-hole qualifier. True to form, Danecki didn't break a hundred. He shot a 108 for the first eighteen and 113 for the second. He might have made the papers to show his friends back home at the post office, but it was an embarrassment for the officials to be shown up by a system that had allowed a golfer trying to qualify for the British Open to come in at 221, a whopping 71 over par.

"I can't get into a lot of tournaments in my part of the country," reasoned Danecki, "so I thought I would come over here and win a big one. Then they would have to let me in the others."

Walter Mitty was certainly alive and well in the mind of Walter Danecki.

On September 25, 1974, **Michael Hoke Austin** was playing at the US National Seniors Open Championship in Las Vegas, Nevada. At 6-foot-2, 210 pounds, Austin was a powerful golfer off the tee, but that day featured a tricky wind on the course. The 64-year-old golfer from Los Angeles stepped up to the fifth hole at the Winterwood Golf Course and placed his ball on the tee at the par 4, 450-yard hole. Austin hit a good drive with a 35-mile-per-hour tailwind. The ball hit the green near the hole, bounced, and kept on going, coming to a stop 65 yards beyond the green. All in all, Austin had hit a 515-yard drive, the longest ever. (John Daly once unleashed a 360-yard drive on an airport runway that bounced another 450 yards, but even he would have been hard pressed to get off a 515-yard drive.)

In 1982, **Matt Pace** of Houston was playing a tournament at the El Dorado Country Club in Humble, Texas. On the front nine he certainly was humbled, shooting a 64 on the 6,583-yard course. His best hole was a bogey (one over par). But picking up the pace, he hit only one bogey on the back nine to go with six pars and two birdies (one stroke under par) to give him a 35. The round of 28 strokes over par coupled with the round of one under par is a difference of 29 strokes—a record for tournament play.

Bagging The Ace or Hole In One

> *"The perfect round of golf has never been played. It's eighteen holes in one. I almost dreamt it once, but I lipped out at eighteen. I was mad as hell."*
> —Ben Hogan

In 1931, **R. W. Bridges** placed his tee and then his ball at the 196-yard hole at the Woodlawn Country Club in Kirkwood, Missouri, and then using his putter to mystify his playing companions, sank a hole in one.

What would be the likelihood of a golfer making eleven holes in one in one year? **Dr. Joseph O. Boydstone** accomplished this feat in 1962. In fact, on October 10 he had three holes in one at the Bakersfield (California) Golf Club, going from tee to tin cup on the third, fourth, and ninth holes.

The Miracle Hills Golf Club in Omaha, Nebraska, couldn't be better named for what happened there on October 7, 1965. **Robert Mittera**, a 21-year-old student, possessed a two handicap and the ability on occasion to unleash a 250-yard drive.

Stepping up to the tenth hole tee, Mittera looked toward the flag fluttering 447 yards away. Not only long, the hole also sported a tricky drop-off halfway. The five-foot-six, 165-pound Mittera hit a drive that was engulfed by a strong 50-mile-per-hour wind. The ball sailed over the 290-foot drop-off, hit the turf, and rolled over 150 yards into the cup. Robert Mittera had bagged the longest hole in one ever.

The Fribley family has a tradition of playing the Pana Country Club in Pana, Illinois. They also have a tradition of scoring a hole in one on the par-3, 186-yard seventh hole. The one who started it all was **John Fribley**, a 65-year-old, in 1971. Next was John's 16-year-old grandson, **Scott Fribley**, in 1975. The last was **Joseph Fribley**, John's son and Scott's father, who sank an ace on the seventh in 1991.

Yoshiaka Ono was not your average golfer. Not by a long shot. In 1981, Ono was playing at the Singapore Open. He was having a decent round, but on the seventeenth Ono hit a hole in one. That would be good news anytime, but at this tournament the seventeenth had been designated the magic hole. Anyone making a hole in one would be awarded $50,000 in cash and a $40,000 car. Great you say. Take the money and run. Well, most of us would, but not Yoshiaka Ono. This son of an electrical contractor in Japan loved to play in amateur tournaments. If he were to accept, he would no longer be an amateur. After wrestling with his dilemma for hours, Ono finally made his decision. He would not accept. He loved to play amateur golf too much.

Jim Taylor lost both his hands as a kid, trying to steady himself on a roof by gripping a 7,000-volt wire.

But he survived and in 1986 even started playing golf, by using a type of rubber band to hold the clubs to the hooks he has instead of hands. "Imagine trying to hold a golf club and not feel it," Taylor remarked, "then swing your whole upper body to force the club in an arc." Three years later, Taylor hit his first hole in one at the Golf Green Golf Center in Longview, Washington. "When I got back to the clubhouse, the word had spread and I became an instant local celebrity."

Since that day, Taylor has hit seven more holes in one. "Jim plays a great game of golf," appraised club pro Skip Manke. "He just happens to have no arms."

But one of the youngest in this club is **Scott Statler**, who at 4 years and 172 days, hit his tee shot into the cup on the par 3 seventh hole of Statler's golf course in Greensburg, Pennsylvania.

At the other end of the age scale, 93-year-old **George Miller** hit a hole in one at the 116-yard eleventh hole at the Anaheim Golf Course in 1970.

Tom Hayden of Long Island regularly plays the Lake St. Catherine Golf Course in Poultney, Vermont. The third hole is only 143 yards long, but it's tricky because it's up a steep hill. You can't see the green, only the flag. It was a green that Hayden had landed on from the tee only once or twice in years of playing there. One day in the summer of 1996 he hit a one wood toward the green. When he got to the top he looked all over: it wasn't in the trap; it didn't seem to be in the nearby woods. His partner was the one to find the ball in the last place Hayden would have thought of looking.

"It's a moment you'll never forget as long as you live," recalled Hayden. "I guess everyone has their moment of fame, and that one was mine."

A hole in one during a career of golf dates is not bad, but how about three during one round of golf? Dr. Joseph Boydstone did just that on October 10, 1962. (see p. 222) The **Reverend Harold Snider** topped that in Phoenix, Arizona, on June 9, 1976. Snider not only hit three, but two were in a row (the thirteenth and fourteenth holes). Don't these professional guys have to work?

Playing a round at the Lake Venice Golf Club in Venice, Florida, in 1974, **Fred Class** played two balls on the eleventh because the course wasn't busy and it felt like one of those days. After a great drive on the par-4, 357-yard hole, this native of Kitchener, Ontario, hit another. The second ball was almost in the same place on the fairway. Drawing a nine iron from his bag, Class lofted the ball straight onto the green and into the cup. Ditto the second shot with the nine iron. Two eagles, same hole. What class!

Doglegs are difficult enough, but for hitting holes in one they are nigh impossible. Yet, that's what **Shaun Lynch** pulled off at the Teigh Valley Golf Club in England on July 24, 1995. Teeing up his ball at the seventeenth hole, Lynch played the 496-yard hole with a result that once again proves that the shortest distance between the tee and the cup is a straight line.

Kenneth E. Schrieber is more challenged by golf than many others, for this man is legally blind. But on May 9, 1997, everything came together just right at the Beacon Woods Golf Club in Bayonet Point, Florida, on the tee for the twelfth hole. For it was there that Schrieber smacked the ball perfectly to go into the tin cup 135 yards away.

Holes In One Are Not Something Foreign to Women Either.

> *"The smaller the ball used in the sport,*
> *the better the book."*
> —George Plimpton

On May 19, 1942, **Mrs. W. Driver** became the first woman to score two holes in one while playing one round. She sank her drive on the third hole and the eighth hole at the Balgowlah Club in New South Wales.

In 1949, **Marie Robie** got off to a hot start at the Furnace Brook Golf Course in Woolaston, Massachusetts. Stepping up to the first tee, Robie hit a 393-yard drive that went into the cup. This is the longest ace on record for a woman.

On May 29, 1977, in Sydney, Australia, **Sue Press** became the first woman to hit holes in one on successive holes. Playing at the Chatswood Golf Club, Press got her aces on the thirteenth and fourteenth holes.

The oldest woman to hit a hole in one was **Erna Ross**. On May 25, 1986, this 95-year-old stroked her ace on the 112-yard seventeenth hole of the Everglades Club in Palm Beach, Florida.

Another woman, **Margaret Waldron**, had more than age to contend with when she hit a hole in one. This 74-year-old was legally blind. On March 18, 1990, she was playing at the Long Point Golf Course on Amelia Island, Florida, with her husband. Pete lined her up at the tee of the par 3, told her that the flag was 87 yards away and how the wind was blowing before handing her a seven iron. Mrs. Waldron then proceeded to hit the ball into the cup.

But this story doesn't end there. Using the same club and even the same ball the very next day on the same par 3 hole at the Long Point, she made another hole in one.

"When we went back to the clubhouse, I was so proud," Margaret Waldron said. "I don't consider myself handicapped. I am challenged to do the best I can with what I have."

One of the youngest girls is **Brittny Andreas**. In 1991, at the age of six, she holed out in one at the 85-yard second hole at the Jimmy Clay Golf Course in Austin, Texas.

At a 1991 tournament at the Arrowhead Country Club in Rapid City, South Dakota, **DeAun West** was so excited when she hit an ace on the 129-yard second hole because she thought she had won the Cadillac. But then she found out that it was only if she were to hit a hole in one on the twelfth hole. When she got to the 148-yard twelfth she drove her tee shot and did it again.

Meanwhile, Back On and Off the Fairways

> *"Golf is deceptively simple and endlessly complicated.*
> *A child can play it well and a grown man can never*
> *master it."*
> —Arnold Palmer

One doesn't usually think of marathons when it comes to golf, but there was an actor from Detroit, **Edward A. Ferguson**, who had more of a claim to fame on the links than on the boards. His first goal was relatively modest: to play Detroit's Ridgemont Golf Course, a nine-hole public course, for a 24-hour period beginning on August 25, 1930. At night a caddie held a lantern and a flashlight to help find the ball painted with luminous paint. After the first day Ferguson felt okay, so he kept on playing.

"I quit on 1 September at 8 o'clock in the morning," Ferguson wrote. "I walked 327 1/2 miles from tee to green, not counting hooks and slices. My hands were covered with soft callouses [sic] and blisters, and I could not control the club. I had played 158 hours, with an average slightly over 86 for each 18 holes."

Ferguson finished with an odometerlike score of 3,999.

* * *

In this day and age there are many odd made-for-TV sports. But back in 1938 a Chicago broker by the name of **J. Smith Ferebee** made an improbable bet, wagering that he could play 600 holes of golf in eight cities across the United States in only four days, and had to break 90 on each round. For his trouble he would win over $180,000. Sleeping only on airplanes between courses and playing at all hours of the day and night, Ferebee played in Los Angeles, Phoenix, Kansas City, St. Louis, Milwaukee, Chicago, Philadelphia, and New York. Ferebee wound up winning more than any golfer on the pro tour that year.

On September 30, 1938, **Ken Bowsfield** shot a 69 for 18 holes at Burnham Beeches in England. The kicker is that Bowsfield played the round in 91 minutes, only five minutes a hole. Try that on foot some day.

Here's a tale of playing through hard to beat. On September 14, 1963, **Floyd Satterlee Rood** hit the first drive and did not finish his last shot until October 3, 1964. In between he took 114,735 strokes. His course? Reed teed off on the shore of the Pacific Ocean and a year and 114 days later chipped into the Atlantic Ocean, a distance of 3,397 miles. And if you think you lose a few golf balls on a round of golf, Rood lost a total of 3,511 balls golfing across the United States

In 1973, **C. Arthur Thompson** of Victoria, British Columbia, became the oldest person to record the same score as his age, carding a 103 on his one hundred and third birthday at the 6,215-yard Uplands Golf Course in Ontario, Canada.

When Thompson was in his early to mid-eighties, he routinely shot in the seventies. When he was 89, he shot an 82. Shortly before his death at 105, this Canadian was still playing nine holes.

In 1977, **Malcolm Miller**, an amateur, bagged a 59 at the Minocqua Country Club in Wisconsin. Only three pros, Al Geiberger in 1977, Chip Beck in 1991, and David Duval in 1999, have ever shot a score as low as 59 for 18 holes in a tournament. Miller was also 59 years old—the lowest score for anyone shooting his or her age for 18 holes. It has been tied only once, by a pro named Bob Hamilton in 1975.

In 1991, **Ronald Kantner** of Wapakoneta, Ohio, hatched a plan to see if he could beat Richard Kimbrough's record of 364 holes played on foot during a 24-hour period. The site was the 3,010-yard, nine-hole Wapakoneta Country Club. The day Kantner chose was not the best of days to make this attempt. The temperature was 93 degrees and the humidity was almost as high when he started out at noon. Still, in the beginning this 30-year-old was practically sprinting, averaging nine holes in less than a half hour. By the time night fell, things got much tougher. The luminescent balls didn't go as far, then in the wee hours of the morning his left knee was killing him and the blisters on his feet made each step painful. But Kantner didn't give up. At noon, he putted out his three hundred and sixty-sixth hole, beating the previous 24-hour record

held by Richard Kimbrough by two holes. Ronald
Kantner had taken 2,134 strokes—giving him an average of 105 per 18 holes. He had also walked almost 80
miles.

A Grab Bag of Fame

"Sweat is the cologne of accomplishment."
—Heywood Hale Broun

On October 24, 1901, **Annie Taylor**, who looked more like the schoolteacher she was than a daredevil, attempted to be the first to go over Niagara Falls in a barrel and survive. Although a weight in the bottom of the four-and-a-half-foot-high, three-foot-wide barrel would keep it from going upside down, the insides were padded, and a pillow was placed over her head before the lid was nailed shut, it was still a dark, scary experience. At five past four the barrel was launched into the swift current. Eighteen minutes later Taylor went over Niagara Falls, plunging 173 feet to the swirling water and mist below. "I was whirled about like a top, and the water seemed to come in on me in bucketfuls," Taylor said later. "Once, for a moment I seemed to lose my senses. I struck rocks three times." Fortunately, she was pulled out safely.

One thing she did with the rest of her life was to try to discourage others from "shooting the falls" in a barrel. "If it was with my dying breath I would caution anyone against attempting the feat," she said. "I would sooner walk up to the mouth of a cannon, knowing it was going to blow me to pieces, than to make another trip over the Falls."

So, why had she done it? "Nobody has ever done that" was what she said for publication, but she was also trying to earn money to pay off a cattle ranch she had bought in Texas. Unfortunately, things didn't work out. Before dying on April 29, 1921, Taylor said: "I did what no other woman in the world had nerve enough to do, only to die a pauper."

At the turn of the century there was a well-known marksman in vaudeville shows named **Adolph Topperwein**. It was one thing to dazzle the audience in a short show, but he wanted to set the shooting world on its ear. He set out to shoot a rifle at two-and-a-half-inch wooden targets thrown high into the air every five seconds eight hours a day for 12 straight days.

The event took place at the San Antonio Fairgrounds in December, 1906. Large crowds gathered on the first day to watch Topperwein hit 6,500 targets without missing. How many of the same spectators were there to see him miss one target the next day out of the 6,600 tossed? Day after day, he shot at a target on an average of every five seconds. An assistant supplied another rifle every 500 shots. After the eighth day, the count was 49,996 targets hit out of a possible 50,000. This feat had become not only mentally tedious but physically difficult as well for Topperwein. He had to battle cramping and exhaustion, but at the end of the twelfth day, Adolph Topperwein had hit 72,491 targets. He had missed only nine times.

Most people find chin-ups difficult. In 1914, **Francis Lewis**, an 18-year-old from Beatrice, Nebraska, pulled off seven chin-ups with the middle finger of his left hand.

Bullfighting is rarely considered a female sport. That's why the events of January 20, 1951, raised more than a few eyebrows. But it also raised olés, for on that date **Patricia McCormick** killed two bulls in the ring at Juarez, Mexico—the first time a woman had donned a suit of lights and fought in a bullring in North America.

When **Lis Hartel** was 23 years old, she was one of Denmark's leading riders in dressage. (Dressage is a complicated form of maneuvers that a horse executes in response to varying pressures of the rider's hands, legs, and weight.) In September, 1944, Hartel was looking forward to the birth of her baby when she was stricken with polio and could barely move. Little by little she regained the use of her muscles. She was not only able to give birth to her child without surgical intervention but also got back on horseback. Although she did not regain the use of her muscles below her knees, by 1945, she was competing again; and in 1952, Lis Hartel represented Denmark in the individual dressage at the Olympic Games in Helsinki.

Hartel did wonderfully well. Some of her most difficult moments were getting on and off her horse, Jubilee, and getting up on the victory stand to receive her silver medal—the first time women were allowed to compete in Olympic dressage. And to top it off, she won another silver medal at the 1956 Olympic Games.

Who of us hasn't tried to hold our breath underwater? Well, few with the determination of **Dr. Robert W. Keast** on July 4, 1958, in San Rafael, California. After inhaling pure oxygen for a half hour, Dr. Keast donned 40 pounds of lead weights and a face mask and sank to the bottom of a pool. There he remained for a record 13 minutes and 35 seconds. Sinking to the challenge on March 15, 1959, **Robert Foster** breathed in pure oxygen and stayed underwater in a San Rafael pool for 13 minutes and 42 seconds.

Another thing no one else had attempted to do was to drive a go-cart around the globe. That's what **Stan Mack** set out to do when he putt-putted out of New York City on February 15, 1961. Twenty-eight countries and 23,000 miles on land later, Mack putt-putted back to New York City. The date was June 5, 1964.

On November 29, 1965, **Dale Cummings** went into the Berry Academy in Rome, Georgia, to see how many sit-ups he could do. The 17-year-old sat down at 11:00 in the morning and was at it until 11:00 that night. When he stopped he had a record 14,118 sit-ups under his belt.

On September 13, 1971, a Marine captain named **Wayne Rollings** upped the ante by logging 17,000 sit-ups in seven hours and 27 minutes. In 1981, he raised the record again by doing 40,000 sit-ups in 16 hours.

In 1965, **Charles Linster** did 6,006 push-ups non-stop. It took the 16-year-old from Wilmette, Illinois, almost four hours. Linster's youth record has since been surpassed by 13-year-old Robert Knecht, with 7,026 nonstop push-ups. But there's more to brag about. Beginning on May 1, 1989, **Paddy Doyle** of Great Britain executed a record 37,350 push-ups in a 24-hour period at Birmingham, England. The current record for push-ups in one day is Jeffrey Warrack's 46,300.

On June 23, 1969, **William Reed**, a student from the University of Pennsylvania, did 106 chin-ups, but he was surpassed by **Lee Chin Yong**, who chinned himself 370 times on May 14, 1988, in Seoul, Korea.

Richard John Knecht, a mere eight-year-old, outdid Dale Cummings and Wayne Rollings on December 23, 1972, at the Idaho Falls High School gym by doing an incredible 25,222 sit-ups in 11 hours and 27 minutes. Not to be shown up by a kid, **Tom Kides** did 125,000 sit-ups in 76 and a half hours from March 9–12, 1989 at Glassboro, New Jersey.

Junko Tabei of Japan had been climbing mountains since she had been in fourth grade. But it wasn't until 1970 that she got a chance to climb one of the Himalayan mountains, Annapurna III. Still, Everest loomed. In 1975 the Japanese Ladies Himalayan Club organized a climb to the summit. After almost meeting disaster in an avalanche, Tabei set off with a Sherpa from the camp they had established for the last push to the top. About noon on May 17, 1975, Junko Tabei, the first woman ever, reached the summit of Everest.

On August 3, 1975, 11-year-old **Karren Stead** adjusted her goggles and hunched over the steering wheel to roll straight and true to first place in the championship run of the National Soap Box Derby. This marked the first time a girl had ever won this annual event. Things would never be the same again at the Stead homestead in Morrisville, Pennsylvania, nor at Derby headquarters.

You could get cold and tired just thinking about the 1,151-mile Iditarod Trail Sled Dog Race from Anchorage to Nome, Alaska. That's one reason why **Libby Riddles** lived in Teller, Alaska. "The weather up here really toughens the dogs' mental attitude," she once said. "It toughens the drivers, too." During the race in 1985, Riddles hatched a plan. As the other mushers slept in the Eskimo village of Shaktoolik, she set off in the middle of the night during a raging blizzard with the temperature hovering at 10 degrees, the wind howling at 40 miles per hour, and the visibility only 25 feet. "You'll never make it," a nearby musher warned. But Libby Riddles, who had never finished higher than eighteenth, desperately wanted to become the first woman ever to win this ordeal of perseverance. After a few hours she let the dogs rest; then they started off again and maintained their lead the rest of the way.

Libby Riddles completed the last 300 miles and won the race in only 18 days.

Mark Wellman was the first paraplegic mountain climber to climb El Capitan in Yosemite National Park. On the tenth anniversary of this 1989 accomplishment, Wellman embarked with Mike Corbett to tackle the more difficult climb of going up the "Nose." Hauling 250 pounds of supplies along with them, Wellman painstakingly pulled himself up using a T-bar system. On July 26, 1999, the two climbers reached the top.

After his successful climb Wellman had these words for others who are disabled. "[It is important] to climb whatever mountain that is the barrier in their life. And that can be anything."

These are words that can well apply to all of us.

Hockey

*"You just keep shootin', and sometimes
they go in and sometimes they don't."*
—Bill "Cowboy" Flett, hockey player

Ivan Mitchell was a goaltender for the Toronto St.
Pats back in the days when there were only four
teams in the league (Toronto, Montreal, Ottawa, and
Hamilton). On January 20, 1920, Newsy Lalonde of
the Montreal Canadiens scored six goals as Toronto
lost to Montreal, 14–7. Only three weeks later, on January
31, the star of the Quebec Bulldogs, Joe Malone,
scored seven goals against Mitchell as the Bulldogs
beat the St. Pats, 10–6. Malone's seven goals is a
record that still stands. Although Ivan Mitchell was on
the St. Pats' roster for three years, he did not have the
luck of the Irish. Not surprisingly, he only played in 21
games.

In December 1926, **Hal Winkler** played in his first
regular season NHL game for the New York Rangers
and scored a shutout, the first time anyone had ever
done this. Before he could enjoy his newly won fame,
he was playing for the Boston Bruins. The Bruins'

rookie goalie, Lorne Chabot, was now playing for the Rangers. The Bruins and Rangers met in the Stanley Cup semifinals with Winkler and Chabot in goal and played to an 0–0 tie.

It was April 7, 1928 and the second game of Stanley Cup play between the Montreal Maroons and the New York Rangers. The Rangers had lost the first game of the best-of-five-game series, 2–0, and now in the opening minutes of the second period their goalie was crumpled on the ice, felled by a puck in the face off the stick of Nels Stewart. As the unconscious Lorne Chabot was carried off on a stretcher and taken to the Royal Victoria Hospital, panic started to set in on the Rangers bench. In those days hockey teams did not have the luxury of reserve goalies. Who could Rangers coach **Lester Patrick** send in?

There were two goalies from other teams in the stands, Alex Connell of the Ottawa Senators and minor leaguer Hugh McCormick from London, Ontario. Patrick asked the Maroons manager, Eddie Gerard, if he could use one of them. The answer was an emphatic no.

Center Frank Boucher turned to the Rangers coach. "How about you playing goal?"

"I'm too old," replied the 44-year-old known as the Silver Fox.

It was true, perhaps, but Patrick was the only one with any goaltending experience on the team and this was the Stanley Cup. (During Patrick's playing days, goalies had to sit out their infractions in the penalty box; Patrick had gained what little experience he had standing in for the penalized goalie.) Well, Patrick agreed to do it if his new teammates would backcheck and clear out all the rebounds. So that was how Lester Patrick started off the evening behind the bench in a suit but wound up in goal wearing a blue jersey.

During the second period the Rangers were short a man three different times but Patrick did not allow a goal. In all, he stopped 15 shots that were fired on goal.

At the beginning of the third period the Rangers took the lead at 1–0, when Bill Cook launched a long shot past Maroons goalie Clint Benedict. But with only six minutes remaining the Maroons' Nels Stewart fired a shot on goal; Patrick stopped it; Stewart fired again; Patrick stopped it; Stewart faked, Patrick went down on the ice, Stewart slipped the goal into the net. That was it for the scoring. The 1–1 tie sent the game into overtime.

If the silver-haired Patrick was tiring, it did not show in the score. He stopped everything that the Maroons hit his way. Finally, seven minutes into overtime Ching Johnson stole the puck, skated the length of the ice, and flipped the puck to Frank Boucher, who slipped it by Benedict to score the winning goal.

Lester Patrick's line score as a goalie in Stanley Cup play is only 46 minutes and a 1.30 average. It may not seem impressive when stacked up against the record of the Montreal Canadiens' Ken Dryden, who played in goal for six Stanley Cups, but Lester Patrick had stopped 17 out of 18 shots on goal.

Emboldened by their coach, the Blue-Shirted Bombers of Lester Patrick went on to win two out of the next three games—with newcomer Joe Miller in goal—to capture the Stanley Cup.

Perhaps **Joe Miller** should receive further mention. Lester Patrick may have swung the momentum to the Rangers in the second game of 1928 Stanley Cup play, but it was Joe Miller who helped make winning the championship into a reality. Patrick recruited Miller from the New York Americans to serve in goal for the final three games. This last-minute fill-in was better than anyone could have expected. After losing the third game, the Rangers came back and won the last two. During his three games, Miller allowed only three goals and recorded a shutout.

Compared to these three games in the spotlight, the rest of Miller's goaltending career was lackluster. During his four years of playing for the Americans, the Pittsburgh Pirates, and the Philadelphia Quakers, Miller's record was 24–90.

Another goaltender, **Clarence Dolson**, played in the NHL for only three years, but his story was different. In 1928–29, he had a terrific rookie season in goal for the Detroit Cougars (the forerunners of the Red Wings). He came up with 10 shutouts in 44 games and his goals-against average was a stingy 1.43, the best in the history of the franchise.

The next year, however, Dolly (as he was known) played in only five games. During the 1930–31 season, he was back, playing 44 games with 6 shutouts and a 2.39 goals-against average.

But that was it. Detroit got Alex Connell for the 1931–32 season and John Ross Roach for the 1932–33 season. Clarence Dolson fell through the cracks and never played again in the NHL.

In 1938, the Chicago Blackhawks luckily found themselves in the finals of the Stanley Cup with the Toronto Maple Leafs. It was lucky because they had only won 14 games during the regular season. But they were unlucky, too, because goalie Mike Karakas had broken his toe before the first game. Frantically, coach Bill Stewart searched for a replacement. At first they tried to acquire New York Rangers goalie Davie Kerr. But the owner of the Toronto Maple Leafs, Conn Smythe, refused to allow that to happen.

So, who did they turn to next but a lowly goalie named **Alfie Moore**? Moore had been kicking around in the minors for years and had appeared in 18 games for the New York Americans. And now, lo and behold, here he was transplanted from one of Pittsburgh's minor league teams smack dab into the middle of the Stanley Cup finals. It promised to be either a dream come true or a nightmare.

Mighty Toronto threw everything they had at the new guy in net, but the unknown goalie stopped practically everything. Only one goal got by him all night. At the other end of the ice, the Blackhawks scored three goals.

In the locker room afterward, Coach Stewart asked what Alfie would like for his night's work.

"Would a hundred and fifty be too much?" the winning goalie asked.

The Hawks sweetened the bargain to $300 and a gold watch.

Unfortunately for Alfie and the Hawks, Moore was declared ineligible to play in any more games. The Blackhawks next found Paul Goodman from one of their Chicago farm teams. Lady Luck frowned this time and the final score was 5 to 1, Leafs. By this time, Karakas's toe had healed enough for him to return and the Chicago Blackhawks took the last two games and the series. It was a major upset and Alfie Moore had played a major role.

On January 28, 1940, 27-year-old **Les Cunningham** of the Chicago Blackhawks had a game to remember. That was when he racked up five points in a single period on two goals and three assists against the Montreal Canadiens. (For perspective, only 10 players in NHL history have ever had five points in one period.) This five-foot-eight, 165-pound center from Calgary had his blowout in the third period, the period in which the Blackhawks scored a total of 6 goals to win 8–1. During his entire 60-game NHL career, Cunningham had only 26 points on 7 goals and 19 assists.

Sam LoPresti was only an NHL goalie two years, the 1940–41 and 1941–42 seasons, but he did something no other goalie had ever done. In net for the Chicago Blackhawks on March 4, 1941, LoPresti made one amazing stop after another—80 stops in all, an NHL record. But two pucks got by the five-foot-eleven, 200-pound goaltender, and the Blackhawks and Bruins found themselves locked at 2–2 in the final period. At

17:29 of the third right winger Eddie Wiseman uncorked a shot that LoPresti could get neither stick nor
glove on and it slid into the corner of the net. Perhaps
stopping 80 shots on goal and still losing would feel
like losing a no-hitter.

In 1942, a lot of hockey players were in uniform, military uniform that is, and the New York Rangers were
having trouble finding a good goalie to replace Jim
Henry. They had already run through two when the
Rangers scouts thought they had found one—**Steve
Buzinski**, playing for an intermediate league team in
the storybook-sounding Swift Current, Saskatchewan.
But what had at first sounded like a press agent's
dream quickly collapsed in front of the blitzkrieg.

The 140-pound Steve Buzinski allowed almost six
goals per game for nine games. One of the sages of the
game, sportswriter Dan Daniel, had these words on the
man from Swift Current: "Steve showed a new technique. He adopted the falling system. Persuaded that
he who drops over the disk need not have fears of it being elsewhere, Buzinski spent more time on the ice
than a mackerel in cold storage."

On one of his worst nights the goalie himself con-
tributed to his losing cause by stopping a shot on goal
and tossing the puck over his shoulder into his own net.

"Steve was a beautiful little guy," said Frank
Boucher, the Rangers coach. "He was earnest and sin-
cere and we all liked him tremendously. There was just
one little problem. He couldn't stop a puck worth a
damn."

Mercilessly, Buzinski stayed in the bigs long

enough to rack up a 2–6–1 record and depart with the monikers The Puck Goesinski and The Human Sieve.

Another rookie who had a short-lived career in the NHL was defenseman **Lloyd Mohns**; but what a full day he had in January of 1943. In the afternoon he played a game for the New York Rovers, a local amateur club. After that, he worked in a date with Sonja Henie, the skating star. In the evening Mohns played a game for the New York Rangers. He neither scored a goal nor made an assist for the Rangers, and never appeared in another game in the NHL.

New York Rangers goalie **Ken McAuley** also had a banged-up debut. Before the first period ended, Murray Armstrong and Bill Quackenbush both scored, making it 2–0 Red Wings.

But then the roof fell in. Detroit scored five goals in the second period and eight in the third. Everyone on the Red Wings got into the act except the goalie and Cully Simon. In all, ten different Red Wings scored— Syd Howe accounted for three goals, Joe Carveth four assists—as Detroit outshot New York, 58–9. "They never even had to clear off the other end of the ice," said "Tubby" McAuley of the Rangers' record 15–0 loss. "It wasn't even marked." As a memento of the evening's demise on ice, Ken McAuley was presented with the overworked red light from behind his net.

A year later, on January 21, 1945, Ken McAuley experienced another nightmare almost as disastrous. In the second period the Boston Bruins scored four goals in only one minute and twenty seconds and went on to thrash the Rangers 14–3.

In 1944, Dartmouth had one of the best collegiate hockey teams and **Dick Rondeau** was one of their best players. One night against Middlebury College he had one of those evenings when he did everything right. For starters he scored 12 goals. Then he made 11 assists. Rondeau's total of 23 points was only exceeded by Dartmouth's 30–0 score.

To say **Eddie Emberg** had a short NHL career is to say little. He never appeared in a regular season game because the regulars were playing so well. However, he did get into two playoff games for the Montreal Canadiens against the Toronto Maple Leafs at the tail end of the 1944–45 season. His moment of fame came on March 29, 1945. It was then, at 6:02 of the first period of the fifth game of this best-of-seven series that this 24-year-old native of Montreal scored a goal, becoming the first player who had ever scored in the playoffs without playing during the season. Montreal went on to win, 10–3, but lost the series in six games. Emberg never skated in the NHL again.

On February 1, 1947, Ranger **Chuck Rayner** tried something new for a goalie. He left the crease and skated toward the Montreal net. Behind 2–1, Rayner was trying to shake things up. Perhaps he was losing the factor of surprise, but he tried it two more times before time expired. The final score was still 2–1.

* * *

There are many players with long careers who never make it to the finals of the Stanley Cup. **Doug McKay** had the opposite experience. The 20-year-old left wing's only game in the NHL came in a Stanley Cup finals. Skating for the Detroit Red Wings against the New York Rangers, McKay's tour of duty lasted only a few minutes. The Red Wings went on to win the 1950 championship.

The Chicago Blackhawks were playing the Rangers in New York on March 23, 1952. It was the final game of the season and neither team was in the playoffs. It was what is sometimes called a "brother-in-law" game. No one wants to get hurt because the game is meaningless. There was no checking; there were no penalties the whole game. Emile "Cat" Francis, the Rangers' backup goalie, had been sent down to Cincinnati, a minor league team trying to get into the playoffs of the American Hockey League. In his place was **Lorne Anderson**, a 20-year-old goalie from the New York Rovers, an amateur team. For Anderson it was a dream come true. He had what he wanted: a chance to play in the NHL. In his first game Anderson had beaten Boston, 6–4; in his second he had lost to Detroit, 6–3. The game with the Blackhawks would be crucial to his future.

The game was in the third period and the hometown team was ahead, 6–2 on Ed Slowinski's hat trick. (Although the term hat trick was borrowed from cricket— taking three wickets on three successive balls won the bowler a new hat—a Toronto haberdasher used to present a hat to the Maple Leaf player who made three goals in a game.) Suddenly, at 6:09, Bill Mosienko, the Blackhawks' right wing, received a pass from center Gus Bodnar and slapped the puck into the net past Lorne Anderson. Bodnar controlled the face-off and hit Mosienko as he crossed the blue line and at 6:20 beat Anderson again. Before the audience had resettled, Bodnar got the face-off again and this time passed to left winger George Gee. Gee took it across the blue line and spotted Mosienko beating his defender. Gee led Mosienko beautifully, and at 6:30 Mosienko beat the hapless Anderson again.

Mosienko had scored the fastest hat trick in history. His three goals in 21 seconds of the third period in a game that the Rangers went on to lose 7–6 proved to be the undoing of Lorne Anderson. Anderson had given up 17 goals during his stint as a Ranger. It was to be the goalie's third and last game in the NHL.

Fred Saskamoose was a Cree from the Sandy Lake Reserve in Saskatchewan. Although this center played only 11 games for the Chicago Blackhawks during the 1953–54 season, his experience with the Blackhawks and later with three minor league teams was to stick with him. When Sasakamoose became the chief of the Sandy Lake Crees, he was known as Chief Thunder Stick.

At one time teams carried only one goalie. That's where a man like **Ross "Lefty" Wilson** came in. Lefty was a trainer and a practice goalie for the Detroit Red Wings who could be pressed into service when the need arose. But only then. As his coach Jack Adams once said, "As a goaltender, the kid makes a pretty good trainer."

Just such a night came on October 10, 1953. Red Wing goalie Terry Sawchuk was hurt with 10 minutes to go. Lefty had to finish up and didn't let anything get by him.

On January 22, 1956, the situation was quite different. The Toronto Maple Leafs' goalie, Harry Lumley, was injured with 13 minutes left in the final period. Lefty had to go into net against his own teammates. The Red Wings, ahead 4–1, tried hard to score, but Lefty worked even harder. He stopped Gordie Howe twice on hard smashes and at one point even turned the net around.

During the '57–'58 season Lefty got into action for the Boston Bruins for Don Simmons in the first period. This was the trainer's longest stint on the ice, 52 minutes, so it's not hard to see how a puck got by him. But that was the only one in his 85 minutes playing for three different teams. His goals-against average was a sparkling 0.71.

Willie O'Ree was the first black professional hockey player. A native of Frederickton, New Brunswick, the 23-year-old O'Ree arrived from the Quebec Aces farm team to play in only two games for the Boston Bruins in 1958. But one was on January 18, the Bruins' victory over the Montreal Canadiens, 3–0, in the Stanley Cup. The Canadiens went on to take the championship, 4 games to 2. In the 1960–61 season, the 5-foot-10, 175-pound left winger returned to Boston to score 4 goals and 10 assists in 43 games. After his 45 games in the NHL, Willie O'Ree was to play out the rest of his career in the minors.

Because of the many injuries to the New York Rangers, the five-foot-ten, 175-pound right winger from South Porcupine, Ontario, **Danny Belisle**, was in a Rangers uniform on Christmas Day, 1960. In his very first game in the NHL, Belisle scored a goal against the powerful Montreal Canadiens. But that wasn't the last of it. The 22-year-old played three more games and scored another goal. Slowly the Rangers regulars were coming back off the injured list.

When Belisle was suiting up for his fifth game, coach Alf Pike told him that Camille Henry was going to play, so he wouldn't be needed. As the rookie was taking off his equipment, Pike told him that it looked like Henry wouldn't be able to go in after all and that he should get ready. Before Belisle was back in uniform, the coach told him that he might not play after all. Why don't you get half-dressed? he suggested.

And that's what Danny Belisle did. On one side he was wearing his street clothes; on the other his hockey uniform. When the players saw this, they hooted and guffawed until Alf Pike looked in to see what was going on. The coach got so mad that he told Belisle he wasn't going to play, not that night, not ever. The next day Belisle was sent down to the minors, never to return to the NHL again.

In 1965 the New York Rangers did something that was a first back then but is commonplace today. They put a player on the ice who was born in Europe and received his training there as well. **Ulf Sterner** could be a listing on a trivia card because he only lasted four games in the NHL and did not score or assist on a goal. He was then given a one-way ticket back to the minors.

On January 13, 1968, **Bill Masterton** was playing in the thirty-eighth game of his career. The 29-year-old rookie center was on the ice for the North Stars against the Oakland Seals in a hard-fought 2–2 game when he was checked hard into the boards. The six-foot, 189-pound Masterton fell to the ice and hit his head. Twenty-four hours later Bill Masterton died of head injuries—the first NHL player to die of injuries received in a game.

Beginning with the year of Masterton's death, the Professional Hockey Writers' Association has presented the Bill Masterton Trophy to "the NHL hockey player who exemplifies the qualities of perseverance, sportsmanship and dedication to hockey."

Who had the shortest career as an NHL goalie? **Robbie Irons**.

Irons was to have a long career in the CHL and IHL, but he had no such luck in the NHL. One reason was that he was playing backup to two of the great ones: Jacques Plante and Glenn Hall. Here's how it happened.

On November 13, 1968, the St. Louis Blues were playing the New York Rangers. Plante was out with a groin pull and was sitting in the stands; and shortly af-

ter the game began the volatile Glenn Hall was called
for a game misconduct. Scotty Bowman told Irons to
warm up slowly and then to pretend that there was
something wrong with his equipment to allow Plante
enough time to get out of his street clothes and into his
hockey gear. With referee Very Buffey issuing a
penalty warning and on the verge of handing out a
penalty for delay of game, Bowman was forced to go
with Irons in net as play resumed. As it turned out,
Irons played a very uneventful three minutes. There
was not a single shot on the St. Louis goal. At 5:01 of
the first period, Jake the Snake went in and Irons re-
treated to the bench. It was the last time Robbie Irons
was on NHL game ice.

After years of playing for the Hershey Bears in the minor leagues, **Barry Ashbee** made it to the NHL to
stay in 1970. He was 34. Although he only scored 15
goals and 70 assists in his 284 games, he made it to a
team that was playing for the Stanley Cup. But on
April 28, 1974, he was hit in the right eye by a puck off
the stick of Dale Rolfe of the New York Rangers in a
Stanley Cup semifinal game.

"I remember a red blob. I felt as if someone had
stuck a poker in my eye. There was a stretcher of some
sort. . . . I felt the chill when I was outside being
wheeled into the ambulance."

Ashbee's vision was greatly impaired and his playing career was over.

"I'm not bitter," he said about the incident. "Some
people strive for sixty years or so to achieve certain

goals in life, and never make it. I got what I wanted at thirty-four."

Three years later Barry Ashbee was dead of leukemia.

Michel Plasse spent 11 years as a goalie in the NHL on six different teams; but oddly, it was what he did in the minors, in the Central Hockey League, that sticks in the memory. It was on February 21, 1971, when Plasse was a rookie on the Kansas City Blues. With time winding down and Oklahoma City trailing 2–1, the Blazers pulled their goalie and had six offensive players on the ice. Forty-four seconds remaining, Plasse cleared the puck, and it slid farther and farther up ice until it landed in Oklahoma City's untended net. Plasse had scored, becoming the first goalie in professional hockey to score a goal.

Ed Giacomin accomplished many things during his long career in goal for the New York Rangers. He was elected to the All-Star team, shared the Vezina Trophy, and was later a member of the Hockey Hall of Fame. But on March 19, 1972, Fast Eddie became the first NHL goalie to get official credit for two assists in the same game. The first was an assist to right wing Bill Fairbairn and the second to center Pete Stemkowski, as the Rangers beat the Leafs, 5–3.

If a person were to play 13 years in the minor leagues and then was released, you might think this person's career was over. That was what happened to **Ross Brooks**, but instead of calling it quits, he did what a recent college graduate might do. He sent out resumes.

Only one team responded, the Boston Bruins, and they sent him to the Oklahoma City Blazers of the CHL. He did all right there, so his next stop was the Boston Braves, where he and Dan Bouchard had an outstanding year. After Bouchard was taken in the expansion draft and the Bruins' regular goalie, Gerry Cheevers, moved to the WHA for more money, the Bruins were suddenly in need of goalies, even a 36-year-old rookie. It was Brooks's moment and he made the most of it.

In the 1973–74 season, Brooks won 16 games (one was a shutout) and lost three.

"A lot of people, especially young people, could look at my story and learn something from it," said Brooks. "After so many years of people doubting I could play well, so many years of people not knowing I was alive out there, after a lot of perseverance and hard work, I finally achieved my goal and proved myself with the greatest team in hockey."

In the next two years, filling in for Giles Gilbert when needed, Ross Brooks posted a record of 37 wins, 7 losses, and 6 ties. His goals-against average was a very respectable 2.64.

At a time when most players would be thinking about retiring, **Connie Madigan** was making his NHL debut. At the ripe age of 38, this defenseman skated for the St. Louis Blues in a 5–1 win over the Vancouver Canucks on February 6, 1973. Madigan's NHL career lasted only 20 regular-season games, during which he made five assists. He capped his career with five scoreless playoff games.

* * *

George Plimpton is known for getting into the thick of a sporting event and writing about it. In the fall of 1977 Plimpton went to the training camp of the Boston Bruins to don the pads of a goalie to find out what that was like. His roommate was Jim Pettie, a goalie in the minor leagues. Plimpton hoped that the combination of practice and guidance from Pettie would get him game ready.

Plimpton had wanted to play in a regular-season game, but Coach Don Cherry said no deal to that idea. Instead the adventuresome journalist would get five minutes during a preseason game. But it was going to be a good one: the Flyers at the Spectrum in Philadelphia. Plimpton was also not going to be sent in during the waning moments of a mopping-up operation; Big George was going to start.

During the first two minutes of play, Plimpton was a spectator, as all the action was down in front of the Flyers' net. But things changed after that, and the Flyers were down on his end of the ice with "that awful black puck, sailing elusively between sticks and skates, as shifty as a rat in a hedgerow." The Flyers' first shot on goal screamed toward the net, and with a last-second correction by Orest Kindrachuk, it was in. After that it only got more fast and furious. The Bruins' Bobby Schmautz drew a penalty, so the author from the Upper East Side found himself facing the Flyers' power play. The Flyers took eight shots on goal: one hit the crossbar but the others all hit Plimpton. Plimpton had withstood the barrage, but he later sheepishly admitted they were not so much saves as he had been "somewhat akin to a tree in the line of flight of a golf ball."

With Plimpton's five minutes ticking away, Mike Milbury threw a stick at a breakaway Flyer. A penalty shot was set up with Reggie Leach versus the rookie goalie. Leach broke quickly and Plimpton journeyed out to meet him. Just as Leach shot, Plimpton fell down. The shot caromed off his skate and sailed into the crowd. The Boston Bruins skated out onto the ice to pick up their fallen goalie and congratulate him. "Of course, they told me Leach was a psychological ruin after he failed to beat me."

Back in the locker room, Plimpton found his tie, socks, and shorts had been treated to the initiatory rites that greet rookies. If there had been any doubt that he had done a commendable job, it disappeared with the toes of his socks.

On February 14, 1977, 21-year-old **Al Hill** was playing in his first NHL game. With the game only 35 seconds old, Hill took his first shot and scored a goal from 45 feet. Before the period was over, he added an assist. At 11:33 of the second period, Hill took his second shot and scored his second goal. He also added another assist that period, and another in the third. In his very first game Hill had scored five points, something no one had ever done before.

Although Hill went on to play 221 regular-season games, he never showed the scoring prowess that he displayed that first night. For the rest of his career he only scored 38 goals and 52 assists.

Jim Stewart had more than 15 minutes of fame. Twenty to be precise. The parent club, the Boston Bruins, had gone to their farm team, Utica, in the Eastern League for a goalie when their two regular goalies went down with injuries. So that was how Stewart found himself in net on January 10, 1980, versus the St. Louis Blues. But it wasn't long before the roof of the Boston Garden fell in, as the Blues scored on three of their first four shots on goal. Stewart remained on the ice until the first period was over and the Blues had scored five goals. (The Bruins came back but still lost 7–4.) Stewart was gone, but his name lives on in the record book. He has the highest goals-against average for all goalies: 15 goals per game.

On February 22, 1980, the scene was set at the ice hockey arena at Lake Placid, New York. It was the Winter Olympics. The team from the Soviet Union, a powerful Russian hockey team that had captured the worlds championship 17 out of 19 tries, was taking the ice for its game against the underdog team from the United States.

"Maybe it's history in the making," **Jim Craig**, the US goalie, had said before the game. "When I was watching them play Canada I found myself rooting for the Russians. If anyone is going to beat them, I want it to be us."

Over the previous six months, the US team had played 61 exhibition games, but the Soviet team had been together for years. Herb Brooks, the American coach, had been instructing his team to play more like the Russians—crisscross playmaking and tiptop conditioning—but it was still a team of players from college and the minor leagues. Compared to the well-groomed

Soviet players, the US team was a ragtag bunch. The Soviets, in fact, had beaten the Americans in an exhibition, 10–3, shortly before the Games began.

Brooks had prepared the Americans as well as possible. "You were meant for this moment," he told them in the locker room before the game with the Soviets. "You were meant to be here. So let's have poise and possession of ourselves at this time."

As Craig had said, "We might all be making history. You never know."

In the first period the Soviets scored first. Buzzy Schnieder tied it. The Soviets scored again. Mark Johnson tied it with a rebound put in of Dave Christian's slap shot. In the second period there was a new goalie in net for the Soviets, Vladimir Myshkin for Vladislav Tretiak. Craig remained in net for the US. The score was 3–2. In the third period Johnson scored again, this time on a power play. The score remained tied until Mike Eruzione scored with 10 minutes left.

The Soviets were changing lines every 40 seconds. The Americans were keeping up; Craig was superb in net. The seconds ticked down the upset, as the Americans beat the USSR to win the semifinal game, earning them a place in the final against Finland.

Comparatively speaking, the final was an anticlimax. In the third period, Finland was leading 2–1. But then the Americans woke up and scored three times for a 4–2 victory.

One of the lasting images was of Craig skating around the rink draped in Old Glory, searching the stands for his father, Don Craig.

"I went from being a kid without a bankbook to an overnight hero," said the American goalie. "I never wanted that role."

Playing before a sell-out crowd in his first game as a pro for the Atlanta Flames, Craig stopped 24 shots on goal as the Flames won 4–1. He played only three more games with the Flames before they moved to Canada. There is little value in an American hero playing for a Canadian team, so Craig went to the Boston Bruins. After 23 games for the Bruins, Craig was sent to the minors. Injuries and problems piled up and in 1981 he was released.

Jim Craig seemed such a natural, but he wasn't. Things haven't been quite right since.

On December 20, 1981, the 25-year-old **Paul Skidmore** from Smithtown, New York, found himself in his first NHL game starting in goal for the St. Louis Blues against the Winnipeg Jets. Before Skidmore even had enough time to appreciate where he was, Doug Smail from Moose Jaw, Saskatchewan, had gone from the beginning face-off to smacking the puck into the net. Only five seconds had elapsed. This was a new record. (It has since been equaled twice.) Smail beat Skidmore again to put the Jets ahead, 4–3, in the third period. The Jets went on to win, 5–4.

Skidmore's second game was on December 29 against the Colorado Rockies. This time there were no surprises in the opening seconds. The goalie was as solid as his six-foot, 185-pound frame as he beat the Rockies, 6–1. It was the last time that Paul Skidmore played in the NHL.

* * *

In January 1982, a high school player scored a hat trick (three goals in a game) that would leave any pro envious. Holliston, Massachusetts was playing Westwood High. With 1 minute, 19 seconds left in the game, **Steve D'Innocenzo** scored. Six seconds later, D'Innocenzo scored again. No more than six seconds had elapsed again when he put the puck into the net a third time. Steve D'Innocenzo had scored three goals in only 12 seconds. (The record in the NHL is 21 seconds, established by Bill Mosienko of the Chicago Blackhawks.)

In his 1981–82 rookie season with the New York Rangers, **Mikko Leinonen** made 20 assists in 53 games. But in a playoff game against the Philadelphia Flyers on April 8, 1982, this center from Tampere, Finland, fed the puck to six different players. It was not only the first time a rookie had ever made six assists, but it was also one of only two times for a player to register six in a playoff game. The other is Wayne Gretzky. Leinonen had a total of 78 assists in 162 regular-season games and only 11 assists in 20 playoff games

Markus Mattsson was at the end of his six-year career in 1984, a year in which he only played in 19 games. But on January 28, 1984, the Los Angeles Kings were playing the Edmonton Oilers with Wayne Gretzky at center. Gretzky was having a phenomenal year; he had either scored or made an assist in 51 straight games. (The Great One's scoring for those 51 games was an incredible 61 goals and 92 assists).

Having one of the better games of his career, Mattsson shut down Gretzky. With two seconds left and the Kings leading 4–2, Wayne Gretzky got off one final shot. Mattsson fell on the puck in front of the net. The streak was over.

Steve Penney played in only four games for Montreal during the 1983-84 season, but he had three shutouts in the playoffs, a record for rookies. It was the beginning of what looked like a spectacular career.

But the next year Patrick Roy joined Montreal and he was in goal when the Canadiens won the Stanley Cup in 1986. During the rest of Penney's five-year NHL career for Montreal and Winnipeg, he played in a total of 91 games. His four shutouts during the playoffs and only one during the regular season mark the only time that a goalie has had more shutouts during the playoffs.

Ray Staszak seemed like a sure bet to a lot of teams in the NHL. No fewer than eighteen teams tried to get the six-foot, 200-pound right winger who had scored 37 goals his senior year at the University of Illinois-Chicago. Scouts thought he would have the same impact that Bob Nystrom had once had for the New York Islanders. The winner in this bidding war was the Detroit Red Wings, landing Staszak with a five-year-$1.3 million contract.

Staszak lasted exactly four games. He left an imprint of no goals and one assist for one point and seven penalty minutes, before disappearing.

*   *   *

Steve Smith had a long career (461 regular-season games and 105 playoff games), but there was something that took place in the seventh game of the 1986 Stanley Cup that casts a flickering shadow. The date was April 30, 1986, and the Edmonton Oilers and the Calgary Flames were deadlocked at three games apiece in the Stanley Cup finals. It was the seventh game, the score was a 2–2 tie and five minutes were gone in the third period. Smith, the big defenseman (six-foot-four, 215 pounds) from Scotland, tried to make a clearing pass for Edmonton, but it struck the skate of Grant Fuhr, the goalie for Edmonton, and popped into their own net. The goal was officially listed as made by Perry Berezan of the Flames, but that's not how it happened. Unfortunately for Smith, there was no more scoring. The Calgary Flames won the game, 3–2, and the Stanley Cup, 4 games to 3.

Chris Kontos had made only two goals in his seven games of the 1988–89 season for the Los Angeles Kings, so no one looking at the charts could expect too much from him in the Kings' playoff series with the Edmonton Oilers. But were they ever surprised. Kontos cracked six power-play goals during the series— more power-play goals than anyone had ever scored in a single series—to help the Kings upset the Oilers in seven games. Over the course of his seven-year career at left wing and center, Kontos only scored a total of 27 goals in the regular season and 11 in the playoffs.

* * *

No goalie had ever scored a goal in playoff competition until April 11, 1989. In the fifth game of the Patrick Division semifinals between Philadelphia and Washington, the Capitals were down 7–5, with the seconds and opportunity ticking away. Philadelphia had lost a man to a penalty, so Washington pulled their goalie, Pete Peeters, in order to have one more offensive skater. The action was in front of the Flyers' net; their goalie, **Ron Hextall**, had the puck on his hockey stick and he flung it 180 feet into the Capitals' unguarded net. The Flyers won it, 8–5.

In November of 1991, **Manon Rheaume**, a young woman goaltender for the Trois-Rivieres Draveurs, a junior A hockey team in Quebec, made her first appearance in net for the Draveurs. It happened in the second period and she played for 20 minutes. Deflecting seven shots, she allowed three scores. She would have stayed in the game longer, except she had to come out for stitches when a puck hit her face mask.

Her career, however, did not end there. On September 23, 1992, Rheaume appeared in an exhibition game for the Tampa Bay Lightning against the St. Louis Blues. Playing for one period, the five-foot-six, 135-pound goalie faced nine shots on goal, stopping seven and allowing two goals, as the Lightning lost to the Blues, 6–4.

"I think she played very well for her first NHL game," said Phil Esposito, the Lightning general manager. "I remember my first game; I was scared to death."

Rheaume's next stop was the Atlanta Knights of the International Hockey League. She played in two games for this Tampa Bay farm team. The second, on April 4, 1993, was for the entire game. Before 15,179 noisy fans, Rheaume and the Knights lost to the Cincinnati Cyclones by the score of 8–6.

As someone who has played against both men and women, Rheaume's comments are noteworthy. "The men are stronger, more physical, and will try to intimidate me by rushing the net," she said. "And the shots are harder. But women players tend to be craftier, and use their stickhandling and skating skills more."

Goaltender **Jeff Reese** may have appeared in 86 regular-season games, but what he did on February 10, 1993, was anything but regular. Playing goal for the Calgary Flames against the San Jose Sharks, Reese in the first period made an unusual play for a goalie. He had an assist. In the second period, Reese had another, and in the third, another. Jeff Reese had made a record three assists (two to Robert Reichel and one to Gary Roberts) as the Flames scorched the Sharks, 13–1.

On October 30, 1993, **Erin Whitten** from Glens Falls, New York, became the first woman goalie to win a game in professional hockey. The five-foot-five 22-year-old had enjoyed a good college career with the New Hampshire Wildcats, but this was a first. Playing for the Toledo Storm in the East Coast Hockey League, Whitten held off the Dayton Bombers, 6–5.

*   *   *

Another goalie, **Kelly Dyer**, who had played for the US in two world championships, received her first chance as a professional in January 1994. In uniform for the West Palm Beach Blaze, the 27-year-old stopped all seven shots in the 10 minutes she appeared. The Blaze went on to beat the Daytona Beach Sun Devils, 6–2, in a Sunshine League game.

Horse Racing

*"A horse doesn't know whether the rider
on his back wears a dress or pants away from the track."*
—Diane Crump, jockey

In 1873 at the Gravesend racetrack in New York, there was a dead heat between two horses, **Bing Aman** and **Mart Jordan**. The owners wanted their horses to race the mile and three-quarters again, and the second time they raced to a dead heat. The horses raced a third time with the same results. Bing Aman and Mart Jordan raced a fourth time, and again they finished in a dead heat. But the track officials had seen enough and they declared Bing Aman had won by a nose. The race patrons would have none of this and practically tore the stands apart.

In 1891, one of the oldest horses ever to appear in an officially sanctioned race galloped his farewell race at the Guttenberg track in New Jersey. The horse's name was **Hickory Jim** and his age was 25.

In 1898, 10-year-old **John Daly** rode ten winners at the Aqueduct racetrack in New York.

* * *

Man o'War won 20 out of 21 starts during the 1919–1920 season. The only horse to upset Man o'War was a two-year-old with a wildly appropriate name. It happened at the Sanford Stakes in Saratoga on August 13, 1919. Although Man o' War, ridden by John Loftus, was an 11–20 favorite to win, an unknown horse ridden by Bill Knapp came out of the blue to beat "Big Red" by a nose. The horse's name? **Upset**.

The description of the race went like this: "Start, poor and slow . . . Upset followed the leader closely from the start, moved up with a rush in the last eighth and, taking the lead, held on gamely when challenged and just lasted long enough to withstand Man o'War's challenge."

Man o'War had defeated Upset earlier in the US Hotel Stakes and defeated Upset five times after this single defeat. "We beat Man o'War only by a head, not a half-length as the chart had it," recalled jockey Willie Knapp. "At the time, Big Red being beaten didn't mean as much as it did at the end of his racing career when people realized that that was the only time he lost."

It just goes to show what racing great Angel Cordero, Jr. later said: "Any horse can be beaten on any given day." After that big win, Upset never won another race of any consequence.

Frank Hayes was a jockey who might have been known as the comeback kid. Even though he saddled a 20–1 long shot, Sweet Kiss, in a July 1923 Belmont steeplechase, Hayes rode like he was the odds-on favorite. The horse must have picked up his rider's verve and confidence because it ran like the wind and finished first. When those at the finish line went over to congratulate the winning mount, they found Hayes was dead. For Hayes, this race had been the kiss of death.

On April 27, 1943, **Judy Johnson** became one of the first women to ride at a track in the United States and the first jockey with a license to ride as a professional. (There was a shortage of jockeys because of the war.) In a steeplechase run at Pimlico Racetrack in Baltimore, Maryland, Johnson placed next to last out of 11 horses, 30 lengths behind. After a few more races, she went back to being a trainer.

On May 6, 1950, a **72-year-old jockey** riding a 14-year-old horse placed second at the Miyazaki racetrack in Japan. As if that weren't stretching things enough, the man had ridden the horse 140 miles to get to the track.

Lester Piggot rode a long shot, Dragon Blood, to victory in the Primio Naviglio on June 1, 1967. How long was the long shot? Would you believe 10,000 to 1? There must have been some serious celebrating that night in Milan, Italy.

After Diane Crump became the first woman jockey in a US horse race, it took a shade over two weeks for a woman to ride home the winner. On February 22, 1969, **Barbara Jo Rubin** wore the silks to ride Cohesian to a close victory at West Virginia's Charles Town racetrack. (Rubin had been ready to ride on February 15, until the other jockeys staged a protest.)

Rubin rode two winners on the same day at Waterford Park in Chester, West Virginia. Then her dressing room window at Tropical Park was broken by a rock. "Horse racing is pretty rank," she admitted. She cut down on some of the insults by wearing cotton in her ears. But at Aqueduct she rode Bray Galaxy, a 13–1 long shot, to victory. The other jockeys showed their acceptance of her by pouring the traditional bucket of water over her head. Then aboard Picnic Fare, Rubin was the first woman to ride at Churchill Downs.

Barbara Jo Rubin's dreams of riding began when she was eight. "I saw Liz Taylor in *National Velvet* on TV," she explained, "and from that time on I had my heart set on riding horses."

The first African-American woman jockey was 17-year-old **Cheryl White**. On June 15, 1971, Ms. White finished last in a seven-horse race at the Thistledown Race Track in Cleveland, Ohio. On September 17, 1971, Cheryl White became the first to win. The horse was Jertola and it was the third race of the day held at the Waterford Park Race Track in Chester, West Virginia.

On October 16, 1973, **Victor Morely Lawson** registered his first win as a jockey, riding his mount, Ocean King, to victory at a track in Warwick, England. Lawson's first trip to the winner's circle came at the age of 67.

* * *

Chris McCarron won 515 races at the age of of 19, but his five hundred and sixteenth race on February 9, 1974, was his biggest. That was the race when he was trying to break the record of 515 wins for one year set by Sandy Hawley just the year before. But in this race for the record, Chris on Ohmylove was racing neck and neck with his 26-year-old brother, Gregg, astride Boston Ego.

"Most of the time, Gregg and I don't pay any attention to each other in a race," said Chris. "But when you are in a stretch battle, there's no doubt about your opposition. Frankly, I don't like to get in these stretch fights with Gregg. For one thing, he is very tough in the last 70 yards and for another, I tend to get careless because I try too hard."

At the finish line, it was Ohmylove by a neck. Chris had the record; the horse had run 7 furlongs in 1:25 2/5.

In her first test against colts, **Genuine Risk** had finished third in the Wood Memorial. The trainer thought that was enough for this filly, but the owners of the horse, the Firestones, wanted to enter her in the Kentucky Derby. It had been 21 years since the last filly ran (Silver Spoon finished fifth in 1959); it had been 65 years since the last filly had won the Derby (Regret in 1915).

On May 3, 1980, Genuine Risk with Jacinto Vasquez on board drew away from the bunched pack at the top of the stretch and won the Churchill Downs classic in 2:02.

* * *

It hadn't been that long since the last filly was victorious in the Run for the Roses at Louisville's Churchill Downs, and here on May 7, 1988, was **Winning Colors** taking the lead in the Kentucky Derby. As the horses turned into the homestretch, the filly was in the lead by three lengths, but she began to tire and Forty Niner and Risen Star made their runs. Winning Colors fought off the challengers to win in the closest finish in two decades.

Twenty-one years after the first woman jockey rode in the Kentucky Derby, **Julie Krone** jockeyed a horse in the Belmont Stakes. The date was June 8, 1991. Two years later, on June 5, 1993, Ms. Krone rode Colonial Affair into the winner's circle of the Belmont Stakes. This was the first time a woman had ever ridden a horse to victory in one of the Triple Crown races.

Running

"The art of running the mile consists, in essence, of reaching the threshold of unconsciousness at the instant of breasting the tape."
—Paul O'Neil, writer

In 1832, a Norwegian named **Menzen Ernst** altered the way you might think about distance running. Ernst did not run around an oval or even stay within the confines of one country. Instead he ran from Constantinople (Istanbul, Turkey) to Calcutta, India, a distance of 5,625 miles.

Now how long do you suppose that would take? A reasonable estimate might be 100 days, 56 miles per day, and that would seem to be pushing it. After all, this gives cross-country running a new dimension. Ernst did his wondrous feat in 59 days. Getting the calculator out, that would be 95 miles a day, or four miles per hour. And that doesn't even allow for eating and sleeping.

The first modern Olympic Games, held in 1896, had been a washout for the host country, Greece. Although there were 14 countries present, a large number of the 245 athletes were Greek. But not one of them had given the crowd in Athens much to cheer about. Of the

11 track and field events, the Americans had won nine, the Australians two.

The last track and field event held was the marathon. The race actually began where the Battle of Marathon had taken place in 490 BC. (A story appeared some 600 years after the battle that a professional runner named Pheidippides had been sent from the Plains of Marathon to Athens to inform the populace that the invading Persian forces had been defeated by the outnumbered Greeks. After reaching Athens and declaring, "We are victorious," Pheidippides dropped dead.)

Seventeen runners started the race. For most of the way, the lead changed between Albin Lermusiaux of France and Edwin Flack of Australia. But as the runners approached the stadium, a cry went up. The leader was a Greek shepherd named **Spiridon Louis**.

Prince George and Prince Constantine, sons of King George, went down to the track to run on either side of Spiridon Louis to the finish line. Louis's time was 2 hours, 58 minutes, 50 seconds. Greece had won a gold medal. The Olympic flame would stay lighted.

John J. McDermott from New York won the first running of the Boston Marathon on April 19, 1897. His time of 2 hours, 55 minutes, 10 seconds was the record until the second Boston Marathon.

In 1904, a medical student by the name of **George Foster** wanted to impress his friends, so he ran up a mountain. The mountain he selected for his timed feat was Mount Washington in New Hampshire. It's not the length of the run that is so daunting—about seven and a half miles—but the fact that this 6,288-foot mountain has an average grade of 11 percent and near the top it's a breath-catching 22 percent. That's a rise of 611 vertical feet per mile. Another obstacle is the notoriously bad weather even in the summertime. In June the weather at the top is freezing and the wind gusts up to 60 miles per hour. Foster's time? One hour and 42 minutes. That was faster than any automobile had ever made it.

The 1904 Olympic Games were held in St. Louis, and anyone who has been there in the summertime knows how hot it can be. Well, on just such a day, August 30, with the temperature dallying with 100, the marathon was held.

At the 16-mile mark **Thomas Hicks** of Great Britain was in the lead, but he immediately realized how he had not paced himself. He was spent and not feeling at all well. After all, he was an entertainer, not a runner, and wanted to pack it in, but his handlers felt otherwise. They whipped up a drink of cognac, egg, and strychnine (thought to be a stimulant). Revived, Hicks continued to the 22-mile mark when again he felt his body falling apart. Again, his handlers gave him more of the same, and Hicks wobbled on to the finish line, finishing six minutes ahead of his nearest competitor in the time of 3 hours, 28 minutes, 53 seconds. Hicks was also understandably finished himself. He collapsed and was taken to the hospital unconscious. It wasn't until a week later that he had recovered enough to receive his gold medal.

* * *

Felix Carvajal was a postman from Havana, Cuba, with the dream of running the marathon in the 1904 Olympics in St. Louis. It was an odd dream for someone to pursue who did not have much experience and had never even run a long-distance race. To raise money for his journey, Carvajal ran around a popular public square in Havana. He collected enough, but when he arrived in New Orleans, he lost his money to professional gamblers. There seemed only one thing to do: run to St. Louis. And that's what he did, begging for food from farmers along the way. It was an odd training regimen, but it seemed to work. The Cuban runner arrived in time to be one of the 31 contestants. Running only 26 miles after covering 700 might have been a relief. Not only was he one of 14 runners to finish the race, Felix Carvajal also finished fourth.

Here is one last tale about the marathon held at the 1904 Summer Olympics. **Fred Lorz**, who trained with the Mohawk Athletic Club, was one of the marathoners for the United States. Lorz got off to a fast start and soon was in the lead. The heat was as difficult as the pace, and it wasn't long before there were fewer than the original 31 runners. At the 10-mile mark Lorz still led, but he dropped out when he reached halfway. The heat, the pace, and his leg cramps had done him in. Someone in an automobile traveling along the route offered him a ride. He hopped in. He would ride in style instead of run to the Olympic Stadium. With five miles to go, the auto conked out. Back on his feet, Lorz started running again. Maybe he hadn't started out with this idea, perhaps it had just come to him when he realized that the other runners were behind him and he was in the lead, but he ran into the Olympic Stadium to the cheers of the crowd. What a rush it must have been. It wasn't until he was climbing onto the pedestal to receive his gold medal that the hoax was discovered. Hopefully, that moment of experiencing what it was like to win a gold medal at the Olympics would be enough to last him the rest of his life, for Fred Lorz was banned from ever running in an amateur race again. However, after convincing others that it had all been a joke, he became the US marathon winner in 1905.

Bloomingdale's is often known today for those chic bags that many shoppers carry around. But back in 1908 Bloomingdale's was also known for the running around of one of its employees. Here's how it happened.

One day, Alfred Bloomingdale got wind that one of his clerks, **John J. Hayes**, was a good marathoner. The owner had a track built on top of the New York department store so that the 19-year-old Hayes would be able to train regularly and still put in a day's work.

Hayes lived up to his billing and made the US team in the marathon. He was immediately given a paid vacation so he could go over to the Olympics in London. But at best, Johnny Hayes was a longshot. The two favorites were Tom Morrissey, a Bostonian who had won that year's Boston Marathon (Hayes had finished close behind him), and Charles Hefferon, a South African.

The marathon was run on July 24, 1908. In the three

previous modern Olympiads the distance had been set at 24 miles. This time the distance was to be 26 miles, 385 yards. The reason for this odd measurement wasn't because that was the distance Pheidippides had run from Marathon to Athens to announce the Greek victory over the Persians (that was 24 miles) but rather that this was the distance from the lawns of Windsor Castle, where King Edward VII and Queen Alexandra were celebrating a birthday party for a grandchild, to the finish line on the track in White City Stadium.

At the start of the race, three runners from England took turns setting the pace. It was a fast pace, too fast for the July heat, and they soon fell back into the pack. The next front-runner was Hefferon, with Morrissey on his heels. But the pace and the heat proved too much for the Bostonian as well. Hefferon ran alone in the lead for most of the race. At the 20-mile mark, the famous wall of marathon running, Hefferon appeared tired and began to slacken his pace. A runner who had not been given much hope for the gold, the candy maker from Capri, Dorando Pietri, a 22-year-old who had won the Paris Marathon the year before, was now gaining on the front runner. The more difficulty Hefferon was experiencing—his pace was half what it had been earlier—the easier time Pietri seemed to be having. At the 22-mile mark, Pietri passed Hefferon, and following behind into second place was the surprising Johnny Hayes. Hayes kept gaining, so that by the time Pietri had reached White City Stadium, the Italian was only 600 yards ahead. Pietri entered the stadium. He had only 385 yards more. But not the way he was going. He was headed the wrong way. Race officials

formed a wall so he had to turn around and go the right
way. Then Pietri fell and got up four times. British officials and Italian spectators finally ran out and helped
"Dorando the Great" cross the finish line. With the race
seemingly over, Hayes entered the stadium and ran to a
second-place finish. Next was Hefferon, then two more
Americans. However, it soon became apparent that the
Italian's finish had been against the rules. A runner
cannot be aided as he had been. When things were
sorted out, Hayes was declared the winner in 2 hours,
55 minutes, 18 seconds, the first American ever to
come in first in the marathon in the Olympic Games.

So Hayes won the gold medal and Bloomingdale's
procured a ransom's worth of goodwill. Upon Hayes's
return to the States, he became the manager of sporting
goods.

Unfortunately for Hayes, the story doesn't end
there.

There remained so much enthusiasm for the two
men to race again that a promoter persuaded both
men to turn pro and run the marathon again on
Thanksgiving Day in the old Madison Square Garden
in New York City. Quickly, it became one hot ticket.
Long before the fourth Thursday of November all
15,000 seats were sold out, so that on the day of the
race 100,000 people showed up for seats that were
unavailable. A riot broke out. Hundreds of policemen
were called in to restrain the crowd, but even so,
thousands were trampled and hundreds were hurt. It
would be difficult for the real foot race to be anything
but anticlimactic.

And it was. Most of the competition seemed to be in

the stands between the Irish and the Italian spectators. On the track, however, "Dorando the Great" was unstoppable. He beat the American soundly in the deafening din of the Garden.

On March 4, 1928, the promoter who had Red Grange do star turns around the country turned to running. Charles C. Pyle's idea was to have a large group of men race across the United States for $48,500 in prize money. One hundred ninety-nine started out in Los Angeles, but before they had gone more than 16 hot miles, 76 runners had dropped out. And that was only the beginning of the promoter's problems, a man nicknamed "Cash and Carry." What had been billed as a "titanic struggle between the greatest long-distance runners of the entire world" had disintegrated into "The Bunion Derby."

But in the midst of the logistical and financial nightmares, a race blossomed. **Andrew Payne**, a 19-year-old from a farm in Claremore, Oklahoma, became the front-runner for a brief time in Arizona and then took over first place again in Oklahoma. "Part Cherokee and all heart," Payne stretched his lead to 17 hours and 28 minutes in Ohio, and held onto it all the way to Madison Square Garden. It took Andy Payne 573 hours, 4 minutes, 34 seconds to run the 3,422-mile race. Although Pyle was besieged by money problems, he did pay Andy Payne his winner's purse of $25,000, and John Salo collected $10,000 for second place.

One of the runners in the 1946 Boston Marathon was not only from Greece, **Stylianos Kyriakides** was running to make the plight of so many of his country-men known to the rest of the world. Malnutrition had seized Greece after World War II as if it were a punishment sent down from Mount Olympus.

John A. Kelley led the race until Kyriakides caught the leader with one and a half miles to go. After running together for a time, Kyriakides pulled away and won in 2:29:27. At the post-race interview, Kyriakides talked about the situation in his country and Kelley cried, not about losing but about the conditions in Greece—conditions that the world was now aware of. Stylianos Kyriakides had scored a double victory.

On December 16, 1963, **Merry Lepper** jumped into the marathon at Culver City, California, after it had started. (She had been hiding behind some bushes with fellow runner Lyn Carman.) Carman made it to the 18-mile mark, but Lepper continued to the end, finishing in 3 hours, 37 minutes, 7 seconds. This time bested Violet Piercy's longstanding world record of 3 hours, 40 minutes, 22 seconds set in London on October 3, 1926. (Women had been officially banned from long-distance running from 1928–1960.) Compared to Piercy, Lepper's record was short-lived; it only lasted for five months when on May 23, 1964, England's Dale Greig surpassed it in the time of 3 hours, 27 minutes, 45 seconds.

Sometimes athletes are thought of as something else first. Black quarterbacks used to be black first and quarterbacks second. The same was true with women marathoners. They were women first and runners second. This was certainly true in the Boston Marathon run on April 19, 1967.

One of the entries was a 19-year-old sophomore from Syracuse University, K. V. Switzer. At the start of the race this runner wore a hooded sweatshirt. As the race wore on, the weather warmed and the runner pulled off the sweatshirt. The K stood for Kathy. (By hiding in the bushes near the starting line, Roberta Gibb was also running in 1967 and had run the year before; however, Switzer was the first official entry.) Two miles into the race, race director Will Cloney attempted to tear her number off her sweatshirt, but other runners around her came to her rescue. Later, Boston Athletic Association trainer Jock Semple tried to remove her from the race, until Tom Miller, her running partner, pushed him away.

This was not an easy race for **Kathy Switzer** in other ways as well. At 20 miles she hit the wall and felt so tired she ran part of the time with her eyes closed. But Ms. Switzer toughed it out and finished the race. Her time that day wasn't much to brag about—4 hours and 20 minutes—but what she had accomplished certainly was. "Women can run," she said, "and they can still be women and look like women." Since 1972, there has been a women's division in the Boston Marathon.

At the 1968 Olympic Games in Mexico City, Abebe Bikila, the great Ethiopian runner, was trying to make it three Olympic marathon victories in a row. Bikila took the early lead and after running a third of the race, he suddenly stopped. Few others knew that he was running with a hairline fracture of his right foot. Bikila thought he might be able to do it, but the pain had become too intense. Immediately, his teammate, Mamo Wolde, took over the lead and maintained it right to the finish line.

But long after the excitement of the race, long after everyone else had finished, there was a runner still out on the course, a runner who was moving with a funny hop-run-step, a runner whose right leg was bandaged at the knee and calf, a runner who was laboriously making his way toward the finish line. Traffic had resumed, the streetlights were coming on, and still this man kept coming. The runner in last place was number 36, **John Stephen Akhwari** of Tanzania.

There was no longer a throng of spectators when Akhwari entered the stadium. But as this tall, thin, dignified man dressed in a yellow runner's shirt and green shorts striped in white made his way around the track, applause erupted from the few who remained and followed him all around the track.

Apparently, it had never occurred to John Stephen Akhwari to drop out. "My country did not send me to Mexico City to start the race," he said, his voice laced with thoughtful patience. "They sent me to finish the race."

Heroes don't necessarily come in first; sometimes they come in last. As is stated in the Olympic Creed:

> The most important thing in the Olympic Games is not to win but to take part, just as the most important thing in life is not the triumph but the struggle. The essential thing is not to have conquered but to have fought well.

On February 28, 1970, a total unknown to the track world, **Caroline Walker**, set the world record in the marathon. Running at Seaside, Oregon, the 89-pound 16-year-old ran in the time of 3 hours, 2 minutes, 53 seconds. This was to be her first and last big race.

Gene Roberts was a wheelchair competitor in the Boston Marathon in 1970. A double amputee from the Vietnam War, Roberts had to get special permission to enter. But why did he want to do it? "I guess I felt I owed God something for letting me live," said Roberts. (Five members of his company had died when a shell from a 105mm howitzer had landed in their midst.) Not only did Roberts wheel his chair, he also walked three miles on his hands—hand jockeying, he called it—so, his time wasn't all that good. Roberts finished in 6 hours and 7 minutes.

Oftentimes marathoners don't try the marathon until they have finished with their shorter events and marathoners often don't hit their prime until their thirties. So what do you think about a five-year-old girl going the distance of 26 miles, 385 yards? This is what **Jennifer Amyx** of Woodsboro, Maryland, did in Johnstown, Pennsylvania, in November 1975. Her time was 4 hours and 56 minutes.

Another five-year-old, **Bucky Cox** of Texas, also completed a marathon in 1978. Her time was slower, 5 hours and 29 minutes; however, two years later she tackled the event again and shaved almost two hours off her time, finishing in 3 hours and 40 minutes.

* * *

For another runner it was a long time between birth and his last marathon on October 10, 1976. **Dimitrion Yordanidis** was 98 years old. Through the streets of Athens, people cheered this runner on. It did not matter that the leaders had finished long ago, because in this land that reveres family and regards the elderly with respect, Yordanidis was definitely a winner in the time of 7 hours, 33 minutes.

On October 15, 1977, **Donald Ritchie** set a world record for running 100 miles at the Crystal Palace in London. The 33-year-old finished the century in 11 hours, 30 minutes, and 51 seconds.

Of the many reasons why a person might take up running, for **Mike Newton** of London, England, it was simply because he was overweight and could no longer fit into his favorite suit. For some, running is a necessary drudgery. Not for Mike Newton. For him it was sheer pleasure. In fact, it seemed he could never get enough. The more he ran, the more he wanted to run. He entered a marathon. For many runners this would be the ultimate running experience. Not for Newton. For him it didn't seem long enough. In 1976 he got wind of a 40-mile race in Epsom. He won it easily in 4 hours and 4 minutes. Was that enough? Not for Newton. He expanded his sights to a 200-kilometer race and won in the world record–setting time of 16 hours and 40 minutes. But he wanted an even longer race.

Mike Newton worked as a security officer; he could

work at night and run during the day. But even with that schedule, he had to take off from work. He ran a 24-hour race and covered 158 miles. He ran a 48-hour race and racked up 227 miles. But it wasn't until 1981 that Newton found the event that could finally satisfy his lust for running: the Nottingham Six Day Race. Day after day Newton ran around the track at Harvey Hadden Stadium. Stopping only to rest, to eat, to use the toilet, to take care of his feet, Mike Newton won the event by logging 505 miles. He not only set a world record for the event but won the *Observer* newspaper's Sports Nut of the Year award. One of the keys to happiness is to find what you are meant to do. Mike Newton was born to run.

On March 19, 1977, 19-year-old **Terry Fox** of Canada received some bad news. A malignant tumor in his right leg required his leg to be amputated six inches above the knee. For some people this would have been the end, but not for Terry Fox. By February 1979, he had begun to train for a run across Canada to raise money for cancer research. Amazingly, this man with an artificial leg jogged some 3,000 miles preparing for his Marathon of Hope. "I'm not a dreamer," Fox told the Canadian Cancer Society. "I'm not saying this will initiate any kind of definitive answer or cure to cancer, but I believe in miracles." By April 12, 1980, Fox and the rest of Canada were ready. Terry Fox began in St. John's, Newfoundland, running about 23 miles each day, as people all over the world began to follow his progress. Unfortunately, after 143 days and 3,339 miles, chest pains forced Fox to stop near Thunder

Bay, Ontario. Once again, he received bad news. Cancer had invaded his lungs. Terry Fox may have stopped running, but his dream of the Marathon of Hope continued. By early 1981, $24 million had been raised, one dollar for each Canadian. Even after Terry Fox's death on June 28, 1981, his legacy is carried on with the Annual Terry Fox Run.

If the name of **Rosie Ruiz** were associated with chutzpah, that would be one thing. But no, it is more like cheat and deceit. When she seemingly won the Boston Marathon on April 21, 1980, there was celebration as the wreath was placed on her head for her 2-hour, 31-minute, 56-second finish. But lo and behold, no one had seen her on parts of the course. It even turned out that her qualifying race, the New York Marathon, had also been bogus. She had been on the subway during the running of the race that she claimed to have finished in 2 hours, 56 minutes, 27 seconds. So after the officials at the Boston Marathon talked to eyewitnesses and pored over thousands of photographs, the real winner was announced, Jacqueline Gareau from Montreal.

World records for both men and women in the six-day race were set in 1984. Twenty-eight-year-old **Yiannis Kouros** from Greece covered 635 miles, 1,385 yards, while 37-year-old **Eleanor Adams** from England completed 500 miles, 1,452 yards.

At the age of 35, **Priscilla Welch** of England took up running to help her quit smoking and to keep her future husband company during his daily workouts. Four years later she ran a 2:28.54 marathon to place sixth at the 1984 Olympic Games. In 1986, Welch placed third at America's Marathon in Chicago; and in 1987, she won the New York City Marathon. At 42, Welch was the oldest person ever to win a major marathon.

But her struggle and accomplishments did not end there. In 1993 Priscilla Welch was diagnosed with breast cancer. "In the time I've got left," she said, "I'll approach running more sensibly. I also hope this has made me a better person—that I'm a bit more compassionate, that I listen to people and that I appreciate life a bit more." Priscilla Welch has gone on to be a writer and inspirational speaker.

Soccer

*"The rules are basically very simple.
Basically it's this: If it moves, kick it;
if it doesn't move, kick it until it does."*
—Phil Woosnam, soccer Hall of Famer

It is reported that the Aztecs had a soccer-type game in which the captain of the winning side was beheaded. Teams would play hard to win, for to win even if it meant to lose one's life in victory was considered a great honor.

Fast-forward to 1942 in Nazi-occupied Russia. Kiev had once sported a crack soccer team known as Dynamo. This once-proud team, now mostly prisoners of war working as porters at a Kiev bakery, formed a new team called **Start**. When the Germans heard about this new team they organized a match between these Ukrainians and a local German military outfit. Start won. Next the Nazis lined up a game for Start with PGS, a much better German team. This time Start won 6–0. "The fact that our team lost," noted the local newspaper, a voice of German propaganda, "must not be regarded as an achievement on the part of members of the Start team."

Two days later, on July 19, 1942, it was arranged that Start should face a good Hungarian team known as MSG Wal. The Ukrainians won 5–1. In a return match they won by a closer margin of 3–2.

The German high command was incensed. The next team to play Start would be the undefeated Flakelf. At the half, Start led by only 2–1. But by game's end the Ukrainians had found the range and run up the score to 5–1.

Afterward, a German officer went to the locker room to tell the Ukranians that they would face Flakelf again in three days, except this time the result would be different. "If you do not lose the game," he told the Start team, "you will be shot."

The next game opened with Start on the attack. They had the Germans on the defense and as the minutes wore on, it became obvious that Start was not going to lose, at least not on the field. The referee blew his whistle. The game was over. The Ukrainians were bused to Babi Yar, where they were lined up and shot. The Start team lay undefeated in a ditch.

On June 29, 1950, the United States did the improbable: they defeated England, 2–1, in World Cup play. **Joe Gaetjens** shot the winning goal after 38 minutes of the game in Belo Horizonte, Brazil. Until then, the US squad with a record of 1–14–1 in international matches had little to brag about. It would be almost 40 years before the US would qualify for another World Cup final round.

On November 19, 1989, the US made it to the World Cup final round with a 1–0 victory over Trinidad and Tobago. The tie was broken in the 31st minute when **Paul Caliguri** netted the winner from 30 yards out.

Swimming

"I swam my brains out."
—Mark Spitz, winner of seven Olympic gold medals
in 1972

For long-distance swimmers, the English Channel has loomed like an aquatic Everest. In May 1857, Captain **Paul Boyton** made the journey in an inflatable bathing suit in just under 24 hours. But the American's suit was so good at keeping him afloat that few considered that the Channel had been conquered by a swimmer.

The next to try to swim the English Channel was 27-year-old **Captain Matthew Webb** of England. A magazine offered a prize, but when the English stock exchange got wind of this merchant captain's ambition, they sweetened the pot considerably.

Webb's first attempt ended in failure. He did not time the tide right, so he found himself being swept along parallel to the shore. The next time he plunged into the water off the Admiralty Pier in Dover, Webb was able to get away from shore and was on his way. He covered over five miles in the first three hours. After that Webb swam the breaststroke at a steady 23 strokes per minute, one mile per hour, until he ran into the jellyfish. In pain, he swam back to the boat and downed some brandy. Swimming wide around the area, he settled back into his rhythm.

At three in the morning Webb had some broth. He floated on his back for some minutes, then fell back into his rhythm. By midmorning it was a tired Webb who struggled toward the French shore. The tide had taken him from his intended destination of Cape Griz-Nez toward Calais. His strokes were down to 15 per minute and he was only making a half mile an hour. But he wasn't giving up. At 10:41 on the morning of August 25, 1875, Webb stumbled ashore. "La Manche" (French for *sleeve*) had been conquered. Webb had swum the 21-mile expanse of water between England and France (actually, he had swum closer to 38 miles) in 21 hours and 45 minutes.

Immediately, this Englishman's fame was launched. Captain Webb was in great demand for public appearances on both sides of the Atlantic. While touring in the United States, Webb was challenged by Paul Boyton. The contest would be a race of 25 miles off Newport, Rhode Island, and the winner would receive $1,000. The two swimmers themselves sweetened the pot by wagering $500.

Webb showed up at the beach at the appointed time wearing his swim trunks; Boyton was wearing a wetsuit that would keep him not only warm but also afloat. All went well for each swimmer for the first 10 miles. Then Webb suffered leg cramps. The cramps were so severe that he had to be pulled into the boat. Boyton paddled on to victory.

Not taking into account the cold-water conditions of the race—a rubber suit versus swim trunks—Captain Matthew Webb felt deeply humiliated. Wanting to reclaim his honor as well as to make money—the point of his worldwide tour—Webb needed something to capture the imagination of the public. He hit upon the solution: Niagara Falls.

Two miles below the main falls were roiling waters with waves that could reach 30 feet. Just beyond these Whirlpool Rapids churned the whirlpool itself. It was a place no less treacherous than Charybdis. And in trying to brave this expanse of water, Webb, like Odysseus, found himself caught between a rock and a hard place.

"At noon today [July 1883] he went to Niagara Falls with the avowed intention of swimming the Whirlpool Rapids," wrote a reporter assigned to Webb's attempted crossing. "The announcement that he would undertake so perilous a feat was not credited, and very few persons paid any attention to it. There were no more visitors at the Falls than on ordinary days."

With a boatman experienced in these treacherous waters alongside, Matthew Webb waded into the waters at a couple of minutes past four. Immediately, he was swept downstream. His head would disappear and then he would reappear still swimming. Again and again, he would disappear and then reappear. But as Captain Webb passed by the first bridge, the "excited spectators watched in breathless suspense. They looked below, to the sides, and all about, but could see no sign of him. They rushed down the riverbank as far as they could go, but saw nothing of the strong swimmer. They looked at each other and said, 'The man is lost.' " Indeed he was. At 4:19 the official search for Webb ended. Four days later the body of Matthew Webb was found washed up in Lewiston, New York.

In 1882 Gerald K. Fox and Washington La Brie bet $250 that no one could swim across the East River in New York City with his feet bound together and his hands tied behind his back. The swimmer selected to attempt this was **Marquis Bibbero**. Taking into consideration the unpredictability of the river, the swimmer would have three chances.

On May 31, 1882, Marquis Bibbero smeared himself with lard and porpoise oil. Once in the water he swam "like a porpoise, with his knees." Halfway across the river, the current began carrying him quickly toward the Battery. After being in the water for an hour, Bibbero signaled that it was over for him that day. An assistant jumped into the water to free his hands and feet.

The next attempt came three weeks later. This time Bibbero tried starting from the Brooklyn side and smeared his body with turpentine and goose grease. "He wriggled like an eel," but again the tide caught him and wore him out. It was a cold Bibbero who was helped into the boat.

The final swim was scheduled for July 3. Fortune smiled on the final swim scheduled on July 3, for the tide was not strong. In only 20 minutes Bibbero was approaching the other bank. However, there was the problem of boat traffic. So many people had turned out to witness the figure in the river that "passing steamers churned up the water and sent waves over Bibbero. . . ."

Ten yards from the pier he had to be pulled into the boat. After a short discussion, the wager was settled and Bibbero was rewarded with a hundred dollars.

The swimming events at the first Olympics in 1896 were not held in a pool but in the open sea, the Bay of Zea, not far from the Grecian port of Piraeus. A man from Budapest under the name of **Alfred Hajos** (his real name was Guttmann) won the 100-meter freestyle in the slow time of 1:22.2 (slow, until you take into account the 12-foot-high waves and the water temperature of 55 degrees Fahrenheit).

In the 1,200-meter freestyle (the forerunner of the 1,500), Hajos won again. Although at 18:22.2, he was two and a half minutes ahead of the second-place winner, Jean Andreou of Greece, Hajos was not dreaming of Olympic glory.

"I must say that I shivered from the thought of what would happen if I got a cramp from the cold water," Hajos said. "My will to live completely overcame my desire to win. I cut through the water with a powerful determination and only became calm when the boats came back in my direction, and began to fish out the numbed competitors who were giving up the struggle."

In 1920, **Ethelda Bleibtrey** became the first woman to win a gold medal at the Olympic Games. (Officially, that is; see Margaret Abbott under Golf.) Bleibtrey's event was the 100-meter freestyle.

In March 1928, **Lottie Schoemmel** beat by an hour the swimming endurance record set by Edith Johnson in 1881. Schoemmel swam for 32 hours at the Deauville Pool at Miami Beach.

In 1930, **Fred Newton** swam the length of the Mississippi River—all 1,836 miles of it. It took Newton six months to accomplish this Herculean task. In 2001, Martin Strel waltzed all over this record by swimming the 1,878-mile Danube River in only 58 days.

On April 20, 1931, **Myrtle Huddleston** floated in the water at Bimini Plunge, New York, for 87 hours and 47 seconds. She had only known how to swim for five hours when she established her record. Mrs. Huddleston was a natural; she later set several long-distance swimming records.

Greta Anderson, a housewife who swam, in October 1932 swam the 22 miles from San Diego to Catalina Island. But then she accomplished something that no one had done before. She swam back. Her time for the 44-mile swim was 26 hours, 53 minutes, 28 seconds. Greta Anderson had become a swimmer who did housework.

In the 1940s, **Charles "Zimmy the human fish" Zibelman** caught the public's imagination. Zimmy was a swimmer with no legs. In Honolulu he established a record by swimming for 100 hours straight. And the feat that hit all the newspapers was when he swam the Hudson River from Albany, New York, to New York City, a distance of 147 miles.

* * *

In 1947, **Thomas Blower**, a bloke from Nottingham, England, became the first person ever to swim across the Irish Sea. Entering the water at Donaghadee, Northern Ireland, Blower swam 25 miles to the shore of Scotland, a wee bit from Port Patrick, in the time of 15 hours, 25 minutes.

On July 22, 1948, a Peruvian named **Daniel Carpio** became the first person to swim the 8 miles of the Strait of Gibraltar from Spain to Morocco in 9 hours, 20 minutes. Nowadays the ferry only does it twice as fast.

On September 11, 1951, American **Florence Chadwick** swam the English Channel from England to France in 16 hours and 22 minutes. The year before she had swum from France to England. Chadwick was the first woman to swim the English Channel in both directions.

On September 9, 1954, **Marilyn Bell** set off from the shore of Lake Ontario with the goal of becoming the first person ever to swim the 32 miles across this Great Lake. Twenty hours and 56 minutes later, she reached the other side—cold, exhausted, and victorious.

In 1958, **Robert F. Legge** entered the water of the Panama Canal to swim its length of 28 and a half miles. After braving the heavy shipping in the locks, the 53-year-old US Navy doctor reached Balboa 21 hours and 54 minutes later.

*   *   *

Diane Struble never swam competitively until 1958, when the 26-year-old swam the 42-mile length of Lake George in 35 and a half hours, a world record for a freshwater distance. In June 1959, she swam Vermont's Lake Champlain during its worst storm in 20 years. Struble also swam around Manhattan, a distance of 27 miles, in less than 12 hours, and swam the Boston Harbor in 13 hours and 24 minutes.

Having already swum the English Channel three times, **Antonio Abertondo** longed to do something more phenomenal: to make a round-trip swim of the Channel. On September 20, 1961, the 42-year-old Argentinean waded into the water off the Dover coast of England and began swimming. Arriving 18 hours, 50 minutes later at a beach near Calais, France, Abertondo rested only long enough to gulp down a cup of hot coffee before starting the swim from Cap Gris Nez, France, back to England. The return journey proved even more difficult as the tides threatened to drag him out to sea; he also began to hallucinate, imagining huge fish surrounding him. On September 21, after a total of 43 hours, 5 minutes in the water, an exhausted Abertondo staggered onto English soil and collapsed.

When the thought of swimming the English Channel comes up, the image is often of a swimmer coated in grease braving the choppy water with a boat cruising nearby. Forty-four-year-old scuba diver **Fred Baldasare** of Cocoa Beach, Florida, sank this image. Baldasare wanted to become the first person to swim the channel underwater. Having learned about currents and the difficulties of doing this in two previous attempts, Baldasare entered the water in July, 1962 near Cap Gris Nez, where many who attempt to swim the Channel begin. He followed a cage dragged by a boat because it is easy to get disoriented when swimming underwater. Even so, the currents took him off course and he wound up swimming about 42 miles. (The measured distance is 22 miles.) Still, he made it to shore at Sandwich in Kent, England, in just a shade over 19 hours.

Until 1975, no one had swum Lake Erie from Long Point, Canada, to Presque Isle, Pennsylvania. Not until November of that year. It was then that **Pat Bundy**, a senior from Cathedral Preparatory High School in Erie, Pennsylvania, swam the 31-mile distance in 25 hours, 52 minutes.

In 1975, **Diana Nyad**, a student at New York University, swam around Manhattan (beginning and ending in the East River at a pier near Carl Schurz Park) in the record time of 7 hours, 57 minutes for the 28 miles. That year Nyad also swam across Lake Ontario in 20 hours, and in 1979 the appropriately named Nyad set the nonstop swimming record of 102.5 miles.

On September 7–8, 1977, **Cynthia Nicholas**, a 19-year-old from Canada, swam a double crossing of the English Channel in only 18 hours, 55 minutes, the fastest round trip ever. She broke her own record in

1982 with a swim of 18:51, and crossed the channel 19 times in all.

One of the most difficult of all places to swim is the ocean. The waves, the tides, the weather, the unforeseen danger—it all adds up to unpredictability and trouble. This did not deter **Walter Poenisch**; he relished the challenge. His objective? To swim from Cuba to the United States. As those who have set out in makeshift boats from Cuba for the States have shown, this can be a treacherous journey.

On July 13, 1978, this 64-year-old American entered the waters off Havana. One variable was controlled. He was swimming inside a shark cage. And there was something else in his favor. He was swimming with ocean currents, not against them. Now comes the hard part. Poenisch swam for 34 hours and 15 minutes until he reached Little Duck Key, Florida. From Havana to Little Duck Key is 128 miles. That's almost four miles per hour. Impressive at any age, but at 64? (In 1997, Australian Suzie Mahoney shattered this record by swimming from Cuba to the US in 24 and a half hours.

Swimming the Bering Straits from the two volcanic islands of Little Diomede, Alaska, to Big Diomede in Russia is not a great distance. It is only 2.4 miles. But no boats had been in these waters since 1948 and no one had ever attempted to swim it. It is especially difficult because of the changing tides, the strong currents, and the frigid water temperatures.

On August 7, 1987, a 30-year-old American, **Lynne**

Cox, entered the ocean water off Alaska at 9:30 in the morning. The water of the Arctic Ocean was extremely cold, varying from 34 to 44 degrees Fahrenheit, and the strong current made it a difficult six-mile swim. There were also sharks patrolling this stretch of water that crosses over the International Date Line, but Cox would not swim inside a shark cage or even don a wet suit. She would be accompanied by two canoes, one carrying three doctors and the other five journalists. The main task for the doctors was to monitor her body temperature (she had swallowed a capsule before the swim so a reading could be taken every 20 minutes). It was important that her temperature not go below 93 degrees. As Cox approached land, she realized that the place that the Russians were waiting for her was half a mile down the shore. She spent the additional time to swim there even though it meant more time in the freezing, turbulent water. She finally went ashore on Big Diomede; the swim had taken 2 hours and 6 minutes and her temperature had dipped to 94 degrees.

Months later, Soviet leader Mikhail Gorbachev said: "It took one brave American by the name of Lynne Cox just two hours to swim from one of our countries to the other. We saw on television how sincerely amiable was the meeting between our people and Americans when she stepped onto the Soviet shore. She proved by her courage how closely to each other our peoples live."

Tennis

*"A champion is afraid of losing.
Everyone else is afraid of winning."*
—Billie Jean King

In 1877, **Spencer Gore** won the first Wimbledon singles championship. He cut through the field with a daring brand of volleying and an underhand service that capitalized on a "double dose of cut." The next year Gore lost in the challenge round to Frank Hadow. Gore then disappeared from the tennis scene.

Frank Hadow had a tea plantation in Ceylon, but he also found the time to play tennis. When on holiday in England in 1878, he entered Wimbledon. During the whole tournament, Hadow did not lose a single set. One of this English righthander's best weapons was the lob. This was the first time anyone had ever seen this stroke and Hadow used it to topple the first Wimbledon champion, Spencer Gore, a serve and volleyer. Frank Hadow did not take a vacation to England the next year, so he did not defend his crown. As a matter of fact, there is no record that he ever played tennis again.

* * *

After hearing about the reinstitution of the Olympic Games in the modern era from Thrasyvoalos Manaos, a Greek classmate, **John Boland**, a student at Oxford, decided to travel to Greece. After the Irishman's arrival, Manaos, who was also the official secretary of the organizing committee, entered Boland in the tennis competition. Without much stiff competition, Boland made it to the final with Demis Kasdaglis of Greece. Boland won the gold medal in straight sets, 7–5, 6–4, 6–1.

The winner of the 1901 US women's singles tournament, **Elisabeth Moore**, had not only played a five setter with Myrtle McAteer (6–4, 3–6, 7–5, 2–6, 6–2) for the championship but had also played a match with Marion Jones the day before that had also gone five sets (4–6, 1–6, 9–7, 9–7, 6–3). Shortly afterward the US Lawn Tennis Association decided that women should not play five-set tennis anymore. This so infuriated Moore (the US singles champion in 1896, 1901, 1903, and 1905) that she wrote to the USLTA that "Lawn tennis is a game not alone of skill but of endurance as well, and I fail to see why such a radical change should be made to satisfy a few players who do not take the time or do not have the inclination to get themselves in proper condition for playing." This "radical change" persists to the present day.

In 1905, **May Sutton** became the first American to win the women's singles title at Wimbledon. With three older tennis-playing sisters in her family, Sutton for quite some time hadn't even been the best player in her family.

* * *

In August 1917, **Lucy Diggs Slowe** won the women's singles title at the first American Tennis Association tournament held in Baltimore. Slowe was the first African-American woman to win a tennis championship.

The 1950 national championship at Forest Hills put two unlikely candidates for champion across the net from each other. One was **Herbert Flam**, a player who often challenged but never quite got to the top because he lacked an all-around game and was especially handicapped by a weak serve and forehand. But what he lacked in an all-around game, he partly made up for with a huge degree of hustle. That year in the semifinals Flam had met Gardner Mulloy in the semifinals. There was one point in particular that showed Flam's assets and deficiencies. After Flam had charged the net, Gardner hit a lob that bounced on the baseline. Gardner turned around and walked slowly to the service line. Flam hustled back, got to the lob, and hit a cross-court winner. Across the net from Flam in the final was **Art Larsen**. Having survived a landing at Omaha Beach in World War II that had wiped out most of his unit, Larsen had developed a ton of tics after this experience. He was left to wonder, Why had he survived? He did a lot of things the same way every time after that. When he returned to the States, he also returned to tennis. But the compulsive behavior followed him onto the court.

"I wouldn't step on any kind of chalk line," Larsen said. "I always had to have the winning ball to put back in play. I'd cross on the opposite side of the net from any opponent, tiptoe over baselines, even in competition, tap the baseline three times before serving, stand for a second with my back to the court. The doctor told me my 'jinxes' were 'compulsory suggestiveness' and he convinced me of one thing: I was wasting a heck of a lot of energy on them."

Flam and Larsen went to five sets. By the end Larsen was still going strong and going through his routine to victory, while Flam was so spent he was having trouble standing up.

At the US Nationals on August 29, 1951, **Earl Cochell** started out making a nuisance of himself, then a fool, and finally he became a detriment to the game. Tied with Gardner Mulloy at one set each, Cochell had fallen behind 4–1. Time after time Cochell stopped play with verbal fusillades directed at the chair umpire, Ellsworth Davenport. The crowd got into the match, got on Cochell's case, and the American tried to climb up to Davenport's chair to wrestle the microphone away from him and explain himself to the crowd. Cochell settled down enough to go on to lose the match to Mulloy, 4–6, 6–2, 6–1, 6–2. But Earl Cochell was to lose more than just the match. For his unsportsmanlike conduct the USTA took the extreme measure of banning Cochell for life. Even though they later rescinded his ban and reinstated him, Earl Cochell's career was kaput.

Playing at Wimbledon in the early 1970s, **Cathy Lee Crosby** of the US lost her singles match in the first round as well as her doubles with sister Linda Lou in the first round. Ms. Crosby may not have been a wonder woman at the tournament, but in 1974 she starred in a made-for-TV movie called *Wonder Woman*, about the comic book character.

The date: May 26, 1975. The place: the Surrey Championships at Surbiton, England. The players: **Anthony Fawcett** of Rhodesia and **Keith Glass** of England. What they did: Fawcett and Glass played a game that lasted 80 points.

Australian **Chris O'Neil** was a five-eleven serve and volleyer who surprised the experts at the 1978 Australian Open. Ranked one hundred and eleventh and unseeded in the tournament, the 22-year-old right-hander breezed through her side of the draw to meet Betsy Nagelson in the final. (Nagelson was ranked only sixty-eighth.) O'Neil won, 6–3, 7–6, to pick up the winner's purse of $6,000. (Compare that to the appearance fees available to the pros today.) Although she would go up in ranking to number 80, Chris O'Neil would never win another important professional tournament.

Ricky Tolston and **Jeff Sutton** may not have been names on the tote boards at a major tournament, but they did do something that no number-one player has ever done. On May 7, 1979, they began play at the Bill Faye Park in Kingston, North Carolina. On May 11, 105 hours later, they were still playing. It is the longest singles match ever played.

* * *

At Wimbledon in 1980, **John Austin** teamed up with his wunderkind sister, Tracy, to win the mixed doubles championship against Mark Edmondson and Dianne Fromholtz. (Tracy Austin was coming off an unprecedented win at the US Open the year before.) The Austins' score was 4–6, 6–4, 7–5.

On March 12, 1988, **Will Duggan**, age 42, and **Ron Kapp**, age 39, were playing a match at the Santa Barbara Municipal Stadium in California. The two of them fell into a groove and staged a rally that went on for a total of 6,202 shots. How long would a rally like this take? Over three and a half hours. After the rally was over, Duggan outlasted Kapp to take the set by the score of 6–2, 3–6, 7–5.

On June 29, 1991, **Nick Brown** of England pulled off a major upset at Wimbledon. In fact, Brown is the lowest-ranked player ever to unseat a seed at Wimbledon. Brown was ranked below 590 when he ousted Goran Ivanisevic from Croatia, the tenth seed, 4–6, 6–4, 7–6, 6–3. After that sterling match, Brown resorted to form and lost to Thierry Champion, 7–6, 1–6, 7–5, 6–3.

On February 8, 1998, **Petr Korda** found himself at the end of a long uphill battle to return to a Grand Slam final. It had been six years since he had been in the finals of the 1992 French Open, where he lost to Jim Courier in straight sets. After operations on his thighs to repair a muscle problem and an operation on his sinuses (acute sinus trouble had forced him to withdraw from the 1997 US Open after beating Pete Sampras in the fourth round), Korda was feeling better than he had in years and feeling younger than his 30 years. The six-foot-three, 160-pound Korda had outlasted Sweden's Jonas Bjorkman in five sets in the quarterfinals and gotten by Karol Kucera of Slovakia in four sets in the semifinals.

"I know the time for me now is five until midnight," said Korda on the eve of the finals with Marcelo Rios of Chile, "but sometimes those five minutes can last a long time."

Korda's years of preparation in Czechoslovakia paid off. "I was ready, you know, to spend five hours on the court." Eighty-five minutes was more like it. Petr Korda manhandled Marcelo Rios, 6–2, 6–2, 6–2.

It may have been his last hurrah, but for Petr Korda, who fell to his knees at the last point, it was long and sweet.

Track and Field

"My head was exploding, my stomach ripping, and even the tips of my fingers ached. The only thing I could think was, 'If I live, I will never run again.' "
—Tom Courtney, 800-meter gold medalist in 1956

The first person to run the 100-yard dash in 10 seconds was Philadelphian **Horace Lee**, who set the magical mark in 1877.

Before Jesse Owens, there was **John Owens**, the first person to break 10 seconds. On October 11, 1890, John Owens ran the 100-yard dash in 9 4/5 seconds at the AAU Track and Field Championships in Washington, DC.

Ray Ewry didn't go to the Olympics until he was 27 and before he was through he had won 10 gold medals. Ewry didn't compete in events that are still around today. His specialties were the standing high jump, the standing long jump, and the standing triple jump. He won three gold medals at both the 1900 Olympics and the 1904 Olympics. After that the standing triple jump was eliminated, so he won only two gold medals at both the Intercalated Games of 1906 and the 1908 Olympics. His personal bests were 5 feet 3 inches in the standing high jump, a world record 11 feet 4 and seven-eighth inches in the standing long jump, and 34 feet 8 and a half inches in the standing triple jump. (The standing high jump and the standing long jump were dropped from the Olympics after 1912.) He also held the amateur record of 9 feet 3 inches for the backward standing long jump.

It was amazing that Ray Ewry was even able to compete in sports. As a youth he had polio and was confined to a wheelchair. It was only through his determination not to be paralyzed for life and his strenuous exercise regimen that he was able to become an athlete.

At the 1904 Olympic Games in St. Louis, **Joseph Stadler** of the United States became the first African-American athlete to win an Olympic medal. After tying Lawson Robertson in the standing high jump at 4 feet 9 inches, Stadler won the jump-off for the silver medal.

Paul Pilgrim wasn't even on the US team that journeyed to the 1906 Olympic Games in Athens. (Known as the interim games, these games are not recognized as official although they did help continue the Olympic movement.) Pilgrim traveled on his own, but once there was allowed to complete. This member of the New York Athletic Club surprised everyone by winning the 400 meters. His slow time of 53.2 spoke to the tightness of the turns of the track. The next day Pilgrim won the 800 in 2:01.5. These were the only two major races that Paul Pilgrim ever won.

* * *

John Baxter "Doc" Taylor Jr. became the first African American to win a gold medal at the Olympic Games as a member of the winning 4 × 400-meter relay team in 1908. Taylor ran the third leg and helped open up a 25-yard lead. The US team's winning time was 3:29.4. The 24-year-old Doctor Taylor succumbed five months later to typhoid on the eve of opening his medical practice.

Also at the 1908 Olympic Games was a theology student named **Forrest Smithson**. Disliking the idea that there were events scheduled for Sunday, this hurdler protested by carrying a copy of the Bible in his left hand. It didn't slow him down, however, as Smithson won the finals of the 110-meter hurdles. Smithson's 15 minutes of fame was even shorter on the track, winning the event in a world record–setting time of 15.0 seconds.

Using the scissors kick, the best that Stanford University graduate **George Horine** could do in the high jump was 5 feet 1 inch. But when his family moved to Palo Alto, the high jump area that he set up behind the house necessitated that he make his approach from the left and take off with his left foot. Consequently, he had to roll over the bar, and his heights increased dramatically. In 1910, he jumped 6 feet 1 and a half inches; in 1911, 6 feet 4 inches; and at the Olympic trials on May 18, 1912, George Horine leaped 6 feet 7 inches for a new world record. Unfortunately, at the 1912 Olympics Horine could only do 6 feet 2 and a quarter inches for a bronze medal.

* * *

Betty Robinson was only a 16-year-old high school girl from Riverdale, Illinois, and she was representing the United States in track and field at the Olympic Games in Amsterdam. This was amazing for two reasons, both personal and historical.

"I was running for the train that took me to school one day. The coach of the track team watched out of the window of the train as I caught up to it and suggested that I should develop my talent. Till then I didn't even know there were women's races."

In the second track meet of her life, Robinson tied the world record of 12 seconds for 100 meters. Her fourth meet took place at the 1928 Olympic Games.

The historical reason was that before 1928 there had never been a track and field event for women in the Olympics. That year there would be five: 100 meters, 800 meters, 4 × 100-meter relay, discus, and high jump.

The final of the first event, the 100 for women, was held on July 31. There were six women lined up at the start: three Canadians, two Germans, and one American. False starts claimed a Canadian and a German runner. That can be very upsetting for the other runners, but it didn't seem to bother Betty Robinson. (Her crisis had occurred earlier when she discovered she had two left shoes and had to return to the locker room at the last minute.) When the runners finally broke clean, she ran strong from start to finish, and by her upraised arms and the smile on her face it was evident that she knew she had upset the favorite, Fanny Rosenfeld from Canada. A couple of days later Robinson added a silver medal by anchoring the relay team that came in second to the Canadians.

The story could have ended right there with a curtsy to royalty and a hero's welcome back in Illinois, but it didn't. Life often works out to be more messy than that. Robinson had wanted to be in the 1932 Olympics, but a plane crash the year before left her in a coma for seven weeks. It was two years before she was even able to run again.

In 1936, Betty Robinson made the Olympic team in the 4 × 100 relay. In the finals, she was running the third leg, running about 10 meters behind the world-record German team, about to hand off to Helen Stephens, the anchor for the US team, when the fourth runner for the German team threw up her hands. Germany's Ilse Dorffeldt had dropped the baton. Stephens, the winner of the gold medal in the 100, cruised to victory. After all that hardship and hard luck, Betty Robinson had won her second gold medal.

Sixteen-year-old high jumper **Jean Shiley** came out of nowhere when she went to the Olympic trials held in Newark in 1928. She wasn't even on a team; she just represented herself. She had trained, though, with Lawson Robertson, the University of Pennsylvania track coach. After qualifying in Newark, Shiley went by ship with the rest of the US team to the 1928 Olympic Games in Amsterdam. On the day of her event, Shiley placed fourth in the high jump.

Comparatively speaking, Jean Shiley was a seasoned veteran for the 1932 Olympics in Los Angeles and was even named captain of the women's team. At the trials she had tied with Babe Didrikson. It was the same thing at the Games. Shiley went head to head with Babe Didrikson, an athlete whose fame was increasing daily. The other women were rooting for Shiley (Babe could be boorish about being the best), so they were probably disappointed when they tied at 5 feet 5 inches. But the officials spotted something illegal about Babe's form. You had to take off with one foot and land with the other, and your shoulders could not go over the bar before the rest of your body. In any case, the jump-off did not continue, and Jean Shiley had won the gold medal.

Jean Shiley should have been the favorite at the 1936 Games, but she had given some swimming lessons and done some lifeguarding, so the US officials decided that this made her a professional.

The date of June 29, 1932 was one that shined brightly for **Zygmunt Heljasz** of Poland. That was when he put the shot 52 feet 8 inches in a meet between Poznan, Poland, and Vienna, Austria, to better the existing world record by one-half inch.

After that day there seemed to be only disappointments. One of the favorites in the 1932 Olympics, the Polish shotputter registered a disappointing 47 feet 6 and a half inches for ninth place. At the European Championships in 1934, Zygmunt Heljasz improved somewhat to 48 feet 6 inches, but still finished in ninth place. He was never to come close to his one moment of glory.

*   *   *

Why not let me compete? was the plea of **Duncan McNaughton** to the Canadian Olympic Association. "I'm good and I'm in Los Angeles anyway," reasoned this Canadian high jumper, who was attending the University of Southern California. Eventually the officials gave in and McNaughton was able to participate in the 1932 Olympics. McNaughton even made it to the finals with a leap of 6 feet 5 inches, but so did three other jumpers. As the bar was raised and lowered, as it was done in those days to decide a winner, Cornelius Johnson of the US and Simon Toribio of the Philippines were eliminated. Then it was down to two friends and teammates at USC, McNaughton and American Robert Van Osdel. Van Osdel missed the height. Van Osdel, who had always coached McNaughton, did not stop now. The American told the Canadian to work on his kick. McNaughton did and cleared the bar for the gold medal.

In March of 1932 Ben Eastman of Stanford University ran 400 meters in 46.4, breaking his world record by a full second. As the world prepared for the Olympic Games, Eastman appeared unbeatable. But that was before he lined up against **Bill Carr** from the University of Pennsylvania at the intercollegiate championships on July 2. Carr seemingly came from nowhere to nip Eastman by two-tenths of a second in 47 flat. Two weeks later at the Olympic tryouts, Carr again stormed from behind to beat Eastman in 46.9, again by two-tenths of a second. Eastman, who also had a chance to medal in the 800, decided to concentrate on the 400 in the Olympics. Eastman won his semifinal in 47.6; Carr won his semifinal in 47.2. In the finals Eastman went out in front and was leading with only 80 meters to go. It was then that Carr turned it on and won by two meters in the world-record time of 46.2, again two-tenths of a second faster than Eastman. "You don't need to sympathize," remarked Eastman afterward. "I know when I'm licked by a better runner." Unfortunately, Carr's brilliant career was cut short by a broken pelvis suffered in a car crash in March 1933.

Glenn Morris only entered three decathlons in his whole life. The first one was at the 1936 Kansas Relays held in April. He set an American record of 7,575 points. The second was in June, when the 24-year-old won the AAU/Olympic trials with a world record of 7,875 points. The third was on August 7–8 at the 1936 Olympic Games in Berlin. En route to the gold medal, Morris set an Olympic and world record of 7,900 points, a record that stood until 1950.

Next, Morris tried swinging through the trees as Tarzan to bad girl Eleanor Holm's Jane (the swimmer who had been suspended from the 1936 team for drinking) in *Tarzan's Revenge*. He wound up his athletic career playing football for the 1940 Detroit Lions.

Archie Williams was not much of an athlete in high school, but he did show speed, so he went out for track. He didn't win any races, however, until he went to college. First, it was at San Mateo Junior College in California. Under the tutelage of Tex Bird, the track coach, Williams began to cut down on his times in the 400, enough so he could go to Berkeley and make the track team there as a walk-on.

Brutus Hamilton, the coach at Berkeley, was instrumental in turning Williams into a stellar runner. "You can be what you want to be," Hamilton would tell Williams, "and I can't make you do it. I can't run for you. So just get out there and do the best you can."

That spring Williams ran a 49.7. With Hamilton's help, Williams began to believe in himself and his times began to show it. The next fall Williams ran a 48.5. By the following spring he was making everyone a believer by winning the PAC 8 with a 46.8, a meet record. But it was just a warm-up for things to come. He won the Pacific AAU at Stanford in 46.3, and then at the NCAA meet in Chicago, in a semifinal heat, Williams ran a world record 400 meters in 46.1.

"Right out of a clear sky," Williams said. "I still don't believe it. And the funny part of it is you never know when it's going to happen because this was in a trial heat, no pressure. All I had to do was be in the first four. I was just floating along."

After qualifying for the Olympic team at a meet on Randall's Island, it was a boat ride and then on to the Olympics in Berlin. The 400 was held over a two-day period. On the first day the first race was at 10:00 and the second at 2:30. The next day the semifinals were at 3:30 and the finals at 5:00. There wasn't much time to think about it, so Williams ran every race as if it were the final.

In the actual final, Archie Williams and another American, James LuValle, led the field into the last 100 meters. Then Great Britain's Godfrey Brown made his move and caught LuValle with 40 meters to go. Brown was only inches behind when a tired Archie Williams crossed the finish line for the gold in 46.5. Brown was second in 46.7. LuValle was third in 46.8.

"That moment of victory was just something that proved that I could do something," the self-effacing Williams concluded years later. "Forget about being the greatest in the world. You just beat the ones who showed up that day."

Most everyone knows that Jesse Owens won the 200-meter dash at the 1936 Olympics. But finishing only four-tenths of a second behind (at 21.1) was another runner from the United States, **Mack Robinson**. Even guys who come in in second place can be heroes. But in Mack Robinson's case it was made even more difficult because his younger brother would later overshadow this second-place finisher's claim to fame as Jesse Owens had done that afternoon in Munich. For his younger brother was none other than Jackie Robinson.

Heroes can also be people who don't make it to the finals. At the 1936 Olympics was a hurdler named **Tidye Pickett**, the first African-American woman ever to compete in the Olympics, who reached the semifinals in the 100-meter hurdles before being eliminated. (Tidye Pickett and an African-American teammate, **Louise Stokes**, should have been in the 1932 Olympics; however, at race time they were both mysteriously replaced.)

* * *

Louis Zamperini was a high-school miler when he made the 1936 US Olympic team. But he often made news in other ways. When Zamperini was in Berlin, he tried to steal Hitler's very own flag and was beaten up by Hitler's guards. Still, he did find time to take an eighth in the 5000 meters in 14:46.8. This was 24.6 seconds behind the winner, Gunnar Höckert of Finland, but not bad for a high-school kid. Zamperini's next major move was not long after returning home, when he set an intercollegiate record of 4:08.3 for the mile.

But Zamperini's political life did not end in Berlin. (His life sometimes sounds like something from Voltaire's *Candide*.) During World War II he was shot down in the Pacific and floated on a raft in the sea for 47 days. Then he spent two and a half years in a prison camp, where he was starved and beaten. When the prison camp was liberated at the war's end, Zamperini weighed only 77 pounds. After becoming a missionary, he returned to Japan, located his prison guards, and forgave them.

It was 9:00 in the evening of August 5, 1936, at the Olympic Games in Berlin, and there were three competitors left in the pole vault: Earle Meadows of the United States and two athletes from Japan, **Shuhei Nishida** and **Sueo Oe**. The bar had been set at a new Olympic record of 14 feet 3 and a quarter inches. On their first attempts, all three missed. On their second jumps, Earle Meadows cleared the height. Nishida and Oe missed on their second and third attempts. They would continue to vault for the silver medal. (Today, that would be determined by who had fewer misses.) But it had become impossible to continue in the darkness. The two Japanese friends returned to the Olympic Village thinking that they had tied for second.

The next day they discovered that for some unknown reason Nishida had been awarded the silver and Oe the bronze. Both friends were upset by this decision. They agreed that when they returned to Japan they would have each medal cut in half and made into two silver-bronze medals. These medals have come to be called the Medals of Eternal Friendship.

Twenty-two-year-old **Ilsebill Pfenning** placed sixth in the women's high jump at the 1938 European Championships. The winner, Dora Ratjen, also set a world record with a jump of 1.70 meters. But it turned out later that Ratjen was not a woman after all, so the record was bogus as well.

But for some strange reason, officials forgot about Ratjen's disqualification, so that when Pfenning leaped 1.66 meters in 1941, it was not hailed as a world record as it should have been. No, it wasn't until 1976, 35 years later, that Ilsebill Pfenning was officially recognized for having held the world record. The sanguine 60-year-old's response? "Better late than never."

At the 1948 Olympics in London, high-jumper **Alice Coachman** became the first African-American woman to win a gold medal and the only American woman to garner a gold that year. Her Olympic record of 5 feet 6 and one-eighth inches stood until 1956, when it was topped by three and a quarter inches by Mildred McDaniel of the United States.

Lindy Remigino wasn't even supposed to make the team. He had squeaked into the Olympic tryouts with a fifth at the NCAA and then onto the team with a photo finish. Also, he was running because the leading US sprinter, Jim Golliday, was hurt. Then in the Olympic semifinals, one of the favorites, Arthur Bragg of Morgan State, had pulled a hamstring and was out of the running.

So there was the improbable 21-year-old Lindy Remigino, a Manhattan College student from Hartford, Connecticut, in lane three in the finals of the 100 meters at the 1952 Olympic Games in Helsinki. The favorites were Jamaica's Herb McKenley on his left in lane two (McKenley was the world record holder in the 400 but was running the 100 because it seemed wide open) and Great Britain's McDonald Bailey in lane five. To Remigino's immediate right in lane four was his US teammate Dean Smith. At the gun, Smith got a good start; at 50 meters, Remigino was in the lead; at 90 meters, McKenley passed him.

"I was sure I had lost the race," said Remigino. "I started my lean too early . . . and I saw Herb McKenley shoot past me. I was heartsick. I figured I had blown it."

Remigino congratulated a happy McKenley, but the judges couldn't tell who the winner was. For them it looked like any of four runners might have won. It wasn't until 20 minutes later, after they had studied a photo of the finish, that the results were posted on the scoreboard. First place and the gold went to Remigino; second and the silver to McKenley; third and the bronze to Bailey; and fourth to Smith. Remigino was one inch in front of McKenley and only fourteen inches in front of Smith. All four runners were clocked in 10.4 seconds.

Lindy Remigino also ran the third leg on the 4 × 100 relay. In the finals, Dean Smith ran first, Harrison Dillard second, and fourth was Andrew Stanfield, who had opened up a two-meter gap over a Russian runner for the victory in 40.1 seconds. So, Lindy Remigino, a guy who wasn't even supposed to make the team, had wound up with two gold medals.

There were two favorites in the 1500 meters at the 1952 Olympics in Helsinki: Germany's Werner Lueg, a co-holder of the world record at 3:43.0, and Great Britain's Roger Bannister. But that's not how things worked out.

For the first lap of the race Norway's Auden Boysen held the lead; Germany's Rolf Lamers led the second lap, until Werner Lueg took over for the third lap and stayed in front during the fourth lap until the final turn. Then, Luxembourg's **Josef "Josy" Barthel**, followed closely by the United States's Robert McMillen, ran all the way from last place to overtake the tiring Lueg 50 meters from the finish.

"Five meters to run, the victory is mine, and just as I had always dreamed in secret, I raised my arms, I smiled and I crossed the finish line." Barthel was first in the Olympic record of 3:45.1. McMillen was second in 3:45.2. Both runners had exceeded their personal bests by over three seconds. Lueg was third in 3:45.4.

As fourth place finisher Roger Bannister commented while watching Luxembourg's first gold medal winner crying in joy: "I had found new meaning in the Olympic words that the important thing was not the winning but the taking part—not the conquering but the fighting well."

The favorite in the 400 meters at the 1956 Olympics in Melbourne was Louis Jones of the US, who had set a world record of 45.2 at the US Olympic tryouts. It certainly wasn't **Charley Jenkins**, the third-place finisher. At the Olympics, Louis Jones took a no-sweat approach, running only as fast as he needed to get into the finals. It took Jenkins, on the other hand, great determination to finish third in his first and second heats, not to mention winning his semifinal. (Jenkins's semifinal was so fast that a runner who had posted a 46.2 was eliminated.) In the finals Louis Jones took the lead as expected and ran seemingly effortlessly, though he didn't hold much of a lead. With 60 meters to go, Ardalion Ignatyev of the Soviet Union surprised Jones by taking over first place. With 25 meters to go Jenkins surprised the Soviet runner. At the tape Jenkins barely held off the hard-charging Karl-Friedrich Haas of Germany, who had come all the way from last to first in the final 100 meters. Charley Jenkins won in the relatively slow time of 46.7. Haas was second in 46.8.

Don Bowden was a junior at the University of California whose best time in the mile was 4:09.9. Nothing prepared the track world for his race on June 1, 1957, in Stockton, California. The six-foot-three, 160-pound runner not only beat the American record of 4:00.5 set by Wes Santee in 1954, but he even threatened John Landy's world record of 3:58.0, also set in 1954. Bowden's time was a spectacular 3:58.7, topping his previous best by over 10 seconds.

Whenever **Al Cantello** hurled the javelin, he attracted attention because he threw himself along with the javelin, ending up on all fours. It was a distinctive style all right, and one that was effective enough to win the AAU meets in 1959 and 1960 and on a sunny day in Compton, California, on June 5, 1959, a world record. During his early throws, Cantello just couldn't get his mechanics right. But then on his third and final throw, everything came together and he uncorked a throw that sailed 282 feet 3 inches. It was one of those beautiful individual moments in sports. At the 1960 Olympics in Rome, Cantello disappointed everyone, most particularly himself, with a throw of 245 feet 1 inch for a tenth-place finish.

The 10,000-meter race at the 1964 Olympics turned out to be one of the most exciting races ever. No track expert could have predicted the outcome. Going into the event were three favorites: New Zealand's Murray Halberg, the defending champion in the 5,000 meters; the Soviet Union's Pyotr Bolotnikov, the defending champion in the 10,000 meters; and Australia's Ron Clarke, the world record holder in the 10,000 meters.

Clarke's strategy was simple: to surge every other

lap, thereby throwing runners off their pace and running them into the ground. After 5,000 meters only four runners were still vying for the gold: Tunisia's Mohamed Ghammoudi, Ethiopia's Momo Wolde, Japan's Kogichi Tsuburaya, and the United State's **Billy Mills**. The race had become particularly difficult because many of the runners being lapped insisted on staying in the inside lanes. In the words of Ron Clarke, the race was "like a dash for a train in a peak-hour crowd."

The final lap found Clarke on the backstretch hemmed in between a lapped runner on the inside and Billy Mills on the outside. Clarke motioned for Mills to move, but he didn't, so Clarke pushed him. Mills veered to the outside and Clarke moved ahead. At that moment Ghammoudi squeezed between Clarke and Mills and shot ahead by ten yards. Clarke took chase and caught him at the top of the homestretch. But Mills was coming on fast, sprinting like a person possessed. It was Billy Mills, running 46 seconds faster than his personal best, who hit the tape ahead by three yards in 28:24.4. Second was Ghammoudi in 28:24.8. Third was Clarke in 28:25.8.

A Native American, an officer in the Marines, a man who had started out to be a boxer—Billy Mills could not stop smiling. "I'm flabbergasted," he exclaimed. "I suppose I was the only person who thought I had a chance."

Dick Fosbury originated his unique way of going over the high-jump bar during a high-school meet his sophomore year. "As the bar got higher," remembered

Fosbury, "I began to lean back further and further, making my back more parallel to the ground." By his sophomore year in college, Fosbury had set a record at Oregon State University of six-foot-ten. And at the Olympic trials the next year he jumped seven-foot-three and qualified for the team. On October 20, 1968, Fosbury flopped his way to the gold medal in Mexico City. His height of seven-foot-four and a quarter set both American and Olympic records.

More importantly, though, Dick Fosbury had set the track world on its ear. No longer would high jumpers practice the Eastern and Western rolls that had been the approach for years. Now all world-class high jumpers would copy Fosbury's headfirst, faceup method of flopping over the bar and collapsing into the pit. They would all use the Fosbury Flop.

The 1968 Olympic Games might have been remembered for the controversy surrounding the Black Power salute of American sprinters Tommie Smith and John Carlos on the victory stand, if it hadn't been for one of the most amazing feats in Olympic history. No one had ever broken 28 feet in the long jump. It was a barrier similar to what four minutes in the mile had once been. But that was before the six-foot-three, 160-pound **Bob Beamon** sprinted down the runway with his 9.5 speed for the 100.

In the preliminaries, Beamon fouled twice and was one foul away from being eliminated. Ralph Boston, the man who had broken Jesse Owens's 24-year-old long jump record, walked over and told Beamon to make a mark a few inches before the board. Beamon did and qualified. (Unlike the other jumpers, Beamon did not make any marks along the 134-foot runway.

Things were different in the finals. Beamon kept telling himself, "Don't foul, don't foul," and he didn't. On his first jump Beamon hit the takeoff board perfectly and sailed six feet above the ground. As he landed, he fell forward out of the pit. "It felt like a regular jump," said Beamon afterward. But the other long jumpers knew it was special, even if Beamon didn't. As the optical measuring device moved to the spot where Beamon had landed, it fell off the track the jump was so long. A tape measure showed that Beamon had not only broken 28 feet, but he had crashed 29 feet as well. His jump of 29 feet 2 and a half inches had shattered the previous world record by 21 and three-quarter inches.

The other jumpers, a dispirited lot, stared at the pit.

"Compared to this jump, we are as children," said the Soviet long jumper, Igor Ter-Ovanesyan, who had held the world record with a jump of 27 feet 3 and a half inches in 1972.

"I can't go on," said Lynn Davies from Great Britain. "What is the point? We'll all look silly."

"It's over for me," said American Ralph Boston, whose longest jump ever was 27 feet 5 inches. "I can't jump that far."

And as it turned out, neither could Bob Beamon. He tried a second jump and only managed 26 feet 4 and a quarter inches. He passed his four other jumps. The silver medal went to East Germany's Klaus Beer, who jumped 26 feet 10 and a half inches; Boston managed 26 feet 9 and a quarter inches for the bronze.

That day, October 18, 1968, remains a magical one in the annals of track and field. After that one amazing jump, Bob Beamon could never even break 27 feet. Beamon's record lasted until 1991, when Mike Powell leaped 29 feet 4 and a half inches.

Dr. Delano Meriwether caught the track world's fancy in the early 1970s. Not only had he not run in high school, not only had he not run in college (he had sprinted through the course work at Michigan State in three years), the sprinting doc didn't take up running until he was 27 years old and finished with medical school at Duke. He took it up for relaxation, but he cut quite a figure on the indoor track circuit in 1971 when he showed up decked out in gold track shorts and striped suspenders.

The first time he ran a timed 100 yards he finished in 9.6 seconds. One of the next times out he lowered it to 9.4 and beat Jean-Louis Ravelomanantsoa of Madagascar, a runner who had finished eighth in the 100 meters at the 1968 Olympics in Mexico. In one of his first 220s, Meriwether was timed in 21.1, beating Ed Roberts, a runner who had finished fourth in the 200 meters in Mexico City. And then on January 8, 1971, Meriwether won the 60-yard dash at the CYO National Invitational Track Meet at College Park, Maryland. His time was six seconds flat.

When Dr. Meriwether wasn't running that year, he was putting in long hours as head of the swine flu program and trying to get as many citizens inoculated as possible.

* * *

Lee Evans had set the world record of 43.68 in the 400 at the 1968 Olympics and would have been a favorite at the 1972 Olympics if he hadn't pulled his hamstring. Instead the favorites were teammates John Smith and Wayne Collett. The third US runner was **Vince Matthews**. All three made it to the finals, so it looked like there might be another sweep by the US, as there had been in 1968. But that was before John Smith pulled up lame after 80 meters. Coming off the curve Matthews was in first, Collett second. Matthews held Collett off to win by four meters in 44.66. Collett was second in 44.80.

Unfortunately, this delicious moment quickly turned sour. Matthews and Collett seemed to be disrespectful on the victory stand. Not only were they talking and moving around, when they stepped down, Matthews twirled his medal around his finger. Matthews later explained that he had not been considered worthy to compete in place of the injured Evans. "A lot of people had forgotten about me and given up on me. I took it off to tell them this was my medal."

At five-foot-eight **Franklin Jacobs** didn't look like a high jumper. He also didn't consider himself a track athlete; he was a basketball player, and a good one, a guard who had led his team at Eastside High to the New Jersey state championship. After the basketball season was over his senior year in high school, Jacobs stopped by at track practice and on his first jump cleared 6 feet 1 inch. A few weeks later he won the New Jersey state championship at 6 feet 8 inches.

Jacobs entered Fairleigh Dickinson University in

the fall of 1976 and worked on his technique with Walt Marusyn, the track coach. Marusyn asked Bill Monahan to work with him further, and together they worked out a 13-step approach that curved toward the bar and capitalized on Jacobs's great ability to leap. Jacobs had a vertical leap of 44 inches; he could touch a basketball rim with his head.

Jacobs was a college sensation and the Millrose Games in 1978 was one of the first national showcases of his talent. Eventually it became a contest between Jacobs and Dwight Stones, the world-class jumper and Olympic medalist from California. Long into the night of their contest, Stones suggested that the bar be raised to 7 feet 8 and a quarter inches, a world-record height, and Jacobs agreed. It was a smart move for Stones because if both jumpers failed to clear it, Stones would win on fewer misses. And both did fail on their first two attempts. But Jacobs had jumped high enough, so Monahan suggested he lengthen his approach by a step to get more speed. On his final try, the bar trembled for the longest time, but it didn't fall. Franklin Jacobs had cleared 7 feet 8 and a quarter inches, a new indoor world record. The bar fell quickly on Stones's third jump.

Franklin Jacobs became the number-one high jumper in the world and was undefeated through 13 straight meets during 1979. Things were looking good for his winning a gold at the 1980 Olympics. When it appeared all but certain the US would boycott the Olympics, Jacobs lodged a silent protest at the Olympic trials by not jumping until the bar was 7 feet 3 inches. He missed on all three attempts. Jacobs was out of track until a friend at the YMCA where he worked suggested in 1984 that he try out for the Los Angeles Olympics. With only a month's work Jacobs cleared 7 feet 4 and a half inches in an indoor meet. But he had hurt his knee, so his dreams of gold were over.

The name Franklin Jacobs remains in the record book, however. His Millrose Games indoor record still stands and he is listed in the Guinness Book of World Records for clearing a height 23 and a quarter inches above his head.

On April 3, 1981, **Arnie Boldt** of Canada high jumped 6 feet, 8 and a quarter inches in a track meet in Rome, Italy. Amazingly, Boldt has only one leg.

Carl Joseph was born with only one leg. For most people, that would end any thoughts about athletics but not Carl Joseph. Joseph won 13 letters in high school football, basketball, and track.

"As long as I can remember," he said, "it's never been a problem for me. But I don't think about having one leg. If you start thinking too much, it makes you wonder what might have been, and that does you no good. I just always try to think positive."

At one time he played football with an artificial leg, but that could be hard on his opponents' heads. So, he began playing without it. He must have been one of the few one-legged players in the country. But that didn't mean he wanted to be treated special by his own players or by his opponents.

"I'm just a natural person," Joseph reasoned. "I want what I earn. I don't want somebody to just give me something. If you're going to be somebody, you've got to make it on your own."

Besides, he sometimes found his lack to be an asset. It made him try harder. "This way, you have to keep driving yourself." And with all the tongue in cheek available to him, he added, "I'm good at blitzing because the blockers are going to miss one of my legs right off."

One afternoon at a high school track meet in 1982, the usual person who high jumped was not available and Carl Joseph was asked to fill in for him. Although his usual events were the javelin and the discus, Joseph was not the sort to say no but to rise to a challenge.

When Joseph began, the bar was set at 5 feet 4 inches. Joseph missed his first two attempts. Then on the third jump, he cleared it. The bar was raised to 5 feet 6 inches. Again, Joseph cleared it. Five-eight looked like it was going to be troublesome, but he cleared that, too. The bar was raised to 5 feet 10 inches.

People started to file over to the high jump pit to watch. After all, it's not every day you see a one-legged person high jumping. It was a bit like what Samuel Johnson, the great English lexicographer, once said about a dog walking upright on its hind legs: It's not so much that it can walk well, but that it can do it at all. But Joseph turned that on its ear; he could do it well, too.

Joseph cleared 5 feet 10 inches. The bar was finally set at five-eleven. Who could not be rooting for him?

Even an opponent would be half on his side. Joseph successfully high jumped the height. The crowd broke into cheering and applause.

Joseph had not only won the event but the hearts of all around him as well. Not surprisingly, Carl Joseph was a shoo-in for the Philadelphia Sportswriters Association's 1982 Most Courageous Athlete award.

Walking

"I like long walks, especially when they are taken by people who annoy me."
—Noel Coward

Tired of racking up frequent flier miles? **Edward Payson Weston** took an old-fashioned approach to travel. For a bet of a bag of peanuts, he walked from Boston to Washington, a journey of 478 miles in 10 days in order to attend Abraham Lincoln's inauguration on March 4, 1861. He got there too late for the swearing-in ceremony but not too late to go to the ball that night.

In 1867, when he was 28 years old, Weston upped the ante to $10,000 that it would take him only 26 days to walk from Portland, Maine, to Chicago, Illinois. Amazingly, he completed the 1,326-mile journey in 25 days and 22 hours. Think about that the next time you're waiting for a bus.

In 1876, Weston lined up England's great walker, a chap named Perkins, and challenged him to a 24-hour walking race. Perkins was through after 16 hours; Weston continued to the end.

But even more astounding was what Weston did at

the ripe old age of seventy. On March 15, 1909, he set out on foot from New York for San Francisco. The 3,795-mile journey took him just 104 days and 7 hours. Then to top it all off, the next year this septuagenarian walked back to New York—3,600 miles in just 76 days and 23 hours.

Mary Marshall was a professional pedestrian. Odd as it may sound, that was all the rage at the time, and it was something both men and woman took part in. But until three nights beginning late in 1876, men and women had never competed against each other in an organized sporting event in the United States.

It was then that Marshall, a five-foot-three, 135-pound professional pedestrian from Chicago, challenged a male pedestrian named Peter Van Ness, from Philadelphia, to a contest. The goal was to walk 20 miles each night; the winner would be the one who completed the 20 miles first two out of three nights. Neither was considered the best walkers of the men and women, but they were both willing to participate for the $500 prize.

The Central Park Garden was packed with onlookers the night of November 17, 1876, as the two walkers began pacing themselves around the 240-foot oval dirt track. Van Ness took the early lead and was averaging 10-minute miles, until he tired and stopped to rest. Although Marshall was averaging 14-minute miles, she continued until she had completed 10 miles. After a lengthy rest Van Ness reentered the 22-lap-per-mile track and again began walking 10-minute miles. But after four more miles he became tired and stopped. After another long rest, he began walking again. But this time he couldn't catch up and Marshall, steady as a tortoise, won by over a mile.

The next night Van Ness was determined not to make the same mistake of resting too long. "He walked rapidly away from her at the start, and made his first six miles in one hour and seven minutes, before she had completed her fifth mile," ran the account in the *Sun*, a New York newspaper. "He continued to increase his lead until the end of the tenth mile and then he retired from the track much exhausted, two and a quarter miles ahead." But Van Ness did not rest as long as he had the night before and he was able to defeat Marshall.

The showdown was held on Saturday night. Again, Van Ness got out in front early and had a commanding lead of more than two miles by the time he stopped to rest at the ten-mile mark. Again, Marshall continued and caught up and passed him during the 45 minutes he was off the track. Van Ness resumed walking and caught her after 13 miles. He continued until the 15-mile mark, at which time he dropped out to rest. But Van Ness was spent. His win the previous night had taken too much out of him and he could not pull off a come-from-behind victory. Ninety-seven years before Billie Jean King beat Bobby Riggs in "The Tennis Match of the Century," Mary Marshall had outwalked Peter Van Ness.

* * *

On January 23, 1881, a six-day race was held on a one-eighth-mile oval at the American Institute Building in New York City. From the outset a total unknown by the name of **John Hughes** went into the lead. His pace was so steady that there arose speculation that he might beat Frank Hart's six-day American record of 565 miles set only a year before. During the middle of the race the number of spectators slacked off, but by the end of the sixth day there were 4,000 people on hand.

By this time there were only seven of the original 30 contestants still in the race for the O'Leary Belt, and the leader was none other than John Hughes. Moving gingerly, Hughes was nothing if not determined. A roar went up from the crowd when he beat Hart's mark, but Hughes was not finished. Charles Rowell's world record of 566 miles was within reach. John Hughes walked 567 miles before calling it quits.

At the 1948 Olympic Games in London, **Norman Read** watched Sweden's John Ljunggren win the 50-kilometer walk and realized a desire to become a walker. This was not a popular sport in England, so in 1954 Read emigrated to New Zealand. As the 1956 Olympic Games in Melbourne approached, Read tried to get on the British team but was rejected. Next he tried the New Zealand team. They refused at first, but after reviewing his record of recent wins accepted him and Read became a naturalized citizen.

The favorite in the 50,000-meter walking race was the Soviet Union's Yevgeny Maskinskov. On the day of the race, Read got lost in the maze of tunnels underneath the stadium and got to the starting line just as all the walkers were waiting for the gun. Maskinskov went to the front of the pack and stayed there, until Read made his move with 8,000 meters to go.

"When I caught up to Maskinskov he had the blank look of surprise and perhaps shock," said Read. "At that point I think we both knew that the race was mine."

Norman Read won the gold medal in a time of 4 hours, 30 minutes, 42.8 seconds. Two minutes behind was Yevgeny Maskinskov, the silver medal winner. And almost five minutes behind was bronze medalist John Ljunggren.

In 1960, **Barbara Moore** walked from Los Angeles to New York in 86 days, establishing a new record for women.

David Ryder was an Englishman who walked on crutches because of a bout with polio. In 1969, Ryder set out to cross the United States. In only 106 days he crutched 2,960 miles. That's an average of almost 28 miles a day.

Another Englishman, **John Lee**, broke the record for walking from Los Angeles to New York. Starting out on April 13, 1972, Lee finished on June 6 after 53 and a half days.

The 10-mile walk has been an annual contest held on the boardwalk of Coney Island since 1908. But no woman had ever won. All that changed in April 1976 when 16-year-old **Eileen Smith** of Seaford, New York, the only woman entry, won the event in 1 hour, 37 minutes, 12 seconds.

Water Sports

*"There is nothing—absolutely nothing—half so much
worth doing as simply messing about in boats. . . ."*
—Kenneth Grahame, *The Wind in the Willows*

On June 6, 1896, **George Harbo** and **Frank Samuelson** left New York in an 18-foot rowboat bound for France. During their 3,000-mile voyage, the two Americans were battered for three days by a storm that eventually capsized their boat. When the storm subsided, they righted the boat and made it to the Scilly Isles, before rowing up the Seine River and reaching Paris on August 6.

On August 26, 1900, at the Olympic Games in Paris, the rowers of the Netherlands team, Francois Brandt and Roelof Klein, determined they had lost their opening heat to the Societe Nautique de la Marne because their regular coxswain, Hermanus Brockmann, was too heavy. As the hour of the finals drew near, the crew of the *Minerva* from Amsterdam asked **a seven-year-old boy** who was fishing nearby if he would help them. He did and the Dutch team won the gold medal. Before their young coxswain could be officially recognized and receive his medal, the youngster had slipped away into the crowd. The boy has never been identified.

* * *

Bill Havens was one of the favorites to win the gold medal in single and four-man canoeing at the 1924 Paris Olympic Games. There was one hitch, however: his wife was due to have their child sometime during late summer. Should he go? Being in the Olympics was a once-in-a-lifetime opportunity. On the other hand, what is more important in a person's life than having a child? Back and forth he went, wrestling with his decision. Then it all fell into place. He would give up his place on the Olympic team so he could be with his wife during the birth of their baby.

On August 1, 1924, four days after the Olympics was over, their son was born. Bill Havens would have missed the birth because the team traveled by ocean liner and the trip across the Atlantic took two weeks.

Havens felt he had made the right decision. Still, sometimes, he would have second thoughts. Yet, in a sense, there did come a second chance. His son took up his sport and became very good at it. Good enough to qualify for the US Olympic team in the 10,000-meter canoeing event and be in the Helsinki Olympic Games. And then one day in the summer of 1952, there arrived at the house this telegram:

Dear Dad,

    Thanks for waiting around for me to get born in 1924. I'm coming home with the gold medal you should have won.

Your loving son,
Frank

Geoffrey Pope and **Sheldon Taylor** paddled a canoe from New York City to Nome, Alaska. Setting out on April 25, 1936, the 6,000-mile trip took a total of 1 year, 3 months, and 17 days.

On March 6, 1947, for the first time anywhere, water-skier **Dick Pope Jr.** was successful in getting up on his bare feet and staying there at Lake Eloise, Florida.

Ann Davison was the first woman to sail across the Atlantic Ocean alone. Setting out from Plymouth, England, on May 18, 1952, on her 23-foot *Felicity Ann*, this Englishwoman made stops in France, Spain, Africa, the Canary Islands, and the West Indies, before sailing into Miami on August 13, 1953.

On April 21, 1959, **Alf Dean** of Mildura, Australia, was fishing in Denis Bay off the coast of South Australia, near Cedura, using a regular rod and reel. What happened next was anything but regular. Dean landed a 17-foot great white shark that tipped the scale at 2,664 pounds.

When **Anita DeFrantz** enrolled at Connecticut College in New London, she decided to go out for a sport. Not having been an athlete in high school, she chose rowing because it was a new sport for her as well as for the school. During her college years DeFrantz improved so much that upon graduation she chose to go to law school at the University of Pennsylvania because it had a good rowing program. DeFrantz not only qualified for the US women's eight-oared shell with coxswain at the 1976 Olympics in Montreal, but she also helped the Americans win the bronze medal. (The Germans were first in 3:33.32; the Soviets second in 3:36.17; the US women were third in 3:38.68.) Four years later DeFrantz was training for the 1980 Olympics when President Carter withdrew the United States from the Moscow Olympics. So what did Anita DeFrantz do? She sued the International Olympic Committee. The committee was so impressed by her that it ended up giving her a job. DeFrantz finally got her double by becoming the first American woman and the first African American to be a member of the IOC.

The fastest speed for a woman on water skis was achieved by **Donna Patterson Brice** of the United States. On August 21, 1977, she got up to 111 miles per hour at Long Beach, California.

The first woman to sail around the world by herself was **Krystyna Chojnowska-Liskiewicz**. Starting out from the Canary Islands on March 23, 1976, this Polish woman sailed her 32-foot sloop west. She completed her voyage just shy of two years later, on March 26, 1978.

A barefoot **Paul McManus** once set a record of 1 hour 30 minutes, and 19 seconds. If your first thought was that this Australian had run the 30,000 meters, you're all wet. He had set an endurance record for water-skiing without water skis. **Billy Nichols** of the

US beat this record on November 19, 1978 by skiing barefoot on Lake Weir in Florida for 2 hours 42 minutes and 39 seconds. A barefoot Paul McManus also once skied backward for 39 minutes.

Christopher Michael Massey of Australia has the claim of going the fastest on water skis. He got up to 143 miles per hour on the Hawkesbury River in Australia on March 6, 1983.

If jumping is your thing, the longest jump on water skis is 205 feet. **Sammy Duvall** of the United States hit it on July 24, 1988, at Shreveport, Louisiana. **Deena Brush Mapple** of the United States set the women's record: 156 feet at Charlotte, Michigan on July 9, 1988.

Lawrence Lemieux was at the 1988 Olympic Games to compete for the gold in the Finn class of sailboats. The day of the fifth of seven races for medals in his class, the wind was very treacherous in the waters near Pusan, Korea, gusting from 15 to 35 knots per hour. As this native of Edmonton, Canada, was reaching the halfway point, Lemieux spotted two sailors from Singapore in a nearby 470-class race capsized in the choppy water. Lemieux sailed over to rescue Joseph Chan, then tacked over to reach Shaw Her Siew. As soon as the patrol boat came by to pick them up, Lemieux continued with his race. Although by this time he was no longer second, but twenty-second, he finished anyway. The International Yacht Racing

Union decided Lemieux should be awarded second place for the race.

At the end of the seventh race, Lemieux had not won any medals, till he was honored by Juan Antonio Samaranch, the president of the International Olympic Committee, at the medals ceremony: "By your sportsmanship, self-sacrifice and courage, you embody all that is right with the Olympic ideal."

Italy's **Giovanni Soldini** was competing in the Around Alone, the 27,000-mile sailboat race around the world that begins and ends in Charleston, South Carolina. He was on the third leg, Auckland to Punta del Este, Uruguay. (The other legs are Charleston to Cape Town, South Africa; Cape Town to Auckland, New Zealand; Punta del Este to Charleston.) Suddenly, a bulletin was broadcast to him on his 60-foot sailboat that France's Isabelle Autissier, his closest competitor, was in trouble. Immediately he changed course and ploughed through the heavy seas in her direction.

"The problem is that these positions aren't precise," said Soldini, "and it won't be easy to see Autissier's boat. Visibility is always poor, and in any case I'll need some luck."

Lady Fortuna must have smiled, for on February 16, 1999, almost 24 hours after he had altered his course, Giovanni Soldini could see the white hull of her capsized boat. He called out her name as he passed her boat twice, but there was no response. On the third pass, he threw a hammer at the hull. A groggy Isabelle Autissier appeared. The Frenchwoman got into her rubber raft and the Italian man threw her a line. After she was safely on board, Autissier exclaimed that she was "on an Italian cruise now, and not unhappy about that."

Weightlifting

On April 15, 1895, the stage was set at the Bijou Theatre in Hoboken, New Jersey. **Josephine Blatt** came out and using a hip and harness contraption lifted a total of 3,564 pounds. This is a record for women that has lasted to the present day.

Sometimes we may be told we should do something, but it can be years before we ever get around to it. Although she wasn't big—she stood a mere four-feet-eleven inches and weighed only 118 pounds—**Minnie Roberts** had always been known as strong. But it wasn't until 1984 that she received any official recognition for her strength. It was then that Roberts entered the Michigan State Championships in weightlifting. She was in the women-over-40 class. And was she ever. This grandmother was 66 years old. But that didn't stop her. Roberts won first place by heaving almost twice her weight.

Winter Sports

*"I do not participate in any sport
with ambulances at the bottom of a hill."*
—Erma Bombeck, humorist

Terry McDermott was lucky to have made the US Winter Olympic team in 1964. He was even luckier to be skating in the 500 meters, for he had forgotten his skates. Fortunately, his coach had a pair to lend McDermott, so that on February 4, 1964, the 23-year-old barber from Essexville, Michigan, was able to skate his heart out in Innsbruck, Austria, shaving a tenth of a second off the old record en route to a gold medal and a new Olympic record of 40.1.

When McDermott tried to defend his medal at the 1968 Olympics in Grenoble, he had to skate last, when the ice was mushy from the warm temperature and the 23 other pairs of skaters who had preceded him. Still, McDermott came in second. "What he did today was just sheer guts," said the winner, Erhard Keller of Germany. "If he had started in the earlier heats while the ice was still good, I'd have lost. It's as simple as that."

Michael Edwards was a plasterer from England. Not the sort of occupation or country that is often associated with ski jumping. But that's what he was during the 1988 Calgary Olympics: the British entry in the 70-meter ski jumping event. Edwards may have been a joke to the other competitors on the small hill, but he seemed to become bigger than life for the guy hanging onto a beer can and wondering what it might be like to whizz down the ski jump, fly off the end, and soar through the air. Eddie the Eagle brought that experience home. "When I looked from the top of the jump," admitted Edwards, "I was so frightened that my bum shriveled like a prune." Edwards may have finished last at the Olympics, but not in the hearts and minds of many viewers. He even parlayed this brief brush with fame into a career as a motivational speaker and a celebrity to meet at openings.